C. Paul Smith

# THE PROPHET JOSEPH SMITH

*Restoration Issues*

ARCHWAY
PUBLISHING

Archway Publishing books may be ordered
through booksellers or by contacting:

Archway Publishing
1663 Liberty Drive
Bloomington, IN 47403
www.archwaypublishing.com
1 (888) 242-5904

Photo on the cover is of statues of Joseph and Hyrum Smith, in front of
the Nauvoo Temple in Illinois. Statues are the work of Stan Watts and Kim
Corpany. This photo is the author's. Unless otherwise indicated, all photos are
those of the author. Photos of artwork are used with permission of owners.

ISBN: 978-1-4808-6944-8 (sc)
ISBN: 978-1-4808-6945-5 (hc)
ISBN: 978-1-4808-6943-1 (e)

Library of Congress Control Number: 2019904204

Print information available on the last page.

Archway Publishing rev. date: 06/26/2019

# CONTENTS

Abbreviations.................................................................xi

About the Author ..........................................................xiii

Preface..........................................................................xv

**Part I – Plural Marriage** ..............................................1

Chapter 1   A Brief History of the Restoration of Plural
Marriage (1831-44)....................................... 7

Chapter 2   Joseph Smith's Plural Marriages ......................... 57

Chapter 3   Oliver Cowdery and Sidney Rigdon .................. 66

Chapter 4   The Character of Joseph Smith ....................... 73

**Part II—Succession in the Presidency** ..................................... 81

Chapter 5   All Priesthood Keys Were Conferred upon the
Twelve prior to the Prophet's Death ................................... 83

Chapter 6   Three LDS Splinter Churches ........................... 105

**Part III—Doctrines and Prophecies**..................................... 135

Chapter 7   The Book of Abraham .............................................137

Chapter 8   Blacks and the Priesthood—God Controls When
the Priesthood Is Bestowed ............................................. 179

Chapter 9   Alleged False Prophecies of Joseph Smith ........214

**Part IV—Joseph Smith, the Messenger of Jesus Christ ... 241**

Bibliography .......................................................... 251

Index........................................................................ 259

# EXPANDED CONTENTS

Abbreviations...........................................................................xi
About the Author ...................................................................xiii
Preface...................................................................................xv

**Part I – Plural Marriage** ......................................................1
  Legality of Plural Marriage......................................................4
Chapter 1  A Brief History of the Restoration of Plural
    Marriage (1831-44)..............................................................7
  Planning to Implement Plural Marriage.......................................7
  The Vision of Heaven.............................................................10
  Marriage to Fanny Alger .........................................................13
  Oliver Cowdery....................................................................14
  National Recession – Apostasy.................................................18
  Restoration of Additional Doctrines...........................................20
  John C. Bennett.....................................................................23
  Introduction to the Twelve and Others ........................................25
  Hyrum Smith ......................................................................26
  Emma Smith.........................................................................27
  Orson Hyde and Nancy Marinda Hyde......................................29
  William Smith, John E. Page and Lyman Wight..............................30
  Orson Pratt .........................................................................32
  Sidney Rigdon and Nancy Rigdon.............................................34
  Presidential Campaign ...........................................................40
  William Law.........................................................................41
  Nauvoo Expositor .................................................................44
  Initial Secrecy.......................................................................45
  Quorum of the Twelve Assume Leadership..................................48

Increased Practice of Plural Marriage .................................... 49

Practice of Plural Marriage Is Suspended ........................... 50

   Appendix A: Other Men Having Plural Marriages
       Prior to Death of Joseph Smith ............................ 53

   Appendix B: Writing of Joseph Smith to
       Nancy Rigdon ............................................................ 54

   Appendix C: Wives of Joseph Smith ......................... 56

Chapter 2   Joseph Smith's Plural Marriages .......................... 57

Marriage to a 14-Year-Old ......................................................... 58

Sealings to Women already Married ....................................... 60

   Appendix D Alleged Children of Joseph Smith of
       Married Women Sealed to Joseph Smith ........... 65

Chapter 3   Oliver Cowdery and Sidney Rigdon ................... 66

Chapter 4   The Character of Joseph Smith ........................... 73

**Part II—Succession in the Presidency** ..................................... 81

Chapter 5   All Priesthood Keys Were Conferred upon the
Twelve prior to the Prophet's Death ................................... 83

Sealing Keys Restored ................................................................. 85

Temple Ordinances Restored ................................................... 86

First Endowments Performed ................................................... 87

All Ordinances and Keys Conferred upon the Twelve ....... 89

Church Conference of August 8, 1844 ................................... 97

Chapter 6   Three LDS Splinter Churches ........................... 105

   I. True Church of Jesus Christ of Latter Day Saints .......... 106

   II. The Reorganized Church of Jesus Christ of Latter Day
Saints ............................................................................................ 110

      Doctrines ............................................................................. 116

      Other Facts of Interest ......................................................... 118

         A. The Kirtland Temple Case ................................... 119

         B. The Independence Temple Lot Case .................. 123

      A Visit to Nauvoo – RLDS Church Properties ............ 127

   III. The Church of Christ – Temple Lot .............................. 131

**Part III—Doctrines and Prophecies** ..................................... 135

Chapter 7   The Book of Abraham ......................................... 137

   I. Background of the Book of Abraham ............................. 138

   II. Addressing Five Criticisms of the Book of Abraham ... 147

1. Allegation that the papyrus writings are not the actual writings of Abraham .............................. 147

2. Allegation that the plural renditions of "Gods" is wrong.................................................................. 151

3. Allegation that Facsimile No. 1 was wrongly completed ...................................................................... 151

4. Allegation that "explanations" for the facsimiles are mistranslations ............................................. 152

5. Allegation that the Book of Abraham is a fraud...... 157

    -Omission.......................................................................159

    -First Assumption. ...................................................160

    -Second Assumption .................................................165

    -Third Assumption ...................................................165

    -Fourth Assumption .................................................166

    -Fifth Assumption......................................................168

    -Final Comments on Dr. Ritner's

        Conclusions...................................................... 169

III. Other Evidence Supportive of the Book of Abraham ...................................................................... 171

    Facsimile No. 1 ......................................................... 174

    Facsimile No. 2 .........................................................175

    Facsimile No. 3 .........................................................176

    Facsimile No. 1: A Comparison of Joseph Smith's Explanations with Those of Theodule Deveria (1860) .............................................................177

Chapter 8  Blacks and the Priesthood—God Controls When the Priesthood Is Bestowed .............................................. 179

I. Equal Opportunity for Exaltation................................ 181

II. God Chooses Who Will Receive His Priesthood.......... 185

    A. "Ye Have Not Chosen Me, But I Have Chosen You." ......................................................................... 185

    B. Special Blessings for Abraham's Seed. ..................... 187

    C. The Long-Awaited Day. ........................................... 189

III. Racial Relations in America ............................................. 190

    A. The Original National Sin. ...................................... 191

    B. Separate But Equal. ................................................. 192

    C. Racism in Sports Reflected National Attitudes....... 193

      1. Baseball—Jackie Robinson .............................. 193
      2. Basketball and Football ................................. 194
   D. Racism in Entertainment. ................................ 195
   E. Brown v. Board of Education. ................................ 196
   F. The 1960s. ................................ 196
   G. Heightened Racial Tensions beginning in 2012. .... 200
IV. Jesus Declined to Participate in Volatile Political
Movements ............................................................. 201
   A. The Church of Christ Is Not a Political Activist
      Organization. ................................ 202
V. Statements of Joseph Smith Regarding Slavery,
Blacks and the Priesthood ................................ 203
   A. Priesthood in the Abrahamic Covenant. ............... 203
   B. Racial Problems in the Early Days of America. ...... 204
   C. Newly Revealed Ancient Scriptures Comment on
      Who Could Hold the Priesthood. ................... 208
   D. Limited Scope of Missionary Work in
      the 1800s. ................................ 210
   VI. Conclusion ................................ 212
Chapter 9   Alleged False Prophecies of Joseph Smith ........ 214
   The One Mistake Test ................................ 217
      1. "Fifty-six years should wind up the scene." ............ 222
      2. Wars shall be poured out upon all nations. ........... 224
      3. "In a few years the government will be utterly
         overthrown." ................................ 225
      4. "Congress will be broken up." ................... 231
      5. Death of the wicked. ................................ 233
      6. Temple to be built in Missouri in this
         generation ................................ 237
   Conclusion ................................ 240

**Part IV—Joseph Smith, the Messenger of Jesus Christ ... 241**

Bibliography ................................ 251
Index ................................ 259

# ABBREVIATIONS

Some names and titles are used so much in this text that I have chosen to routinely use the abbreviations for them listed below. For other sources identified in the text and footnotes, those sources are fully identified the first time, and thereafter are identified by the author's name. The sources that are frequently identified by abbreviations are:

D&C  *Doctrine and Covenants* – collection of revelations and inspired writings of the Prophet Joseph Smith and his successors.

HC  *The History of the Church of Jesus Christ of Latter-day Saints,* ed. B. H. Roberts, 7 vols. (Salt Lake City: The Church of Jesus Christ of Latter-day Saints, 1902-1951). It contains many writings and words of the Prophet Joseph Smith.

JD  *Journal of Discourses* — discourses of Church apostles and prophets (1854-1886)

LDS  The Church of Jesus Christ of Latter-day Saints

RLDS  Reorganized Church of Jesus Christ of Latter Day Saints (now known as "Community of Christ")

# ABOUT THE AUTHOR

C. Paul Smith is an ex-
perienced trial lawyer
in Maryland, where he
has practiced law for 40
years, beginning in 1978.
He graduated from the J.
Reuben Clark School of
Law at Brigham Young
University in 1978, after
also receiving a Bachelor of

Arts Degree there in English in 1974. Paul is married to Terry
Thompson Smith, and together they have twelve children and
35 grandchildren.

Paul has operated a general law practice, handling primarily civil matters in state and federal courts, including family
law, real estate, bankruptcy, personal injury, wills and estates
and probate matters. Paul was elected Frederick City Alderman
(2006-2009) and was elected Vice President of the Board of
County Commissioners of Frederick County (2010-2014). He
has been an active leader in the Boy Scouts of America for 45
years, and he was awarded the Silver Beaver Award in 2013. He
coached youth baseball and basketball teams for many years.

Paul has served in many positions with The Church of Jesus
Christ of Latter-day Saints, including bishop, high councilor,
stake young men's president, stake mission preparation teacher,

ward young men's president, scoutmaster (5 times), missionary to France (1970-72), and most recently (2017-2018) with his wife Terry as full-time missionaries in the Texas Ft. Worth Mission.

Paul has authored several books: *The Fetal Right to Life Argument* (1977); *I Will Send My Messenger* (1988, 2019); *The State of the Constitution* (2002); *The Life of J. Russel Smith* (2016); and *The State of the Constitution--2017* (2017). For several years Paul also published the newsletter, *Constitutional Law Updates* (2001-2017).

# PREFACE

*The Prophet Joseph Smith—Restoration Issues* addresses some historical and religious issues about the Prophet Joseph Smith that continue to fuel debate today, 175 years after his death. This book provides answers and insights to six of these issues.

The church founded by Joseph Smith in 1830, The Church of Jesus Christ of Latter-day Saints (Mormon Church), is a significant force in America and around the world. In America it is the fourth largest denomination (behind Catholicism, the Southern Baptist Convention and the United Methodist Church). Some of the nation's most powerful politicians are Mormons: former Presidential candidate Mitt Romney and former Senate Majority Leader Harry Reid. Mormons comprise a large percentage of the population in Utah, Idaho, Wyoming and Nevada. Hall of Fame NFL quarterback Steve Young is a popular football analyst. Bill Marriott heads the world's largest hotel chain. And television star Marie Osmond continues to charm television viewers, as she promotes her dieting product. Thousands of Mormon "Helping Hands" are routinely part of our nation's emergency relief efforts, including participating in the cleanup following the hurricanes in 2017 that ravaged Texas and Florida.

In a day when traditional Judeo-Christian values are incessantly challenged and attacked, the Mormon Church stands out as a strong and unflinching defender of traditional marriage, chastity outside of marriage, the sanctity of unborn life, and strong families. The Church maintains a world-wide missionary force of 65,000 missionaries serving around the world—comprised mostly of young men and young women ages 18-22, who are responsible to fund their own missions.

Mormonism attracts about 250,000 converts each year—primarily the result of the Church's phenomenal missionary effort. Church doctrines also play a key role in this continuing growth—especially the doctrine of "eternal marriage," the teachings that "families can be together forever"—meaning after death, in the resurrection—and the teaching that God is an immortal, exalted man and that it is the purpose of our eternal existence to become like Him.

But Joseph Smith and Mormonism have always had their detractors and critics, and attacks on Mormon doctrines and on Joseph Smith continue to pummel the Church in the 21$^{st}$ century. The Church's former practice of plural marriage (polygamy) continues to be assailed; some accuse the Church of racism for its former practice of not extending the priesthood to blacks for many years; some people contend that Joseph Smith was an imposter and a false prophet because they argue that his "translation" of the Book of Abraham (from some Egyptian papyri) is a fraud; and they argue that some of his "prophecies" never came to

Statue of Joseph Smith in front of Zion's Mercantile store, in Nauvoo, Illinois. Sculpture by D. J. Bawden.

pass. Because these attacks against the Prophet Joseph Smith and Mormonism continue to be aggressively waged, a response to these allegations is both timely and warranted. That is what this book is—a response, an explanation, a defense, and in some instances a refutation of many of the attacks that are currently being made against Joseph Smith and Mormonism.

Joseph Smith is revered and esteemed by millions to be a virtuous, brave prophet of God. But he is considered by others to be an evil manipulator and a fraud. How can this be? These opinions are polar opposites—both cannot be true. A thorough study of the life and words of Joseph Smith, including many accusations made against him, leads me to conclude that he was a virtuous man of great faith, and that he was indeed a prophet of God.

Joseph Smith has been criticized and maligned when he delivered messages that he said God revealed to him. Joseph Smith proclaimed that God had called him as a prophet to restore the fullness of the gospel of Jesus Christ. As Joseph Smith became effective and successful in his mission, this evoked fierce opposition from some of those who disagreed with him. Like many prophets of God throughout the history of the world, he was hated, misrepresented and killed because he boldly declared the word of God.

Joseph Smith disrupted the religious world in America and around the world. His teachings were at odds with the status quo of current Christianity, but many of the world's best people embraced his teachings and joined with what he said was the "restored gospel of Jesus Christ." This caused many pastors of other churches in the world to unite in attacking and condemning Joseph Smith—for as he converted people away from them, this was an implicit criticism of some of their teachings, and it jeopardized their very livelihood.

Joseph Smith dared to teach not only that males and females were created in the image of God, but that the eternal potential of man is to become gods and goddesses. While there is support for this doctrine in the Bible, many people accused Joseph of blasphemy. And when Joseph said he was restoring the biblical practice of plural marriage, many people called Joseph an immoral and evil man—never mind the fact that some of God's greatest prophets, Abraham, Jacob and Moses anciently practiced this doctrine. The first chapters of this book will discuss this doctrine.

I have studied the life and words of the Prophet Joseph Smith for over five decades. I found him to be a man of virtue, love, great faith, unwavering devotion to God, and unmatched courage. I conclude that the criticisms that he was evil and corrupt are wrong. Joseph Smith's mission was to be the Lord's prophet in restoring all things, in preparing the world for the Lord's triumphal return to reign on earth during the Millennium. I have found that those who disparage Joseph Smith are wrong in virtually all of their criticisms of him. Joseph's detractors are invariably wrong on the facts, wrong in their interpretation of the Bible, and wrong in their assumptions about Joseph's motivations and desires.

Nevertheless, some of the criticisms of Joseph Smith can sound persuasive on the surface, to someone who is not fully versed in history and in the scriptures. Therefore, I believe that it can be helpful to address some of these criticisms and some historical facts about his teachings. That is what I intend to do in this book.

I think it is important to say something about the basis I have for the conclusions I have reached about Joseph Smith. While I am not the world's greatest expert on Joseph Smith, I believe that my knowledge of the life and writings and statements of the Prophet Joseph Smith is superior to most of his critics. I have made a lifetime study of Joseph's life and words. Because of this, I am able to more easily identify and refute most of the false criticisms that Joseph's enemies make. I have read and studied *The Book of Mormon* dozens of times. I have read and studied *The Doctrine and Covenants* and *The Pearl of Great*

*Price* multiple times. I have also read and studied *History of the Church* (7 volumes), *An American Prophet's Record: The Diaries and Journals of Joseph Smith* (Scott Faulring, ed.), *The Restored Church* (by William E. Berrett), *Joseph Smith and the Restoration* (by Ivan J. Barrett), and *The Autobiography of Parley P. Pratt*. I have read many additional books and articles about Joseph Smith, some of which I found helpful in coming to a thorough understanding of him—nine of which I will mention here: *History of Joseph Smith* (by Lucy Mack Smith); *Joseph Smith, Rough Stone Rolling* (by Richard Lyman Bushman); *They Knew the Prophet* (by Hyrum L. & Helen Mae Andrus); *Joseph Smith the Prophet* (by Truman G. Madsen); and *No Man Knows My History* (by Fawn Brodie). The latter book is a classic anti-Mormon book—of course, I know that. But I nevertheless found it to provide some helpful insights. Additional valuable information is found in the biographies of two men who shared some of the Prophet's most spectacular manifestations: *The Voice of One Crying in the Wilderness: Sidney Rigdon, Religious Reformer (1793-1876)* (by F. Mark McKiernan) and *Oliver Cowdery, The Elusive Second Elder of the Restoration* (by Phillip R. Legg). Other insights about the Prophet are provided in *The Life of Heber C. Kimball* (by Orson F. Whitney) and *The Life of John Taylor* (by B. H. Roberts). I mention these books to show that there is a substantial basis for the conclusions I have reached about Joseph Smith.

There are some Mormon scholars whose studies of Joseph Smith have been more extensive than mine. But I doubt there are many critics of Joseph Smith who can match the depth and breadth of my scholarship. Most critics of Joseph Smith are pseudo scholars who cherry pick their criticisms—repeating a few negative-sounding criticisms they have found. This inevitably leads to major flaws in their criticisms of Joseph. Such critics are invariably deficient in a thorough and solid education about the words and actions of Joseph Smith. Thus, while I have received a divine witness of the divinity of the prophetic mission of Joseph Smith, my witness is also confirmed by extensive study of Joseph's words and actions. Joseph's critics typically have neither.

In the meantime, for those who are confronted with accusations about Joseph Smith that present him to be a bad person and a false or fallen prophet, let me make it very clear—I have heard many such allegations and accusations; I have found them to be typically flawed in their factual premises; and I have never found that the facts supported their conclusions. I have always come away with a strengthened witness that Joseph Smith was indeed God's prophet. So, for those who are confronted with anti-Mormon propaganda and who do not know how to find answers to it, it is my hope that the discussions included in this book may help. Frankly, I have never found a critic of Joseph Smith who has an appreciation of the spiritual depth and magnificence of the 872 pages of scripture that he contributed to the world.

With this background, in this book I will address several historical matters pertaining to Joseph Smith and the restored gospel of Jesus Christ. A thorough study of the main specific criticisms made against the Prophet exposes them to be factually flawed or otherwise without justification. A review of these historical matters should be interesting and enlightening.

As I have studied the issues covered in this book I have not found another source that succinctly covers them in the way they are treated here. I believe that the treatment this book gives will be enthusiastically received by those who are asking the same questions I have asked. For example, the chapters on plural marriage (1-4) are unique in their conciseness and thoroughness. Students of history will enjoy reading the chapters (5 & 6) about the Church's initial succession crisis after the death of Joseph Smith and about three groups that broke away from the Church beginning in 1844. The chapter on the Book of Abraham (7) refutes the arguments made by some Egyptologists that the Book of Abraham is a fraud. The chapter on Blacks and the Priesthood (8) presents (i) statements by Joseph Smith on the initial exclusion of blacks from holding the priesthood, and (ii) historical background supporting the timeliness of Official Declaration 2 in 1978, which extended to all worthy males the opportunity to hold the priesthood. The final chapter (9) refutes frequently made allegations that six particular prophecies of Joseph Smith's were false prophecies.

I believe the reader will acknowledge that the information provided in these pages will be helpful to truth-seekers. I believe there is a need for this book, and I believe that the followers of Jesus Christ will be grateful for it.

# Part I – Plural Marriage

There is no more provocative or emotionally charged religious issue than that of the practice of polygamy, or "plural
marriage," in The Church of Jesus Christ of Latter-day Saints."
Because it involves intimate social, religious, legal, historical,
and sexual issues, it is a matter about which almost everyone is
interested in learning. The practice is both illegal and socially
unacceptable today. It is not practiced today in The Church
of Jesus Christ of Latter-day Saints, but it was practiced for
approximately 50 years in the nineteenth century, until it was
suspended in 1890. Some individuals have apostatized from
the Mormon Church and continue to practice plural marriage

today, but this is regarded as a violation of God's commandments. Nevertheless, understanding some basic historical facts
about the practice of plural marriage is essential to understanding many important aspects of Mormon history and doctrine.

## Part of God's Eternal Plan

Plural marriage exists in the highest kingdom of heaven in the
celestial kingdom (D&C 132:37). It is a part of God's eternal
plan of happiness. The restoration of the doctrine and practice of plural marriage was a vital part of the restoration of all
things (Matthew 17:11 & Acts 3:21) that was brought about by
the Prophet Joseph Smith. Its restoration was necessary to do
the work of the Lord on earth, and was also necessary in implementing the great work for the redeeming of the dead—which
includes not only baptisms for the dead, but also vicarious
sealings for deceased husbands and wives. God directed this
restoration. And when commanded by God, the proper application of this principle in this life by people of virtue and faith
could be happy and fulfilling. For those who are privileged to
practice it in the celestial kingdom, it will be a source of incredible joy and glory.

Plural marriage was authorized and practiced in ancient
Israel (see e.g., Deut. 21:15), including being practiced by the
great Hebrew prophets Abraham and Jacob (Israel). Regardless
of any other reasons for its being part of God's gospel,[1] we know
that plural marriage was practiced by some of God's greatest
prophets. Moses also had more than one wife, although most
people are unaware of this. Gideon had several wives. The
prophet Samuel was the son of Elkanah's second wife. David
and Solomon each had many wives; their having multiple wives
was fully acceptable in that day and time. In other words, there

---

[1] While a discussion of God's reasons for plural marriage could be an interesting discussion, it is not within the scope of this writing to enter into an
in-depth discussion of such reasons.

is no question that plural marriage was a practice and a doctrine that existed among ancient prophets, and which was acceptable to the Lord.

In the following pages, I will address a number of issues and historical facts pertaining to plural marriage. In doing so it is my intent to answer a number of questions about plural marriage and how it was practiced by Joseph Smith and the early Mormons. When the Prophet Joseph Smith presented the doctrine and practice of plural marriage to the Twelve Apostles (1842-43), each of them had to deal with his own personal aversion to it, but each of them received the witness from God that it was His will to restore the doctrine and practice.

The discussion here will proceed as follows: **Chapter 1** discusses the history of the restoration of plural marriage during Joseph Smith's lifetime; **Chapter 2** discusses some issues related to Joseph Smith's personal experience in practicing plural marriage; **Chapter 3** discusses some implications from how Oliver Cowdery and Sidney Rigdon both rejected plural marriage, but continued to believe that Joseph Smith was God's prophet; and **Chapter 4** discusses the character of Joseph Smith.

Today it is perhaps possible to ignore or postpone coming to grips with the doctrine of plural marriage. But this was not the case for Joseph Smith, Brigham Young, Heber C. Kimball and the other leaders of the Church in the 1840s.[2] They had to know right then and there. For many today, this review is also important in their personal quest to determine whether Joseph Smith was a prophet of God. As you will see from the following discussion about Joseph Smith's practice of plural marriage, it shows him to be a man of goodness and courage—a man who was determined to do the will of God at all costs. His bold and unflinching commitment to do God's will led to his being

---

[2] One of the best accounts of the introduction of plural marriage in the Church is given in Orson F. Whitney, *The Life of Heber C. Kimball* (Salt Lake City: Bookcraft, 1945, Third edition 1967 [originally published 1888]) pp. 321-28.

assassinated in Carthage Jail at the hands of hateful men. This discussion will demonstrate that Joseph Smith was martyred because of his faithful allegiance to the Lord Jesus Christ.

## Legality of Plural Marriage

Before reviewing some of the history of plural marriage, let us first consider the legality of it in the 1800s. While state laws of Illinois, Ohio and Missouri may have prohibited polygamy, Joseph Smith took the position that the First Amendment of the Constitution gave him a religious right to practice plural marriage, and that this constitutional right superseded any conflicting state or federal laws: "Congress shall make no law respecting an establishment of religion or prohibiting the free exercise thereof...." The United States is a "federal" govern-ment—meaning it is one nation composed of fifty independent states, which means that some aspects of the lives of Americans (including marriage) are regulated by fifty different laws of the fifty different states—subject to constitutional constraints. In any event, inasmuch as marriage and divorce are religious matters, there existed in the 1840s the legitimate argument by churches and individuals that they had controlling rights and liberties over matters such as marriage and divorce. For many years the leaders of the Church took this position—that neither the State nor the federal government had the right to prohibit plural marriage because it was an individual religious liberty protected by the Free Exercise Clause of the First Amendment. Therefore, the Prophet was not subject to Illinois laws regarding divorce and marriage, including determining whether a man could marry more than one wife. There was certainly a reason-able basis to support the Prophet's views on this.

In 1878 the Supreme Court rejected the Mormons' assertion that such a right was an absolute right protected under the First Amendment (*Reynolds v. United States*, 98 U.S. 145). The Court ruled that the state power to regulate conduct that it regarded as detrimental to the state superseded the Mormon's right to the free exercise of their religion. Beginning then, it was clear that God's commandment to practice plural marriage conflicted with laws in the United States of America.[3] Thereafter, until the Lord suspended the practice (in 1890), Church leaders chose to obey God, rather than to follow the law of the land in this matter.

---

[3] The laws in the United States continue to change. Sometimes such changes go into and out of harmony with God's laws. In 2015, in *Obergefell v. Hodges*, 576 U. S. ____, the Supreme Court for the first time ruled that individuals of the same sex have a right under the First Amendment to be married; this marked a significant change in the Supreme Court's interpretation of how individual marriage rights are impacted by the First Amendment. This highlights the fact that while our national laws set standards for right and wrong in our democratic government, those laws sometimes change, and they are not always in harmony with God's will. It is clear that the Prophet Joseph Smith was focused on God's commandments and God's moral standards, and if those standards were different from the laws of either Illinois, Missouri or Ohio, Joseph opted to obey God.

# Chapter 1

# A Brief History of the Restoration of Plural Marriage (1831-44)

## Planning to Implement Plural Marriage

W. W. Phelps wrote that it was on July 18, 1831, in Independence, Missouri, that he first heard from the Prophet Joseph Smith that plural marriage was to be restored in the future.[4] This was the Prophet's first trip to Independence. While there, he identified the site for a temple at Independence—for what was to be the main temple in the center of Zion. Sidney Rigdon accompanied the Prophet on that trip, and Joseph dedicated the temple site on August 3, 1831. Orson Pratt said that it was as early as 1832 that the Prophet first mentioned plural marriage to him, and that Lyman Johnson told him that the Prophet had spoken of it to him in 1831.[5] Joseph said that between 1834 and 1842, an

---

[4] J. Max Anderson, *The Polygamy Story: Fiction and Fact* (Publishers Press, 1979), p. 100, citing *Journal of Discourses*, 13:193; and William W. Phelps to Brigham Young, August 12, 1861, Church Archives, Salt Lake City; and Joseph Fielding Smith, *Doctrines of Salvation*, 3:197.
[5] Joseph Fielding Smith, *Doctrines of Salvation*, 3:197; and "Doctrine and Covenants," *Encyclopedia of Mormonism* (New York: Macmillan Publishing Co., 1992), p. 422.

angel appeared to him three times, commanding him to begin practicing plural marriage—and that the last time the angel threatened him with a sword if he did not obey the commandment.[6] In 1841, the Prophet began his effort to reach out individually to key men and women to establish the practice of plural marriage. Part of this effort involved his teaching "celestial" or "eternal" marriage. On May 16, 1843, Joseph taught the saints that in order to attain the highest degree of glory in the celestial kingdom, one must enter into a celestial marriage (D&C 131:1-4). He then explained, "Except a man and his wife enter into an everlasting covenant and be married for eternity, while in this probation, by the power and authority of the Holy Priesthood, they will cease to increase when they die; that is, they will not have any children after the resurrection."[7]

The success of implementing plural marriage would depend upon several things happening: Joseph would have to set the example; other leaders of the Church would have to both accept the doctrine and also set the example in practicing it; and the Prophet would have to tightly control who would be permitted to practice it. Joseph knew that the enemies of the Church would accuse him and all those who would practice it to be doing so for lustful and licentious reasons. Therefore, those taking plural wives had to be men of pure and unimpeachable character, so that both the Church members and all the world would witness that it was being done only for the most high and noble purposes.

---

[6] "Essay on Plural Marriage," www.lds.org, footnote 9: "See Brian C. Hales, "Encouraging Joseph Smith to Practice Plural Marriage: 'The Accounts of the Angel with a Drawn Sword,' Mormon Historical Studies 11, no. 2 (Fall 2010): 69-70." See also, Orson F. Whitney, *The Life of Heber C. Kimball*, p. 321. See also Don Cecil Corbett, *Mary Fielding Smith, Daughter of Britain, Portrait of Courage* (Salt Lake City: Deseret Book Co. 1966), 154, footnote 8, citing: "Journal History, L. D. S. Church Historian's Office, Salt Lake City, Oct. 9, 1869, containing copy of a letter from Apostle George A. Smith to Joseph Smith, son of the Prophet Joseph Smith."

[7] HC 5:391. "Celestial" marriage applies to marriages between one man and one woman, and to plural marriages.

It was a major undertaking for the Prophet to get the Church leadership and membership on board. While Joseph needed to lead the way in beginning the practice of plural marriage, he also needed to bring the Church to embrace the doctrine and practice. This challenge was obviously a difficult task. Not only was America at the height of its Victorian ideology, but most people in America were of a devout Judeo-Christian background that rejected polygamy. To persuade Mormons to accept and embrace plural marriage was a formidable challenge. The initial reaction of almost every Mormon to the prospect of practicing plural marriage was one of repulsion and opposition. Such a practice violated their cultural norms, and Mormons knew they would invoke the wrath and criticism of the majority of the nation if they did it. But in the face of this, all twelve members of the Quorum of the Twelve Apostles supported the doctrine and practice of plural marriage. Nine out of those twelve had plural wives before Joseph's death, and the other three took plural wives shortly thereafter (see appendix A, at the end of this chapter). This fact demonstrates one of the most difficult but important accomplishments of Joseph Smith: he was successful in convincing the Quorum of the Twelve and other key members of the Church of the divinity of plural marriage and leading them to receive their own individual witnesses from God of its divinity. It was necessary that this campaign be conducted one-on-one, and it took over two years to accomplish it. Early in 1841, no other member of the Twelve was practicing plural marriage, and most did not even know about it. But by the time Joseph was assassinated on June 27, 1844, all of the Twelve were on board with him in this critical doctrine.

## The Vision of Heaven

On February 16, 1832, at the John Johnson farm house, in Hiram, Ohio (above), Joseph Smith and Sidney Rigdon were privileged to see in vision God the Father and His Son, Jesus Christ, after which they also witnessed the marvelous vision of the three degrees of glory in heaven. At the end of the Prophet and Sidney's account of their vision, they wrote:

> This is the end of the vision which we saw, which we were commanded to write while we were yet in the spirit.
>
> But great and marvelous are the works of the Lord, and the mysteries of his kingdom which he showed us, which surpass all understanding in glory, and in might, and in dominion;

Which he commanded us we should not write while we were in the spirit, and are not lawful for man to utter;

Neither is man capable to make them known, for they are only to be seen and understood by the power of the Holy Spirit, which God bestows on those who love him, and purify themselves before him;

To whom he grants this privilege of seeing and knowing for themselves; That through the power and manifestation of the Spirit, while in the flesh, they may be able to bear his presence in the world of glory. (D&C 76:113-18)

These verses state that the Prophet and Sidney did not write all that they witnessed about heaven. In fact, they were commanded not to write about some things that they saw in heaven.[8]

I submit that one of the things that they would have seen (or at least that Joseph saw) would have been evidence of plural marriages in heaven. But at that time he was commanded not to write about it. I believe that this was only a part of the things he and Sidney saw that they were commanded not to write, but I do think it was one of those things. And it is certainly understandable why it would be advisable for him not to write about plural marriage at this time—it would have unleashed

---

[8] The Prophet's language in section 76 is similar to the language used by the Apostle Paul when he referred to a vision of the "third heaven": "I knew a man in Christ above fourteen years ago, (whether in the body, I cannot tell . . .) such an one caught up to the third heaven. And I . . . heard unspeakable words, which it is not lawful for a man to utter" (2 Corinthians 12:2-4). Commenting on this, Joseph Smith said: "I could explain a hundred-fold more than I ever have of the glories of the kingdoms manifested to me in the vision, were I permitted, and were the people prepared to receive them" (HC 5:402, May 1842).

intense persecution upon him and the Church, which could have destroyed the Church in its infancy. When the Church did begin to publicly acknowledge that it practiced plural marriage in 1852, the saints were somewhat insulated from the rest of America and the world by virtue of living in the Rocky Mountains. A premature announcement of such a belief would have been devastating to the Church when it was centered in Ohio, Missouri or Illinois.

While I have no doubt that Joseph saw evidence of plural marriage in the 1832 vision, it is unclear what Sidney Rigdon saw or perceived. Joseph's abilities to observe and understand were certainly superior to those of Sidney, such that Joseph undoubtedly learned more from the vision than did Sidney. But by at least 1842, Sidney knew that Joseph was teaching and attempting to practice it. Sidney Rigdon did not say much specifically about plural marriage while the Prophet was still alive. But he stated his disapproval of it after the Prophet's death, and my reading of Church history makes me believe that he opposed it while the Prophet was alive, as well. But he never practiced it, and I have not read that the Prophet ever asked him to do so. During the 1832 vision, Sidney either did not see the evidence of plural marriage that Joseph must have seen, or he saw such evidence but did not appreciate what he was seeing—or he did not accept what he saw. (More will be said of Sidney Rigdon later, in chapter 3.)

Eleven years later, the Prophet Joseph Smith did write down and publish additional information about heaven, as is currently found in sections 131 and 132 of the *Doctrine and Covenants*. Section 131 explains that there are "three heavens or degrees" in the celestial kingdom, and that in order for a man to obtain the highest kingdom of glory, he "must enter into . . . the new and everlasting covenant of marriage." The Prophet gave this "instruction" to the saints on May 16, 1843.

On May 21, 1843 the Prophet gave two reasons why he did not state all that he knew about the celestial kingdom—the first is that God told him not to, and the second is that the people were not prepared to hear it (HC 5:402). Undoubtedly plural marriage was one of those undisclosed things that Joseph Smith saw. Shortly thereafter (July 1843), the Prophet dictated Section 132, which gives an explanation of "the new and everlasting covenant of marriage." It is also called "celestial marriage," and the Prophet also explained the doctrine of plural marriage, which is a part of celestial marriage for those commanded to enter into it.

## Marriage to Fanny Alger

The first plural marriage to take place in this dispensation was between Joseph Smith and Fanny Alger in Kirtland somewhere between 1833-1836 (probably 1836).[9] Fanny turned sixteen in 1832, so she was 16 or older at the time of the marriage. According to Mosiah Hancock, the marriage was performed by Levi Hancock (Mosiah's father).[10] Levi is the brother of Clarissa Alger, Fanny's mother. Some have argued that no one had authority to perform such a marriage. The obvious answer to this argument is that whoever the Prophet authorized to do it could do it. If someone were to argue that the laws of Kirtland did not authorize someone to perform such a marriage, the obvious counter is that this was a matter of religion and that the Prophet did not need civil authorization to perform a religious ordinance. That was certainly the position the Prophet took. Today I don't believe that such a position would be upheld by the United States Supreme Court, but it was a valid argument then, both legally and spiritually. Another argument made by

---

[9] Some historians place the date as early as 1833, when Fanny would have been sixteen. But my review of the various accounts makes me conclude that it was not before 1834, and probably was in 1836, when Fanny was twenty. Fanny did not come to work as a maid for Joseph and Emma until after they moved into their home, close to the temple in 1834.

[10] Brian C. Hales, "Fanny Alger," *Joseph Smith's Polygamy,* accessed online; see also, Richard Bushman, *Joseph Smith--Rough Stone Rolling* (New York: Alfred A. Knopf, 2005), 323-27.

critics of Joseph Smith is that no one could have authority to perform such a marriage because the "sealing powers" of the priesthood were not restored until April 3, 1836. Whether or not the marriage to Fanny was performed before April 3, 1836, Joseph would have authority to authorize others to perform a plural marriage if God so directed. The requisite sealing could be done later.

Historical documents indicate that in September 1836 Fanny Alger moved away to Indiana, and that she was later married to a Solomon Custer, by whom she had nine children. When Fanny Alger was much older, she was asked by her brother about her relationship with Joseph Smith, and she responded: "That is a matter of my - own. And I have nothing to communicate."[11] This response confirms the high probability that she at one time had a close relationship with Joseph Smith.

## Oliver Cowdery

Whether Emma was aware of the marriage to Fanny Alger, I do not know. But we know that Oliver Cowdery was aware of it. One of the interesting exchanges between Joseph and Oliver addressed the question of whether Joseph had ever committed adultery during the Kirtland period. Joseph extracted from Oliver the admission that Joseph had never admitted to him that he had ever committed adultery. And Oliver acknowledged this.[12] The unspoken implication is that Oliver had been made

---

[11] See e.g., Richard L. Bushman, *Joseph Smith--Rough Stone Rolling*, 327, citing Todd Compton, *In Sacred Loneliness: The Plural Wives of Joseph Smith* (Salt Lake City: Signature Books, 1997), 39-41.

[12] The High Council minutes at Far West for April 12, 1838 report that the council was made aware of the allegation that Joseph was guilty of adultery with a certain girl, and that George W. Harris, David W. Patten and Thomas B. Marsh all testified that Oliver admitted that Joseph had never confessed to him that he was guilty of adultery. See Brian C. Hales, *Joseph Smith's Polygamy: History*, p.370, citing Ebenezer Robinson clerk, High Council Minutes, April 12, 1838, in Donald Q. Cannon and Lyndon W. Cook,

aware that Joseph had married Fanny Alger, and that Joseph said this was a plural marriage, authorized by God, and that therefore any relationship he had with her was not adulterous. But on January 21, 1838, Oliver wrote to his brother Warren, and referred to "a dirty, nasty, filthy affair [or scrape] of his [Joseph's] and Fanny Alger's" (Legg, 120). Oliver knew about Fanny Alger, and he also knew that Joseph had introduced plural marriage.[13] On February 24, 1838, Oliver complained in a letter to his brother Lyman that he (Oliver) was being "denounced" because he was one of those "who refuse to confess those disgusting doctrines lately introduced unto the church."[14] In early 1838 when nine charges were brought against Oliver Cowdery for his membership in the Church, one of those charges was that Oliver had accused the Prophet of adultery (HC 3:16). This was a very sensitive point for the Prophet; for while he did practice plural marriage, he steadfastly denied that he ever committed adultery.

Oliver rejected the doctrine of plural marriage, and he felt justified in challenging the Prophet on this matter. Thus, Oliver presented a challenge to the Prophet that was greater than from anyone else—Oliver, as Second Elder in the Church, challenged Joseph's authority in a more serious way than anyone else could; Oliver was in essence asserting that he had authority to dictate to the Prophet on marriage issues; and Oliver condemned plural marriage. Together these two things only added to the

---

eds., *Far West Record: Minutes of the Church of Jesus Christ of Latter-day Saints, 1830-44* (Salt Lake City: Deseret Book, 1983), 167-68.

[13] Brigham Young said that Oliver Cowdery was made aware of the doctrine of plural marriage in 1829 while Joseph was translating the gold plates, and that Oliver came to a fuller understanding of it in 1832 when Joseph was making his inspired translation of Genesis. "Oliver Cowdery," *Encyclopedia of Mormonism*.

[14] Phillip R. Legg, *Oliver Cowdery, the Elusive Second Elder of the Restoration* (Herald Publishing House, 1989), 122, citing: Letter from Oliver to Lyman dated February 24, 1838 (H.E. Huntington collection, RLDS Archives microfilm #95). Oliver's biographer, Phillip R. Legg, understands that the "doctrines" referred to were "spiritual wifery" or polygamy. Legg, 122-23.

Prophet's burden to do the Lord's will in implementing plural marriage. This challenge became more serious when Oliver wrote and included sections 100 and 101 in the 1835 edition of *The Doctrine and Covenants*. Section 100 (now section 134) was a statement of belief about the role of government in life. Section 101 was a statement of beliefs about marriage. In section 101,[15] Oliver included in it a specific rejection and condemnation of plural marriage: "Inasmuch as this church of Christ has been reproached with the crime of fornication, and of polygamy: we declare that we believe, that one man should have one wife; and one woman but one husband, except in case of death, when either is at liberty to marry again" (verse 4). This was not worded as a revelation from God, but it was nevertheless a statement of belief, and the Prophet would have preferred that the matter not even be discussed[16] because he already knew that the day would come when plural marriage would have to be acknowledged in writing and practiced. Section 101 made this transition

---

[15] Some historians think that W. W. Phelps assisted Oliver in this.

[16] This section was added by Oliver Cowdery, just prior to submitting the book to the printer for publication. Joseph was in Michigan at the time, and was not present when the proposal was made to add section 101. Sidney Rigdon was another member of the committee that was present and approved of Section 101 at the conference when the matter was presented to the Church for its approval (HC 2:243-46). Joseph Fielding Smith wrote this about the inclusion of section 101 in the 1835 edition of the Doctrine and Covenants: "I am informed by my father [President Joseph F. Smith], who got it from Orson Pratt—the Prophet was very much troubled . . . . when the Prophet came back from Michigan, he learned of the order made by the conference of the Church and let it go through." Joseph Fielding Smith, *Doctrines of Salvation*, 3:194. See also Robert J. Woodford, *Doctrine and Covenants Editions*, BYU, Harold B. Lee Library—see: eom.byu.edu/index.php/Doctrine_and_Covenants-Editions. Woodford wrote: "Although Joseph Smith subsequently endorsed the statement on government, there is evidence that he opposed including the statement on marriage from the beginning." Woodford cites "Cook, pp. 348-49, n. 11."

more difficult. Oliver's feeling that he had authority to venture out on his own in this matter was a problem for the Prophet.[17]

On April 3, 1836, Oliver Cowdery was present with the Prophet when the Savior, Moses, Elias and Elijah appeared, and when the keys of the covenant of Abraham were bestowed upon them. The gospel of Abraham included both celestial marriage and plural marriage. Whether or not Oliver Cowdery under-stood this, I do not know. But being a partner with Joseph to this manifestation probably increased Oliver's confidence in the propriety of his counseling the Prophet, and even correcting the Prophet. But once again, as Oliver rejected plural marriage, the growing assertiveness of Oliver presented a problem to Joseph.

When the complaint was filed against Oliver in Missouri in 1838, challenging his membership in the Church, it was not di-rectly brought by the Prophet, but the Prophet was apparently aware of it and was supportive of it. Seymour Brunson brought nine different charges against Oliver (HC 3:16), but the charge of falsely accusing Joseph Smith of adultery was at the heart of the proceeding. Now that many historic documents have come to light, it is possible to reconstruct many of the key events that were the basis for Oliver's excommunication.

Oliver may not have been trying to undermine the Prophet, but he was trying to correct the Prophet, and he voiced to some people his criticism that Joseph's relationship with Alger was adulterous. This is what ultimately led to Seymour Brunson's

---

[17] Some historians have questioned the basis for the premise stated by Oliver--that some or someone in the church had been reproached for "forni-cation" and "polygamy." Oliver was aware of Joseph's encounter with Fanny Alger, but it is unclear who else was aware of it, and it is unclear what other allegations with respect to others had created a public concern about these things. A polygamous man from Maine named Jacob Cochran had joined the Church in 1832, and there were people pursuing him because of this. But it is unclear to whom the allegations of "fornication" and "polygamy" were intended to refer. But the inclusion of this statement created additional problems for the Prophet. There was no need for Oliver Cowdery to include the gratuitous statement that some in the Church were accused of practicing polygamy.

charge that Oliver accused the Prophet of adultery. For Oliver's part, he may not have intended to be working overtly to undermine the Prophet, but that is nevertheless the effect of what he was doing. Oliver was clearly not supporting the Prophet in restoring the doctrine of plural marriage. And Oliver did do several things to interfere with what Joseph was trying to do. Not only did Oliver reject and oppose plural marriage, but he was also acting unilaterally in taking action that the Prophet did not approve, and which was undermining the Prophet.

## National Recession – Apostasy

When the national recession of 1837 hit the saints in Kirtland, the financial troubles for the saints in Kirtland were so severe that it brought wide-spread hardship and criticism and apostasy in the Church. Joseph moved to Missouri in early 1838, and for two months he stayed at the home of George W. Harris. Although unknown to most people at that time, apparently Joseph entered into a plural marriage with Lucinda Morgan Harris in 1838. This marriage was apparently treated by both Joseph and Lucinda as a "next life only" marriage. Today we have documents confirming that this sealing took place, but I am not aware of evidence of any cohabitation between Joseph and Lucinda.

Meanwhile, in early 1838, shortly after Oliver arrived in Far West, Missouri, Seymour Brunson made a complaint to the High Council against Oliver Cowdery for nine different charges. This resulted in Oliver's excommunication on April 12, 1838.[18] David Whitmer was similarly excommunicated the next day (HC 3:19). Oliver Cowdery's being moved out of the way was a big deal, because since Oliver was Assistant President of the Church, the Church regarded him as a near equal to

---

[18] HC 3:17. See also *The Joseph Smith Papers*, Dean C. Jesse, Ronald K. Esplin and Richard L. Bushman, eds. (Salt Lake City: The Church Historians' Press, 2008) 1:253, note 92.

the prophet. Oliver presented a major problem for Joseph in restoring plural marriage in the Church. But with Oliver's excommunication, that obstacle was removed.

Oliver Cowdery and David Whitmer were not the only prominent leaders who were excommunicated in 1838. There was so much criticism and apostasy in 1837 and 1838 that the Prophet felt a need to cleanse the Church of all those critics and dissenters who were in any way undermining him and the work of the Lord. The dissent was so strong and vocal that the Prophet felt a need for a purge of this element. Thus, in addition to Cowdery and Whitmer, the following other leaders were excommunicated: Martin Harris, W. W. Phelps, Thomas B. Marsh, William E. McLellin, Luke S. Johnson, Lyman E. Johnson, and John Whitmer. Orson Hyde was also affected by the Church's critics at this time, and he was dropped from the Quorum of the Twelve on May 4, 1839. But he acknowledged the error of his ways and was re-instated as a member of the Quorum on June 27, 1839. ("Orson Hyde," *Encyclopedia of Mormonism*, Daniel H. Ludlow, ed. (Macmillan Publishing Co., New York: 1992).) W. W. Phelps also repented and sought and obtained re-admission in the Church a little later (1840). But the pride of Oliver Cowdery, David Whitmer and Thomas Marsh was such that they would not readily admit their flaws, as minor as they may have been. (Eventually Oliver Cowdery returned to the Church in 1848, and Thomas Marsh returned in 1857.)

After the excommunication of Oliver Cowdery and David Whitmer in April of 1838, there was reason for the Prophet to think that he and the saints could experience some peace and tranquility in northwestern Missouri. But any such hopes were crushed in the fall of 1838. Whatever the Prophet may have intended to do in introducing plural marriage in the Church at that time was put to an abrupt end. The Missouri extermination order, the jailing of the Prophet for six months, the mass exodus of the saints from Missouri—all of these made refugees of the saints, and set back their peace and prosperity by two years.

It wasn't until 1841, after the saints had begun to make a new settlement in Nauvoo, Illinois that Joseph began to introduce plural marriage to some of the faithful saints.

## Restoration of Additional Doctrines

When Moses, Elias and Elijah restored important priesthood keys to the earth (in 1836), two of these three keys pertained to marriage. The gospel of Abraham (restored by Elias) included the covenant and ordinance of celestial marriage,[19] which blesses participants with a marriage for time and eternity with a posterity as numerous as the sands of the sea shore. The sealing powers (restored by Elijah) involved the power for all priesthood ordinances, including celestial marriage, to make those covenants and blessings for time and all eternity. But while the keys were restored on April 3, 1836, the Prophet's full understanding of those keys and powers was not immediately appreciated by him. It was not until several years later that the Prophet understood and taught the specific ordinances to secure these great blessings. The Prophet introduced the following ordinances to the saints at Nauvoo between 1840 and 1843: The endowment; celestial marriage; and the saving ordinances for the dead, including baptism for the dead.

In the summer of 1840 the Prophet taught the saints about baptisms for the dead, and the first such baptisms were performed in the Mississippi River in August. On January 19, 1841, the Prophet received a revelation (D&C 124: 27-31, 55), commanding the saints to build a temple at Nauvoo, and directing that baptisms for

---

[19] *The Doctrine and Covenants Student Manual*, The Church of Jesus Christ of Latter-day Saints, p. 276, citing Bruce R. McConkie, *Mormon Doctrine* ("Elias"), pp. 219-20. See also Bruce R. McConkie, *The Millennial Messiah* (Salt Lake City: Deseret Book Company, 1982), pp. 119, 268.

On the first floor of the Kirtland Temple, at the west end (to the left), on April 3, 1836, the Savior appeared to Joseph Smith and Oliver Cowdery and accepted the just dedicated temple. Moses, Elias and Elijah then appeared to both of them, and restored the sealing keys of the priesthood for the gathering of Israel and for the performance of eternal marriages.

the dead are to be performed in the temple (v. 29-30), indicating that *God would shortly reveal other ordinances* (v. 40-41), calling Hyrum Smith to be Patriarch and Assistant President (v. 91-95), and commanding the saints to build the Nauvoo House (v. 56-82, 119-22). Construction of the Nauvoo Temple was started in February of 1841. On November 21, 1841, the first baptisms for the dead were performed in the temple in a wooden, temporary font built by Elijah Fordham. The building of the rest of the temple

This is Joseph Smith's Red Brick Store, which was rebuilt in 2002. The first endowments were performed here on the second floor, on May 4, 1842.

continued for another four years. The Prophet introduced the Endowment to a handful of saints on the second floor of the Prophet's red brick store on May 4, 1842. In the spring of 1843 the Prophet began to teach that a man and woman must enter into the "everlasting covenant" of marriage in order for that marriage to continue in the next life (D&C 131:1-5; and HC 5:391 [May 16, 1843]). Shortly thereafter, the Prophet dictated the revelation on plural marriage (D&C Section 132), that explained that this "celestial" marriage sometimes includes plural marriage. "But," Joseph said on July 16, 1843, "on account of the unbelief of the people, I cannot reveal the fullness of these things at present" (HC 5:510).

Several of the Apostles were among those to whom the Prophet administered the holy Endowment, when it was introduced for the first time, on May 4, 1842.[20] By March of 1844, most if not all of the Twelve had received this ordinance. Then in late

---

[20]  HC 5:2. It was not until November 1845 that the first Endowment was performed in the Nauvoo Temple.

March, 1844, the Prophet told the Twelve that he had conferred all keys and powers upon the Twelve to enable them to lead the Church if he should be gone. The Prophet had prepared the Twelve in all the important temple ordinances. The Twelve were prepared to continue the ordinance work that the Prophet had restored. Neither Sidney Rigdon, William Law, James J. Strang nor any of those who apostatized right after the Prophet's death had the authority or the keys to perform this work—only the Twelve possessed this authority and these keys.

While the Prophet was coming to understand and implement the crowning ordinances of exaltation during the years 1840-43, the work of the Church was going forth in Nauvoo and internationally. The Twelve had been sent out multiple times on missions to spread the gospel. And in Illinois, the Prophet attended to the building up of Nauvoo. One of the first items of importance was to secure a charter from the State of Illinois, giving Nauvoo judicial powers, including the right to issue writs of *habeas corpus*, and the power to maintain a police force (the Nauvoo Legion)—both of which could provide protection for the saints.

## John C. Bennett

In June 1840, a man named John C. Bennett came to Nauvoo. He knew Sidney Rigdon from days in Ohio when both had been followers of Alexander Campbell. Bennett was a man with an impressive resume: He was quartermaster general of the Illinois militia; he was a professor, and he was a doctor—a gynecologist. ("John C. Bennett, *Encyclopedia of Latter-day Saint History*, 88.) Joseph was aware of Bennett, and some years previously had invited Bennett to join with the saints. When Bennett arrived in Nauvoo he offered to help the saints secure the charter from the Illinois Legislature, and Joseph accepted his help. Bennett was successful in this. The State granted the Charter, and the Nauvoo government was put into effect in February of 1841. The citizens elected John C. Bennett to be their first Mayor. Bennett was quickly embraced by the Prophet, and in April 1841, Bennett was also sustained as a counselor in the First Presidency. Bennett was flamboyant and dynamic, and was a persuasive person. But he also had some major character flaws that began to surface very quickly. No sooner had Bennett heard some rumors about plural marriage than he began to persuade some young women to engage in immoral acts with him. He used the prestige of his positions as mayor, counselor to President Smith, and gynecologist for his own indulgences. He did not have the Prophet's authority to either preach or practice plural marriage, but he proceeded to have several affairs.[21] In the summer of 1841, information arrived in Nauvoo that Bennett had deserted a wife and children in Ohio, but this information was not confirmed until several months later.[22] In 1842, it became known that Bennett "went to some of the females of the city who knew nothing of him but as an honorable man, and began to teach them that promiscuous intercourse between the sexes was a doctrine believed in by Latter-day Saints, and that there was no harm in it."[23] When Bennett's affairs surfaced in public, he resigned as mayor on May 19, 1842 (HC 5:12). Then on May 25th he was excommunicated (HC 5:18). Bennett left Nauvoo, but he did not go quietly. He proceeded to

---

[21] Multiple sources report such evidence. Hales and Smith conclude that one of them was Sarah Pratt (wife of Orson). Brian C. Hales and Gordon L. Smith, "A Response to Grant Palmer's 'Sexual Allegations Against Joseph Smith and the Beginnings of Polygamy in Nauvoo.'" Sidney Rigdon's biographer Mark McKiernan wrote that Stephen Markham accused Bennett of engaging in sexual improprieties with Nancy Rigdon. F. Mark McKiernan, *The Voice of One Crying in the Wilderness: Sidney Rigdon, Religious Reformer (1793-1876)* (Coronado Press, 1971; Herald House 1979, 1986), 120, citing: George W. Robinson to John C. Bennett, September 1, 1842; Bennett, *History of the Saints*, 248.

[22] F. Mark McKiernan, 112-13. Reportedly, Bennett had abandoned a wife and three children in McConnelsville, Ohio.

[23] HC 5:35-36; see also, McKiernan, 113. McKiernan also reports that Bennett attempted suicide by poison when his adultery was discovered. *Id.*

immediately publish a book (*History of the Saints*) that accused Joseph of adultery and polygamy, and which made other libelous statements about the Prophet and the Church. Bennett's vindictive efforts played a role in the assassination of Joseph in 1844. Bennett perverted the doctrine of plural marriage and took advantage of his positions of authority and of being a gynecologist, and sought illicit relationships with women in Nauvoo. ("John C. Bennett," *Encyclopedia of Latter-day Saint History*, 89.)

## Introduction to the Twelve and Others

In May of 1842, Joseph learned that Gov. Boggs was seriously injured in a failed assassination attempt on his life and that Gov. Boggs was accusing Joseph of the assault. This led Joseph to live in hiding for much of the remainder of that year, until the writ for extradition was dismissed by the court in January of 1843. Notwithstanding this distraction and the Bennett matter, in this same period of time Joseph began individually introducing plural marriage to the members of the Quorum of the Twelve and to a few other faithful saints. The first two members of the Quorum of the Twelve to take plural wives were Brigham Young in June of 1842, and Heber C. Kimball later in 1842. Thereafter, beginning in 1843, seven additional members of the Quorum of the Twelve accepted the doctrine of plural marriage and took plural wives: William Smith; Willard Richards (January); Orson Hyde (in February or March); Lyman Wight (by July); Parley P. Pratt (July 24th); John Taylor (December 12th); and John E. Page. (See appendix A, at end of chapter.) Orson Pratt, Wilford Woodruff and George A. Smith never did take a plural wife before the Prophet's death, but they were taught and accepted the doctrine of plural marriage, and they each took a plural wife shortly after the Prophet's death. Similarly, Amasa Lyman, the Apostle who was not a member of the Twelve, also accepted the doctrine of plural marriage before the Prophet's death, and then took a plural wife shortly after the Prophet's death. There was no opposition to the doctrine of plural marriage from the Council of the Twelve. This unanimous support from the Twelve is evidence that all twelve of these brethren received the divine witness from the Lord of the divinity of this doctrine.

Every one of the Twelve accepted and embraced the restored doctrine of plural marriage, and for most or all of them it was a trial of their faith to do it. Brigham Young stated that when he learned of plural marriage, "it was the first time in my life that I had desired the grave." "I had to pray unceasingly, and I had to exercise faith and the Lord revealed to me the truth of it and that satisfied me."[24] Heber C. Kimball was similarly distraught when he learned about the doctrine, and he only found comfort after his wife Vilate had a manifestation telling her that plural marriage was of God.[25]

## Hyrum Smith

Hyrum was not one of the first saints to be introduced to the doctrine of plural marriage. Apparently, the principle was not presented to him until the spring of 1843. For a year prior to his accepting plural marriage, Hyrum was one of the most vocal critics of plural marriage and anyone who would practice it. Hyrum was one of the nine faithful brethren to whom the Prophet introduced the endowment on May 4, 1842. Later that month, Bennett's immorality was exposed and he was excommunicated. Thereafter Bennett immediately began a campaign to expose plural marriage and to accuse Mormon leaders of

---

[24] LDS Essay on Plural Marriage - Kirtland and Nauvoo Era, www.lds.org, citing: JD 3:266 for first quote, and for the second quote: Brigham Young, Discourse, June 18, 1865, George D. Watt Papers, Church History Library, Salt Lake City; see also JD 3:266 and 11:128.
[25] Orson F. Whitney, The Life of Heber C. Kimball (Salt Lake City: Bookcraft, 1888, 1945), 326-27.

practicing it. Hyrum spoke out against Bennett and against his arguments. But Hyrum did not know that Joseph had been practicing it and introducing it to others. Bennett's attacks certainly delayed the Prophet's plans to introduce plural marriage to others. When Hyrum and others denied that plural marriage was being practiced, Joseph did not correct them. This led some people to accuse Joseph of denying that it existed.

In May of 1843 Joseph said some things in a couple of talks that led Hyrum to believe that Joseph must have been teaching some things to Brigham and the Twelve which he had not taught him. Hyrum took Brigham Young aside, asking him what additional information Joseph may have taught Brigham which had not been shared with him (Hyrum). At the end of this conversation, Hyrum learned that Joseph had already been practicing and performing plural marriages (Ehat, 35-36, 40). At that time, or shortly thereafter, Hyrum became converted to the principle, and then he became a strong proponent for it, including helping Emma to eventually accept it (Ehat, 53-54). Hyrum's first wife, Jerusha, had died in 1837. Later, in December 1837, Hyrum married Mary Fielding. Because of these two marriages, Hyrum contemplated whether he would be with both wives in the next life; this certainly helped him to accept that eternal marriage can properly include more than one wife.

## Emma Smith

The reluctance of Emma to accept plural marriage and her later denial of it after the Prophet's death are well known. Nevertheless, there are many witnesses that she did accept the doctrine during the Prophet's life. It is not known when Joseph first presented the doctrine to her. But in May of 1843, prior to Hyrum's acceptance of the doctrine, Emma gave an initial endorsement to it, with the condition, "if you will let me choose" the plural wives, whereupon she chose Emily and Eliza Partridge as wives for Joseph (Ehat, 37). (Interestingly, these two sisters had already been sealed to Joseph two months earlier. See appendix C, at end of chapter.) After Emma's initial acceptance, she then opposed it again. Hyrum prevailed upon Joseph to write down the revelation, which he did on July 12, 1843, and thereafter Hyrum offered to present the revelation to Emma, as he was convinced that he could get Emma to accept it. Hyrum's initial effort was not successful (Ehat, 43), and resulted in Joseph's telling Hyrum that he was not surprised because he knew Emma better than did Hyrum.[26] Nevertheless, eventually in August of 1843, Emma was brought to accept the doctrine in what appeared to be a total and solid embracement. Maria Jane Woodward reported that one evening in August there was an intense discussion between Joseph and Emma, and that Joseph asked Jane to go and get Hyrum, which she did. Hyrum returned and joined the discussion. The next day, Jane said that Emma told her that she knew that "the principle of plural marriage was right . . . . and is from our Father in Heaven," and she remarked at how persuasive Hyrum was (Ehat, 52-54). Shortly thereafter, on September 28, 1843, Emma and five additional brothers were endowed in an upper room of the Mansion House (Ehat, 45, 55-56). Thereafter, Emma was closely involved in administering part of the endowment to other females, and this was done in the upstairs of the Mansion House (Ehat, 63-64). While the sealing of a husband and wife is a separate ordinance from the endowment, the endowment is a pre-requisite to the sealing. Thus, the prophet taught that if a person would not accept plural marriage then that person was not ready to be endowed.

---

[26] Ivan J. Barrett, *Joseph Smith and the Restoration* (Brigham Young University Press, 1967), 439, citing Brigham H. Roberts, *A Comprehensive History of the Church* (Salt Lake City: Deseret Book Co., 1930) vol. 2, 106-07.

# Orson Hyde and Nancy Marinda Hyde

While Orson Hyde was away on a mission from 1840 - 1842 (the mission that took him to Palestine), on December 3, 1841, Joseph Smith received a revelation instructing him to prepare a better place for Nancy Marinda Hyde to reside, and instructing her to "hearken to the counsel of my servant Joseph in all things whatsoever he shall teach unto her." Joseph's diary includes an entry stating: "Apr 42 Marinda Johnson to Joseph Smith 1843."[27] Some, including Marinda, have characterized this entry as a marriage, but apparently this was to be an "eternity-only seal-ing."[28] Marinda and Orson had not been married for eternity, because their marriage was performed before the ordinance of eternal marriage was restored. In early 1843, Orson returned to Nauvoo, and in Orson Hyde's own words:

> In the month of February or March, 1843, I was married to Miss Martha R. Browitt, by Joseph Smith, the martyred prophet, and by him she was sealed to me for time and all eternity in Nauvoo, Illinois. . . . and in the month of April, I was married . . . to Mrs. Mary Ann Price, . . .

---

[27] Brian C. and Laura H. Hales, *Joseph Smith's Polygamy*, online article about "Marinda Nancy Johnson," footnote 3 which reads: "Photography of hologram in Richard E. Turley, Jr. *Selected Collections from the Archives of The Church of Jesus Christ of Latter-day Saints* (Provo, Utah: Brigham Young University Press, 2002): 1: DVD 20. See also Scott Faulring, ed., *An American Prophet's Record: The Diaries and Journals of Joseph Smith* (Salt Lake City: Signature Books, 1989), 396." See also footnote 30.

[28] *Id.* Hales reports that John D. Lee said that he witnessed this sealing. He said he recalls that Marinda was "sealed to Joseph for an eternal state." Although Lee added, "but I do not assert the fact," whatever that means. Hales gives the citation: John D. Lee and W. W. Bishop, eds., *Mormonism Unveiled, or, The Life and Confessions of the Late Mormon Bishop* (St. Louis: Byron, Brand, 1877), 147.

> while the woman to whom I was first married . . .
> gave her cordial consent to both.[29]

Then, in May of 1843 there was a sealing of Joseph to Marinda.[30] Marinda's sealing to Joseph in May took place two months after Orson's sealing to Martha Browitt, and presumably Marinda and Orson had full knowledge of both. Apparently, it was the understanding of Marinda, Orson and Joseph that the Orson-Marinda marriage was only for time, and that the Marinda-Joseph marriage was only for the next life. In any event, there is no evidence that Marinda was simultaneously married to Orson and Joseph at the same time, nor is there evidence that Joseph ever had any marital relations with Marinda. After this, Orson and Marinda had seven additional children (for a total of eight), and Orson married seven additional women.[31] But in 1870 Marinda and Orson were divorced.[32]

## William Smith, John E. Page and Lyman Wight

Less is known about William Smith's, John E. Page's and Lyman Wight's initial experiences being introduced to plural marriage. William Smith had at least three wives who later came to live in Utah: Precilla M. Smith, Sarah Libby and Hannah Libby.[33] William Smith's excommunication in December 1845 was primarily due to his attempting to take over leadership of the

---

[29] Affidavit of Orson Hyde, September 13, 1869, MS 3423, CHL; affidavit was copied into Joseph F. Smith Affidavit Books, 2:45, published in Joseph Fielding Smith, *Blood Atonement and the Origin of Plural Marriage* (Salt Lake City: Deseret News 1905), 74.

[30] Records do not make it clear whether this was the original sealing of Marinda to Joseph, or whether it was a re-sealing for what was referred to in Joseph's records for April 1842. See also footnote 27.

[31] www.wivesofjosephsmith.org/11-MarindaJohnsonHyde.htm

[32] *Id.*

[33] Joseph F. Smith, Jr., *Blood Atonement and the Origin of Plural Marriage* (Salt Lake City: Deseret News Press, 1905), 49.

Church after his setting apart as Patriarch to the Church.[34] For a short time William participated in the church of James J. Strang. From 1849-1851 William Smith attempted to lead his own church. One of his adherents, Jason W. Briggs, said he left William's church because William practiced polygamy.[35] Eventually, William became a part of the RLDS movement.

Similarly, John E. Page had more than one plural wife. His wife, Mary Eaton, of Independence, told Joseph Fielding Smith in 1904 that she "gave" him "other wives."[36] John E. Page was excommunicated June 27, 1846, due to his continued insubordination; he refused to obey the direction of Brigham Young to move west with the main body of the saints. Following his excommunication, he was involved in four of the different apostate groups.

Lyman Wight's practicing of polygamy is reported in the History of the Reorganized Church.[37] Likewise, Lyman Wight refused to be told what to do by anybody. He stated this to some people, but the Twelve were not sure about his defiance for some time. When they did obtain evidence that Wight had set up his own church, he was excommunicated on February 12, 1849.[38] William Smith, John E. Page and Lyman Wight all apostatized from the Church because of pride and insubordination. Each of them sought to establish themselves as great leaders in their own organizations. It was their pride that led them astray. Their departures were not due to opposition to plural marriage; all of them had accepted this doctrine by 1844.[39] Later they may

---

[34] William Smith also published a pamphlet that was critical of the Twelve. Hoyt W. Brewster, Jr., *Prophets, Priesthood Keys and Succession* (Salt Lake City: Deseret Book Company, 1991), 65.

[35] Joseph F. Smith, Jr., *Blood Atonement*, 49.

[36] *Id.*, 49-50.

[37] Id., p. 49. See also Gary James Bergera, "Identifying the Earliest Mormon Polygamists, 1841-44," *Dialogue: A Journal of Mormon Thought* (2005), 18-19 (for Page), 34-36 (for Wm. Smith), 39-42 (for Wight).

[38] Garr, Cannon & Cowan, "Lyman Wight," *Encyclopedia of Latter-day Saint History* (Salt Lake City: Deseret Book Company, 2000).

[39] Bergera, 18-19 (for Page), 34-36 (for Wm. Smith), 39-42 (for Wight).

have voiced opposition to it, but it was not the cause of their excommunications.[40]

In addition to the nine members of the Quorum of the Twelve who took plural wives before the Prophet's death, there were eighteen other faithful brothers who also took plural wives before Joseph's death. Included in this number were Hyrum Smith, Ezra Taft Benson, William Clayton, Theodore Turley, John Smith (the Prophet's uncle), Erastus Snow and Isaac Morley. See appendix A, at the end of this chapter, for a list of the brethren who took plural wives.

## Orson Pratt

One of the first of the Apostles to be introduced to plural marriage was Orson Pratt. Orson said that he learned about it from the Prophet as early as 1832.[41] In December 1841, when he returned to Nauvoo from his mission in Great Britain, he was immediately confronted with reports that the Prophet Joseph had tried to seduce his wife. It was Orson's wife, Sarah, who made these accusations, so Orson was in a real predicament. He believed his wife, and he did not directly discuss the matter with Joseph. This matter was devastating to Orson. I don't believe Sarah ever recanted her allegations, and neither did the Prophet ever admit to any impropriety. Orson sided with Sarah. Stephen Markham accused John C. Bennett of sexual improprieties with Sarah Pratt. Markham stated in an affidavit

---

[40] These three Apostles each had a history of insubordination and lack of cooperation. None of them went across the ocean to preach the gospel with the rest of the Quorum of the Twelve when commanded to do so (in D&C 118). John Page decided he had better things to do than to go with Orson Hyde to travel to Palestine and dedicate that land for the return of the Jews. See, e.g., Ronald K. Esplin, "Brigham Young and the Transformation of the 'First' Quorum of the Twelve," in *Lion of the Lord – Essays on the Life and Service of Brigham Young*, Susan Easton Black and Larry C. Porter, eds. (Salt Lake City: Deseret Book, 1995), 65, 67, 69 & 74-75.

[41] Joseph Fielding Smith, *Doctrines of Salvation*, 3:197. See also footnote 5.

that he was in the Pratt home when Sarah was ill and that he saw Bennett and Sarah involved in some improper behavior.[42]

Consequently, Sarah Pratt was excommunicated for adultery on August 20, 1842, and Orson was excommunicated also for siding with Sarah. The Church court found that Sarah had an affair with John C. Bennett,[43] and that Sarah and Orson falsely charged the Prophet with attempting to seduce Sarah. Both Sarah and Orson were later re-baptized. Orson changed his views on what had happened pretty rapidly—eventually believing Joseph's version of events. Orson was re-instated in the Quorum of the Twelve on January 20, 1843, causing Amasa Lyman (who had been called to replace Orson, but had yet to be sustained) to function as an Apostle, but not to be a member of the Quorum until the next vacancy.

By the end of 1842 Orson accepted that the time had come to practice the doctrine of plural marriage, but he did not actually take a second wife until after the death of the Prophet. I would speculate that because of the turmoil surrounding Sarah's allegations against the Prophet, that the Prophet did not press Orson Pratt to take a second wife, but the Prophet did request that most of the Twelve take a plural wife. As a post script to the dispute between the Prophet and Sarah—Sarah remained with Orson for many years, but she harbored a severe dislike for plural marriage. She taught her children to oppose it, even though she allowed Orson to have several plural wives, beginning in 1845. But publicly she said very little. Finally, in 1870 she divorced Orson and began to publicly denounce Orson and the Church for plural marriage. She was excommunicated again on October 4, 1874.[44]

---

[42] See footnote 21.

[43] Witnesses of Sarah's affair included Jacob B. Backenstos, Robert Foster, and Stephen and Zeruiah Goddard. ("Sarah Marinda Bates Pratt," *Wikipedia*.)

[44] In 1877, after Sarah Pratt was excommunicated, she publicly criticized the Church and made many statements about the 1841 incident when she said that Joseph asked her to become one of his plural wives, and that she refused. She was publicly quiet about this for about 35 years. Sarah's initial

I mention this incident involving Orson Pratt because it shows the difficulties experienced by Orson Pratt in coming to accept the doctrine of plural marriage. Orson was not a "yes" man who would not think for himself. He took a stance that directly opposed the Prophet. But later, when he learned more about the situation, he changed his opinion about the matter and recommitted to continue his life's work as a valiant disciple of Jesus Christ. Orson Pratt was a very intelligent man, a gifted speaker and writer, and one of the greatest missionaries the world has ever known. He never acquired great riches, and because of his dispute with the Prophet, he lost his position of seniority in the Quorum of the Twelve, such that at the death of Brigham Young, it was John Taylor and not Orson Pratt who became President of the Church. Orson's life demonstrates his powerful witness of the restored gospel of Jesus Christ, and of his determination to serve God with all his heart always. In addition to his several missions in the United States, Orson crossed the Atlantic Ocean and travelled to the British Isles eight different times to preach the gospel there.[45] This required great sacrifice by him and his family. Orson did not rest on his laurels. He was faithful to the end—a witness of the restored gospel of Jesus Christ and of the divinity of the doctrine of plural marriage.

## Sidney Rigdon and Nancy Rigdon

In the spring of 1842, the Prophet Joseph Smith asked Nancy Rigdon, the daughter of Sidney Ridgon, to become his plural wife. Nancy refused, and she told her father of the incident,

characterization of the incident was that of Joseph's attempting to seduce her; years later she described it as Joseph's requesting that she become his plural wife. See "Sarah Marinda Bates Pratt," *Wikipedia*, footnote 14, citing: Van Wagoner, R. S. & Walker, S. C. (1982) *A Book of Mormons*, Salt Lake City: Signature Books, 212.

[45] Susan Easton Black, *Who's Who in the Doctrine & Covenants* (Salt Lake City: Deseret Book Co., 1997), 238.

including sharing with her father a writing that the Prophet gave to her that did not speak specifically of plural marriage, but which did state that it is important to obey all of God's commandments, and that some commandments from God are to do things that would be wrong in other circumstances. (See appendix B, at the end of chapter.) The result of this was a meeting in the Rigdon home on June 28, 1842, attended by Sidney, the Prophet, Bishop George Miller, Nancy, George W. Robinson (Nancy's brother-in-law), and John W. Rigdon (Nancy's brother).[46] Neither Sidney nor the Prophet described the substance of this meeting in detail (HC 5:46), but Robinson gave his version. That version is that Joseph admitted asking Nancy to marry him as a plural wife and that Nancy refused.[47] Robinson accused Joseph of attempting to seduce Nancy, and he described this as an immoral act of debauchery. Shortly thereafter, Robinson left the Church. But Sidney did not leave the Church, and he did not proceed to openly attack the Prophet. It is my opinion that Sidney recognized this as one of the Prophet's attempts to marry a plural wife, but not an effort to seduce Nancy. Sidney opposed plural marriage, but he was not prepared to declare Joseph a fallen prophet for such actions. In fact, in September of 1842, Sidney specifically refuted rumors that he believed Joseph to be a fallen prophet; he confirmed his support of Joseph as the Lord's Prophet in a statement published in the *Times and Seasons*: "I unequivocally state, that I never thought so—but declare that I know he is a prophet of the Lord, called and chosen in this last dispensation, to roll on the Kingdom of God for the last time." (McKiernan, 121; *Times and Seasons*, September 15, 1842.)

This incident shows several things. First, it shows that Sidney

---

[46] In an affidavit dated July 28, 1905, John W. Rigdon describes this incident and the ensuing meeting at the Rigdon home with Joseph, Sidney, Nancy and others. But John mistakenly dates this as occurring in 1843 or 1844. Joseph F. Smith, Jr., *Blood Atonement and the Origin of Plural Marriage* (Salt Lake City: Deseret News Press, 1905), 83.

[47] Legg, 116-19; see also Black, *Who's Who in the Doctrine and Covenants*, 246.

Rigdon was fully aware that Joseph taught and attempted to practice plural marriage. Second, it is evidence that Rigdon did not support the Prophet in this doctrine and practice. Third, it demonstrates that Rigdon did not regard Joseph's belief in this doctrine as something that disqualified him from being the Lord's Prophet. Fourth, the incident left no evidence of any adultery on the part of Joseph nor of any attempt to seduce Nancy or anyone else. And fifth, this incident caused a serious estrangement between the Prophet and Sidney Rigdon. Clearly Sidney did not share the Prophet's concern and urgency to restore the practice of plural marriage. From the Prophet's point of view, Sidney failed the Abrahamic test of obeying God's commandment. When you know the commandment comes from God, like Abraham did, you have to obey it. Sidney failed this test, and this lessoned his ability to help the Prophet. Thus, even though Sidney professed his allegiance to the Prophet in his statement in the *Times and Seasons* on September 15, 1842, the Prophet lost faith in Sidney. And this distrust was increased when John C. Bennett's book, *History of the Saints*, was published in late 1842, which included a rather thorough description of the Nancy Rigdon incident, including Bennett's publishing of the writing that the Prophet had sent to Nancy as a part of his requesting her to become a plural wife.[48] The fact that Bennett had access to so much private information was a reason for the Prophet to have increased distrust for Sidney. Then, in early 1843, Orson Pratt obtained and then shared with the Prophet a letter from John C. Bennett asking Sidney Rigdon and Orson Pratt to help Bennett get Joseph extradited to Missouri to be tried there. It is totally understandable why Joseph sought to have Rigdon released from his calling in the First Presidency.

On March 27, 1843, Joseph wrote a letter to Sidney Rigdon, advising Sidney that his membership in the Church was in

---

[48] See appendix B, at end of chapter. That letter is actually a very beautiful statement about the need to keep God's commandments in order to be happy. See HC 5:134-36.

question because of his dealings with John C. Bennett. (HC 5:312-14; and Legg, 122-23.) Rigdon promptly replied and denied all charges in such a manner that the matter was effectively dismissed (HC 5:314-16). Later, at the Church conference on October 7 and 8, 1843, Joseph again tried to expel Sidney or at least to have him released as First Counselor in the First Presidency (HC 6:47-49). But the Prophet's proposal failed. Ammon W. Babbot and William Law spoke in favor of Sidney (HC 6: 49). When Hyrum suggested showing some mercy for their aged companion, this seemed to tip the scales in favor of Rigdon, and he was again sustained as First Counselor (HC 6:49). Joseph was not happy about this.

But again, this was all setting the stage for the succession conflict that would unfold ten months later. Those close to the Prophet knew that Joseph had lost confidence in Sidney; that Sidney had rejected the doctrine of plural marriage; and that Joseph would not want Sidney to lead the Church.

The most significant aspect of Joseph's rebuffed invitation to Nancy Rigdon to become a plural wife is not that Nancy rejected the proposal, but how Sidney Ridgon responded to it. What is really puzzling is to try to understand how Sidney could continue to support the Prophet Joseph Smith as the Lord's anointed, when Sidney rejected the doctrine of plural marriage that the Prophet was determined to restore, as God had commanded. Sidney began to openly oppose plural marriage **after** the Prophet's death and **after** the saints unanimously voted for Brigham and the Twelve Apostles to succeed the Prophet. But for Sidney to begin to openly oppose plural marriage **after** he lost the leadership battle, is totally inconsistent with his professed commitment to be faithful to the Prophet and to continue leading the Church as the Prophet Joseph would have wanted. Sidney's subsequent rejection of plural marriage revealed him to be unsupportive of the Prophet and an enemy to Joseph's teachings and directions about plural marriage. Nevertheless,

Sidney refused to conclude from this that the Prophet had fallen from being God's prophet.

How could Sidney possibly reconcile such a stance—that Joseph was God's prophet and yet that his direction on plural marriage was wrong? I submit that part of the answer to this is that Sidney regarded himself as the individual spoken of by Isaiah the prophet—that he Sidney was the one who fulfilled the prophecy of Isaiah: "The voice of him that crieth in the wilderness, Prepare ye the way of the LORD" (Isaiah 40:3). When, immediately after his baptism, Sidney Rigdon went from Kirtland to Palmyra to visit the Prophet Joseph Smith, Sidney stayed at the Prophet's home in December of 1830. At that time Joseph received a revelation for Sidney that included the following comment about what Sidney had already done and what he should yet do for the work of the Lord:

> Thou [Sidney] art blessed, for thou shalt do great things. Behold thou was sent forth, even as John, to prepare the way before me, and before Elijah which should come, and thou knewest it not. . . .
>
> I have looked upon thee and thy works. I have heard thy prayers, and prepared thee for a greater work.

(D& C 35:4, 3.) Sidney regarded himself as the one who fulfilled the prophecies of Isaiah and Malachi, and who would be God's messenger (Isaiah 40:3 and Malachi 3:1) to prepare the way for the Second Coming of the Lord. And it was the Prophet Joseph who had stated this connection in the revelation. The whole basis for Sidney's views about who he was, and his important life's mission was inextricably connected with the Prophet Joseph Smith, and Sidney was not prepared to discard the high views he had about his own importance.

After the Prophet's death, when Sidney returned to Nauvoo

to attempt to secure the reigns of leadership in the Church, he spoke to many of the Saints on Sunday, August 4th and told them that he (Sidney Rigdon) "was the identical man that the ancient prophets had sung about, wrote and rejoiced over, and that he was sent to do the identical work that had been the theme of all the prophets in every preceding generation." (Legg, p. 127; see also HC 7:224.) There was certainly some truth to this. When Parley P. Pratt and Oliver Cowdery brought the message of the restored gospel to Sidney and his congregation in the fall of 1830, Sidney had prepared his congregation for the very message that Pratt and Cowdery preached to them: They were looking for a "restoration of the ancient order of things" (Legg, 25). They were also looking for a restoration of the gifts of the Spirit that had existed in the times of the original apostles (Legg, 27). Thus, when Ridgon finished reading the Book of Mormon, he concluded that "Mormonism was truly the apostolic church divinely restored to the earth" (Legg, 35). The conversion of Sidney Rigdon and most of his congregation in late 1830 provided a gigantic boost for the fledgling, restored Church. There were pockets of people around the world who were looking for the Lord to do a great work in preparation for the Second Coming, and they were prepared to receive the messages brought by the Elders of the Church. (Two other examples of this would be the conversion by Parley P. Pratt of John Taylor's organization in Toronto in 1835, and the conversion of a congregation of over 500 people by Wilford Woodruff in England in 1840.) Sidney Rigdon's acceptance of these messages became a great benefit to the growth of God's kingdom in the last days—and was a part of the fulfillment of ancient prophecies. But, however much Sidney Rigdon may have been a part of the fulfillment of biblical prophecies about the restoration—he was only a part of something much bigger than himself; and his role in fulfillment of ancient prophecies was much less significant than that of the Prophet Joseph Smith. And when Sidney rejected the counsel and directions of the Prophet, Sidney's days were numbered. It appears that he came to regard himself as superior to and insubordinate to the Prophet. He did not have the faith to keep up with the Prophet.

## Presidential Campaign

In early 1844, the Prophet had multiple projects that were occupying him. By late 1843 Joseph decided to mount a campaign for President of the United States. He planned to use the Quorum of the Twelve and over 300 missionaries to carry the campaign throughout the states. Joseph enlisted W. W. Phelps to help in this—especially in preparing his platform document, which the brethren would carry with them during the campaign. The political campaign would be coupled with a vast missionary effort. But while Joseph had the capable assistance of Phelps, Sidney Ridgon was not providing much assistance.[49] At the October 1843 General Conference the saints had sustained him again as First Counselor, but this was over the objection of Joseph—this presented a very unusual situation. And though Rigdon was sustained, he proceeded with making plans to move to Pittsburgh. Since Ridgon opposed plural marriage, his utility to the Prophet was quite limited. By early 1844, most of the Quorum of the Twelve had taken plural wives, and the Prophet had also introduced them to the Endowment and to the sealing ordinances. By late March 1844, the Prophet had conferred all priesthood keys upon the Twelve. This last meeting of the Prophet with the Quorum of the Twelve probably took place on March 22 or 26, 1844,[50] where the Prophet confirmed that he had conferred upon them all the keys, enabling them to lead the

---

[49] Sidney Rigdon (who was to become a resident of Pennsylvania) agreed to be Joseph's vice presidential running mate. As required by the Twelfth Amendment, the Prophet's running mate needed to be the resident of a different state than that of the presidential candidate. Despite Sidney's co-operation in this endeavor, he and Joseph had become somewhat distant in their ecclesiastical relationship.

[50] See footnote 93 in Chapter 5 about "Succession."

Church if he should die. Beginning in late March or early April, eight of the remaining ten Apostles left for their missions to the east. Thus, the only Apostles remaining in Nauvoo in June were John Taylor and Willard Richards.

## William Law

The Prophet's major mission-presidential campaign had been planned for several months, and so it was being undertaken right when the Prophet's practice of plural marriage was about to be exposed. In fact, the eruption was already underway before eight more of the Apostles left on missions by May. On August 12, 1843, shortly after the revelation on plural marriage was recorded, Hyrum Smith read the revelation to a majority of the members of the Nauvoo stake presidency and high council.[51] It was received with mixed reviews—stake president William Marks and his counselor Austin Cowles would not accept plural marriage. Shortly thereafter William Law also learned about plural marriage, and he did not accept it either. Law said that he confronted the Prophet about this and attempted to correct him in private. (*Nauvoo Expositor*, 1 & 2.) Initially Law did not publicly oppose the Prophet.

By January, 1844 Law's non-acceptance of the doctrine grew into opposition to it and to the Prophet. Law proceeded to expose the practice that had previously been kept secret, and he began to declare Joseph to be a fallen prophet, and to do so openly. Law's opposition was especially damaging because he had been Second Counselor in the First Presidency for three years. Law was dropped as a counselor in the First Presidency

---

[51] *Nauvoo Expositor*, June 7, 1844, 2; see also, Joseph F. Smith, *Gospel Doctrine* (1975 edition), 490, and Ehat, 53. See also the affidavits of David Fullmer (June 15, 1869) and Leonard Soby (March 23, 1886) printed in Joseph F. Smith, Jr., *Blood Atonement*, 79-81.

on January 8, 1844 (Ehat, 76).[52] Thereafter Law became bitter, and he sought to bring down the Prophet. Law then combined with approximately two hundred others in what turned into a plan to kill Joseph. A couple of teenage boys advised Joseph of the plot in March of 1844[53], and on March 24, 1844, Joseph publicly announced that he knew of the plot to kill him, and he publicly announced the names of several key men involved in the plot—William Law, Wilson Law, Joseph Jackson, Robert D. Foster, and Chauncey Higbee (HC 6:272 and Ehat, 93). The Prophet knew that his secret teaching and practice of plural marriage was about to be blown wide open. It was with this background that the Prophet prepared and on April 7, 1844 delivered his famous King Follett Discourse (HC 6:302-17). In that address, he revealed several doctrines that were both profound and provocative. He taught that God previously went through his own experience in mortality; he taught that the potential of mankind is to become gods; and he taught that there is an intelligent essence in every human being that is as eternal as God, and that God gave us the opportunity to come to earth to obtain a body and to become like Him. These teachings were received with joy and gladness by the faithful saints, but William Law and other apostates immediately attacked the Prophet's teachings, claiming them to be false and of the devil. This served to accelerate Law's plans to depose Joseph Smith and take over the leadership of the Church. But Law's attempted coup was not successful; it only exposed his many flaws to the saints.

---

[52] Joseph wrote that on January 8th: "I also had an interview with William Law in the streets" (HC 6:171). Apparently, this was when Law was advised that he was dropped as a counselor.

[53] The two young men were Dennison Harris and Robert Scott. William E. Berrett, *The Restored Church*, (Salt Lake City: Deseret Book Co., 1961) 169-71, and sources cited therein. The existence of this plot was further confirmed by two other men, neither of whom were Mormons—Dr. Abiathar Williams and Marenus G. Eaton. Andrew F. Ehat, *Joseph Smith's Introduction of Temple Ordinances and the 1844 Succession Question* (Master's Thesis, Dept. of History, BYU 1982), 93.

Law was excommunicated on April 18, 1844,[54] after which he promptly organized his own church[55]—claiming that Joseph was a fallen prophet and claiming that Law's church was carrying on with the truth, but without plural marriage, without celestial marriage, without temple ordinances, and without a belief in man's potential for exaltation. Law's actions also totally disregarded the role of the Quorum of Twelve Apostles. And Law's actions were more bent on criticizing and condemning Joseph Smith for multiple matters, rather than on advancing the work of the Lord. William Law and his wife, Jane, were excommunicated for "unchristianlike" conduct (HC 6:341). Law's actions, including his publishing the *Nauvoo Expositor*, were mostly intended to condemn Joseph and to salvage Law's own reputation. In any event, the vindictive steps taken by William Law never resonated with very many of the saints.[56] On June 16, 1844, Joseph then delivered his "Plurality of Gods" Discourse, which was a bold, public rebuke to William Law for his publicly criticizing what the Prophet taught in his "King Follett Discourse" (HC 6:473-79).

---

[54] HC 6:341. On April 18, 1844 William Law, Jane Law (William's wife), Wilson Law, and Robert D. Foster were all excommunicated. Joseph named Apostle Amasa Lyman to be a new member of the First Presidency (but Lyman was never sustained or set apart). Amasa Lyman had briefly been a member of the Quorum of the Twelve after Orson Pratt's excommunication. But upon Orson's re-instatement, Amasa was dropped from the Quorum until the next vacancy.

[55] Law established himself as "prophet," with Austin Cowles and Wilson Law as counselors. See, e.g., "Austin Cowles," *Wikipedia*.

[56] An interesting post script to this is that later, in 1850, William Law affiliated with a new church that William Smith organized in 1850, where Lyman Wight served as a counselor to William Smith. Hoyt W. Brewster, Jr., *Prophets, Priesthood Keys and Succession*, (Salt Lake City: Deseret Book Company, 1991), p. 65. Since both William Smith and Lyman Wight practiced plural marriage during the lifetime of Joseph Smith, it is interesting to see William Law submitting to their authority in that church, when the practice of plural marriage was one of the main reasons given by Law for declaring Joseph Smith to be a fallen prophet.

## Nauvoo Expositor

William Law called his church the "True Church of Jesus Christ of Latter Day Saints" or "Reformed Mormon Church." William Law combined with his brother Wilson, Robert and Charles Foster, Chauncey and Francis Higbee, Charles Irvins, and Sylvester Emmons (editor) to start the newspaper, the *Nauvoo Expositor*,[57] for the purpose of advancing his church and to publicize the fact that Joseph was secretly teaching and practicing plural marriage, and for the purpose of accusing Joseph Smith of adultery and several other crimes and perceived flaws. In early May, Law announced his intent to publish the new paper.[58] William Law, Robert Foster and Joseph Jackson then filed criminal complaints against Joseph for adultery, perjury and receiving stolen property. Joseph learned of the criminal charges against him on Saturday, May 25, 1844 (HC 6:412-13). The following Monday (May 27th) Joseph responded, with the assistance of his attorneys, and denied these charges and requested a speedy trial. The prosecution then requested and obtained a postponement. (HC 6:413). This matter never came to trial before the Prophet's death.

On June 7th, the first and only issue of the *Nauvoo Expositor* was published. This marked the full eruption of contention and discord and threatenings and open hostilities in Nauvoo. In the *Nauvoo Expositor* Law placed a lengthy statement of the reasons for his conclusion that Joseph was a fallen prophet. By so doing he exposed many elements of his own apostasy. It was not just the fact that Law could not accept the doctrine of plural marriage. Law also attacked the doctrine of the divine potential of mankind to be exalted, which includes the doctrine

---

[57] *Nauvoo Expositor*, June 7, 1844, 1, 2 and 4.

[58] William Law and the other publishers acknowledged that they were "seceders" from the Church, and they published a lengthy "Preamble" setting for the reasons for their forming a new church. *Nauvoo Expositor*, June 7, 1844, 1-2.

of celestial marriage. Law criticized the Prophet for being too hasty in calling for the saints to gather to America. Law accused the Prophet of personally profiting from the saints around the world by taking their monies for his own benefit. These additional criticisms indirectly attacked the need for a temple, and the ordinances of the temple, and the power of the Priesthood. Law criticized the Prophet for attempting to unite church and state—an excessive mingling of religion and government. Law criticized the Prophet for having hostility towards Missouri, and Law called for the repeal of the Nauvoo Charter. All of this exposed Law's own doctrinal flaws and showed that he had allowed his personal criticisms of the Prophet to turn himself into an apostate.

Law's own words showed that he rejected multiple fundamental doctrines of the restored church. Like both Rigdon and Cowdery, Law began to diverge from the teachings of the Prophet. Law saw himself as not only equal with the Prophet, but superior to him. And Law's writings demonstrate that he had gone astray. Law's words and actions showed that he was out of tune with the Spirit of the Lord in many things, not just in his failure to accept plural marriage.

## Initial Secrecy

On more than one occasion the Prophet wrote that he could not state or write some of the things that he saw and knew about heaven because the saints would not be able to handle it. Joseph initially made such a statement at the end of the written account of the vision of the three degrees of glory that he and Sidney Rigdon experienced in 1832 (D&C 76:114-15). Joseph made a similar statement on May 21, 1843, when he said:

> Paul ascended into the third heavens [2 Corinthians 12:1-4], and he could understand the three principal rounds of Jacob's ladder—the

telestial, the terrestrial, and the celestial glories
or kingdoms, where Paul saw and heard things
which were not lawful for him to utter. I could
explain a hundred fold more than I ever have of
the glories of the kingdoms manifested to me in
the vision, were I permitted, and were the people
prepared to receive them. . . . (HC 5:402-3)

In preaching to the saints on July 16, 1843, Joseph made
similar comments again: "[O]n account of the unbelief of the
people, I cannot reveal the fulness of these things at present"
(HC 5:510). The world and many saints were not ready to receive
many truths about heaven that the Prophet knew. And therefore, the Prophet's withholding such information from them
at certain times was the right thing to do. I believe that such
reasoning applies to many things about heaven, but it certainly
applies to plural marriage because the minds of most people are
so set against its morality that they are not able to accept that
under certain circumstances it can be pure and holy, and that
it exists in the highest kingdom of heaven.

The Prophet's two-track approach to plural marriage—practicing it and keeping it secret—led some to accuse him of being a
fallen prophet. Some had accused Joseph of this in 1837-38. And
that episode of dissent led to the excommunication of a number
of people. But the plural marriage matter in Nauvoo caused a
lot more accusations and disruption—plus, the very nature of
polygamy accusations was such that almost everyone was eager
to hear and to talk about it.

For the three years prior to his death, Joseph seemed to be
sending messages that denied the doctrine and practice of polygamy, but secretly among the most devout Mormons, he was
aggressively campaigning to persuade many Church leaders to
believe in and practice it. It was inevitable that this approach
would eventually erupt and create problems—which it did.
One might also have expected this to cause the disintegration

of the Church—but that did not happen. The Church survived plural marriage because the saints were moral and pure, and they accepted and practiced plural marriage for pure and noble reasons, not because of base or impure desires.

Some writers have stated that Joseph Smith publicly denied that he practiced or taught plural marriage. I don't think this is technically accurate. As I have read what the Prophet said and wrote about this—especially in the last three years of his life— he deflected those questions when he did address the subject. Other Church leaders, including Sidney Rigdon and Hyrum Smith denied that plural marriages existed as long as they were unaware of it, and Joseph did not correct them. But I don't believe that Joseph stated that he did not practice or preach plural marriage. All of the statements by Joseph that I have read which are offered to show that Joseph lied about it were not technically lies—they were carefully worded so as not to actually oppose or deny it. For example, on May 26, 1844, Joseph stated that it was absurd to accuse him of being married to several wives when he could only find one (HC 6:411). Some inferred from this that he denied practicing plural marriage, but he actually did not specifically deny it.

Prior to the Prophet's death plural marriage was practiced by Joseph and most of the Twelve Apostles, plus a few other faithful members. But these marriages were kept secret—at least as secret as possible. It was inevitable that some of these secrets would come to light, and this was certainly a factor leading to the Prophet's death. The primary source of such leaks came from men who had been in leadership positions, but who rejected the doctrine of plural marriage, and who then endeavored to expose and destroy Joseph Smith. They were unsuccessful. It was not until 1852—after the saints had settled in the Salt Lake Valley, in Utah, that the Church publicly acknowledged the practice.

Joseph and Hyrum Smith were assassinated while imprisoned in this jail in Carthage, Illinois on June 27, 1844. Statue is the work of D. J. Bawden.

## Quorum of the Twelve Assume Leadership

After the death of Joseph Smith, a conference of the Church was convened on August 8, 1844, where the Church addressed the question of who should succeed the Prophet Joseph Smith. The conference unanimously sustained the proposal of the Twelve Apostles for Brigham Young and the Quorum of the Twelve to lead the Church. The proposal of Sidney Rigdon, that he should lead the Church as "guardian" or "spokesman" was rejected.[59]

---

[59] See also chapter 5. Shortly after this conference, a few men led efforts to establish different churches, arguing that The Church of Jesus Christ of Latter-day Saints had gone astray. But the over-whelming majority of members followed Brigham Young and the Twelve. Sidney Rigdon and James J. Strang were both excommunicated within a month of the August 1844 conference. A year later, William B. Smith also apostatized and formed a new church. John E. Page and Lyman Wight also apostatized and formed

During the four hours of meetings on August 8th, when the leaders discussed the issues related to succession in the Church, no mention was made of the doctrine of plural marriage. And yet that that was one doctrine that hung in the balance as the succession issue was being debated. Sidney Rigdon opposed plural marriage, while the Twelve supported it.

## Increased Practice of Plural Marriage

Following the death of Joseph Smith, the practice of plural marriage continued to be expanded by Brigham Young as new individuals began to take plural wives, including Orson Pratt, Wilford Woodruff, George A. Smith, Lorenzo Snow and others. Also, Brigham Young and Heber C. Kimball began to marry many of Joseph's widows for time only. These marriages were clearly intended to provide support for those of the Prophet's former wives that wanted it. In 1846 the main body of the Church left Nauvoo and headed west. Beginning in July of 1847, the saints began to settle in Utah. Then, in 1852 the Church made public its practice of plural marriage.

Almost all of those who entered into plural marriages during the Prophet's lifetime were discreet in its practice.

---

new churches within a few years. Opposition to plural marriage was not the reason for the forming of these break-off churches. None of these efforts succeeded. After the Church publicly announced its practice of plural marriage (in 1852), some apostates joined together in their disapproval of plural marriage and began a "reorganization" movement, which resulted in the formation of the Reorganized Church of Jesus Christ of Latter Day Saints in 1860, with Joseph Smith, III, as its leader. I have recently noticed that the Community of Christ (formerly the RLDS Church) seems to acknowledge that Joseph did teach and practice plural marriage, but that insist that he repented of this during the last two years of his life. The last half of this position is patently false because it was during this time that he taught this doctrine to dozens of people, that he entered into most of his 33 plural marriages, and that he performed plural marriages for over a dozen other faithful brethren. To contend that Joseph repented of this practice during the last two years of his life is totally false.

Consequently, many people were unaware that it was being practiced, and many people believed that it was Brigham Young who introduced plural marriage into the Church. Thus, you will find that some of the brethren who wrote about Mormon doctrine in the early 1900s devoted writings to make the case that it was Joseph Smith and not Brigham Young who initiated the practice. (See, e.g., Joseph F. Smith in *Gospel Doctrine*, Joseph Fielding Smith in *Blood Atonement and the Origin of Plural Marriage*, and John A. Widtsoe in *Evidences and Reconciliations*.) For 150 years the RLDS Church (now "Community of Christ") refused to accept the fact that plural marriage was instituted by Joseph Smith. Recently the RLDS Church may have come to accept this—but still insisting that Joseph repented of it in the last two years of his life.[60]

## Practice of Plural Marriage Is Suspended

In 1878 the United States Supreme Court issued its ruling in the case of *Reynolds v. United States*, 98 U.S. 145, that Congress had the right to make a law prohibiting the practice of plural marriage, and that this did not violate the First Amendment "free exercise" rights of George Reynolds, a Mormon who had

---

[60] See also footnote 59. On a 2017 visit to the Nauvoo Community of Christ Visitors Center, I found materials indicating that their church now acknowledges that Joseph Smith taught and practiced plural marriage, but that he repented during the last two years of his life. The official Community of Christ website on July 12, 2017 said that plural marriage was a "divisive" issue and that after the Prophet's death "church members who opposed polygamous practice found themselves scattered across the Midwest without a leader or an organized church." In 2017 *Wikipedia* wrote this about the Community of Christ's views about whether Joseph Smith practiced polygamy: "Today, although the Community of Christ has no official position on whether Smith was a polygamist, some members now accept the historical consensus that Smith had multiple wives. Some members have argued that Smith was wrong to introduce polygamy; in any case, most Community of Christ members continue to reject polygamy." In 2018 this statement has been removed from the *Wikipedia* article.

more than one wife. Reynolds was a faithful Latter-day Saint; he was secretary to the First Presidency. He had allowed himself to be arrested, with the intent of appealing his anticipated conviction in order to seek a ruling from the Supreme Court that would uphold his First Amendment right to practice his religious beliefs without infringement by the Congress and the federal government. Reynolds was partly successful, in that his case did make it all the way to the Supreme Court. But the ultimate result was not what he had hoped for. The Court reasoned that the "free exercise" clause is not an absolute right; that Congress can properly regulate conduct; and that laws prohibiting polygamy were within the powers of Congress and were not an infringement upon religious freedom protected by the First Amendment.

The *Reynolds* case was the beginning of the end of plural marriage in the Church. For years—beginning with the Prophet Joseph Smith—the Church had asserted the First Amendment religious freedom to engage in plural marriages, regardless of any state laws that may have prohibited it. And frankly, there was good reason for this interpretation. But the *Reynolds* case changed things. Regardless of whether the ruling was right or wrong, it was nevertheless the law of the land. After the *Reynolds* case the Church continued to perform plural marriages. The Church leadership determined to follow God rather than submit to the law of the land that conflicted with God's commandment. But Congress took notice of the Church's insubordination and passed other laws that imposed penalties on the Church for non-compliance. Eventually, Congress passed the Edmunds-Tucker Act in 1888, which imposed harsh sanctions against the Church for its non-compliance, including empowering the federal government to take ownership and possession of Church properties, including temples. The Church also challenged this law in the Courts, all the way to the Supreme Court. But in 1890, the Court upheld the Edmunds-Tucker Act. This led the Prophet, Wilford Woodruff, to issue the "Manifesto"

(Official Declaration 1 at the end of *The Doctrine and Covenants*), suspending the practice of plural marriage.

Ending the practice of plural marriage caused almost as many problems for the Church as did its initial implementation. Apostles John W. Taylor and Matthias Cowley had differences of opinion with the First Presidency about this matter, which led to both of them being dismissed from the Quorum of the Twelve Apostles In 1905.[61] A full discussion of these matters is not within the scope of this article. But beginning with the Manifesto, the Church was taking a course of full compliance with the law of the land prohibiting further plural marriages.

---

[61] Taylor was excommunicated in 1911. Despite their differences with the First Presidency, both Taylor and Cowley remained believers in the restored gospel of Jesus Christ.

# Appendix A: Other Men Having Plural Marriages Prior to Death of Joseph Smith

(not a complete list)

| Husband | Plural Wife | 1841 | 1842 | 1843 | 1844 |
|---|---|---|---|---|---|
| Hyrum Smith | Mercy Fielding | | | Aug. 11 | |
| | Catherine Phillips | | | Aug. | |
| Brigham Young | Lucy Ann Decker Seeley | June 14 | | | |
| | Augusta Adams Cobb | | | Nov. 2 | |
| | Harriet Elizabeth Cook | | | Nov. 2 | |
| | Clarissa Caroline Decker | | | | May 8 |
| Heber C. Kimball | Sarah Peak Noon | | xx | | |
| John Taylor | Elizabeth Kaighan | | | Dec. 12 | |
| | Jane Ballantyne | | | | Feb. 25 |
| Orson Hyde | Martha R. Browitt | | | Feb/Mar | |
| | Mary Ann Price | | | Apr. | |
| Parley P. Pratt | Elizabeth Brotherton | | | July 24 | |
| Orson Pratt | NONE | | | | |
| William Smith | Mary Ann Covington Sheffield | | xx | | |
| | Mary Jones | | xx | | |
| | Precilla M. | | | | |
| | Sarah Libby | | | | |
| | Hannah Libby | | | | |
| John E. Page | Nancy Bliss (??) | | xx | | |
| | — | | | | |
| Lyman Wight | Mary Hawley | | | by July | |
| | Mary Ann Hobart | | | by July | |
| Wilford Woodruff | NONE | | | | |
| George A. Smith | NONE | | | | |
| Willard Richards | Sarah Longstroth | | | Jan. | |
| | Nancy Longstroth | | | Jan. | |
| James Adams | Roxena Higby Repsher | | | July 11 | |
| Ezra Taft Benson | Pamela Andrus | | | Nov. 19 | |
| Reynolds Cahoon | Lucina Roberts Johnson | late | | | |
| William Clayton | Margaret Moon | | | xx | |
| Joseph Coolidge | Mary Ann Buchanan | | | | xx |
| Howard Egan | Catherine Reese Clawson | | | | early |
| William Felshaw | Charlotte Walters | | | xx? | |
| William Huntington | Harriet Clark | | xx? | | |
| Joseph A. Kelting | Minerva O Woods | | | | xx |
| Vinson Knight | Philinda C. Myrick | | xx | | |
| Isaac Morley | Abigail Leonora Snow | | | xx | |
| Joseph B. Noble | Sarah B. Alley | | | Apr. 5 | |
| John Smith | Mary Aikens | | | | Aug. 13 |
| Erastus Snow | Minerva White | | | | Mar. |
| Theodore Turley | Mary Clift | | xx | | |
| | Eliza Clift | | | | Apr-Mar |
| Edwin D. Wooley | Louisa Chapin Gordon Rising | | | end | |
| | Ellen Wilding | | | end | |
| Lorenzo D. Young | Harriet P. Wheeler Decker | | | | |

This information was obtained primarily from Gary James Bergera, "Identifying the earliest Mormon Polygamists," Smith-Pettit Foundation (2005), published in *Dialogue, Journal of Mormon Thought*.

## Appendix B: Writing of Joseph Smith to Nancy Rigdon

Happiness is the object and design of our existence, and will be the end thereof if we pursue the path that leads to it; and this path is virtue, uprightness, faithfulness, holiness, and keeping all the commandments of God. But we cannot keep all the commandments without first knowing them, and we cannot expect to know all, or more than we now know unless we comply with or keep those we have already received. That which is wrong under one circumstance, may be and often is, right under another. God said thou shalt not kill,—at another time he said thou shalt utterly destroy. This is the principle on which the government of heaven is conducted–by revelation adapted to the circumstances in which the children of the kingdom are placed. Whatever God requires is right, no matter what it is, although we may not see the reason thereof till long after the events transpire. If we seek first the kingdom of God, all good things will be added. So with Solomon—first he asked wisdom, and God gave it him, and with it every desire of his heart, even things which may be considered abominable to all who do not understand the order of heaven only in part, but which, in reality were right, because God gave and sanctioned by special revelation. A parent may whip a child, and justly too, because he stole an apple; whereas, if the child had asked for the apple, and the parent had given it, the child would have eaten it with a better appetite, there would have been no stripes—all the pleasures of the apple would have been received, all the misery of stealing lost. This principle will justly apply to all of God's dealings with his children. Everything that God gives us is lawful and right, and 'tis proper that we should enjoy his gifts and blessings whenever and wherever he is disposed to bestow; but if we should seize upon these same blessings and enjoyments without law, without revelation, without commandment, those blessings and enjoyments would prove cursings and vexations in the end, and we should have to go down in sorrow and wailings of everlasting regret. But in obedience there is joy and peace unspotted, unalloyed, and as God has designed our happiness, the happiness of all his creatures, he never has, he never will institute an ordinance, or give a commandment to his people that is not calculated in its nature to promote that happiness which he has designed, and which will not end in the greatest amount of good and glory to those who become the recipients of his laws and ordinances. Blessings offered, but rejected are no longer blessings, but become like the talent hid in the earth by the wicked and slothful servant–the proffered good returns of the giver, the blessing is bestowed on those who will receive, and occupy; for unto him that hath shall be given, and he shall have abundantly; but unto him that hath not, or will not receive, shall be taken away that which he hath, or might have had.

"Be wise to-day, 'tis madness to defer.
Next day the fatal precedent may plead;
Thus on till wisdom is pushed out of time," Into eternity.

Our heavenly father is more liberal in his views, and boundless in his mercies and blessings, than we are ready to believe or receive, and at the same time is as terrible to the workers of iniquity, more awful in the executions of his punishments, and more ready to detect every false way than we are apt to suppose him to be. He will be enquired of by his children—he says ask and ye shall receive, seek and ye shall find; but if ye will take that which is not your own, or which I have not given you, you shall be rewarded according to your deeds, but no good thing will I withhold from them who walk uprightly before me, and do my will in all things, who will listen to my voice, and to the voice of my servant whom I have sent, for I delight in those who seek diligently to know my precepts, and abide by the laws of my kingdom, for all things shall be made known unto them in mine own due time, and in the end they shall have joy.

*The above statement is supposedly the version that was printed in the Sangamo Journal (Springfield, Illinois, August 19, 1842), which was apparently taken from the document that Joseph Smith gave to Nancy Rigdon on about April of 1842. With a number of minor changes in punctuation and spelling and a few wording edits, this rendition is almost identical to the statement found in HC 5:134-36. See also, McKiernan, Sidney Rigdon, pp. 117-18.*

## Appendix C: Wives of Joseph Smith

### (including those sealed for the next life only)

| Name | Date of Marriage/Sealing | Age at Marriage | Husband (if any) at time of next life sealing |
|---|---|---|---|
| Emma Hale | Jan. 1827 | 22 | |
| Fanny Alger | 1833-1836 | 16-19 | |
| Lucinda Morgan Harris | 1838 | 37 | George W. Harris |
| Louisa Beaman | Apr. 1841 | 26 | |
| Zina Huntington Jacobs | Oct. 1841 | 20 | Henry Jacobs |
| Presendia Huntington Buell | Dec. 1841 | 31 | Norman Buell |
| Agnes Coolbrith | Jan. 1842 | 33 | |
| Sylvia Sessions Lyon | Feb. 1842 | 23 | Windsor Lyon |
| Mary Eliz. Rollins Lightner | Jan. or Feb. 1842 | 23 | Adam Lightner |
| Patty Bartlett Sessions | Mar. 1842 | 47 | David Sessions |
| Marinda Johnson Hyde | Apr. 1842 | 27 | Orson Hyde |
| Elizabeth Davis Durfee | June 1842 | 50 | Jabez Durfee |
| Sarah Kingsley Cleveland | June 1842 | 53 | John Cleveland |
| Eliza R. Snow | June or July 1842 | 38 | |
| Delcena Johnson Sherman | by July 1842 | 37 | |
| Sarah Ann Whitney | July 1842 | 17 | |
| Martha McBride Knight | Aug. 1842 | 37 | |
| Ruth Vose Sayers | Feb. 1843 | 33 | Edward Sayers |
| Flora Ann Woodworth | Spring 1843 | 16 | |
| Emily Dow Partridge | Mar. 1843 | 19 | |
| Eliza Maria Partridge | Mar. 1843 | 22 | |
| Almira Johnson | Apr. 1843 | 30 | |
| Lucy Walker | May 1843 | 17 | |
| Sarah Lawrence | May 1843 | 17 | |
| Maria Lawrence | May 1843 | 19 | |
| Helen Mar Kimball | May 1843 | 14 | |
| Hannah Ells | mid 1843 | 29 | |
| Elvira Cowles Holmes | June 1843 | 29 | Jonathan Holmes |
| Rhoda Richards | June 1843 | 58 | |
| Desdemona Fullmer | July 1843 | 32 | |
| Olive Frost | mid 1843 | 27 | |
| Melissa Lott | Sep. 1843 | 19 | |
| Nancy Winchester | 1843 or 1844 | 14 or 15 | |
| Fanny Young (Murray) | Nov. 1843 | 56 | |

Gary James Bergera, "Identifying the Earliest Mormon Polygamists," Smith-Pettit Foundation (2005) – see www.dialoguejournal.com/up-content/uploads

# Chapter 2

# Joseph Smith's Plural Marriages

Of the 34 women that were sealed to Joseph Smith during his lifetime,[62] most of these sealings were done in the last three years of his life. The chart below shows the years of such sealings/marriages to Joseph Smith, and the number each year:

| 1827 | 1833-1836 | 1838 | 1841 | 1842 | 1843 | 1844 |
|------|-----------|------|------|------|------|------|
| 1 | 1 | 1 | 3 | 11 | 17 | 0 |

The great increase in the number of marriages to Joseph Smith in his last three years shows that something was going on other than the building of a harem for personal gratification. Many of the 28 marriages from 1842-44 were for after-life purposes only. He never lived with most of those wives, which supports the representation that these marriages were for the next life only, and that they were done in compliance with the

---

[62] Historians put the number of marriages as between 34 and 48. Fawn M. Brodie puts the number at 48, D. Michael Quinn at 46, George D. Smith at 38, Todd M. Compton at at least 33, and Richard Lloyd Anderson and Scott H. Faulring at 29. (See "Mormonism and Polygamy," *Wikipedia* on July 14, 2017.) I do not know what the correct number is. Historians dispute the conclusions of Brodie, Quinn and Smith for lack of good evidence for some rumored marriages. For the sake of this discussion I will use the number 34, which is close to the number proposed by Todd M. Compton. For a list of these 34 wives, see appendix C, on the previous page.

Lord's commandment to Joseph Smith. The evidence is that he did not have sexual relations with many of the plural wives, and apparently none with the women sealed to him for the next life, but who were already married. The great number of marriages in the last three years is consistent with his oft-repeated purpose: To obey God's commandment to restore plural marriage. During the Prophet's last three years he set the example, and he spent many hours with several dozen Church leaders and other key individuals, making the case for plural marriage. Joseph said that God threatened to destroy him if he did not do this. Joseph was very bright—he knew that establishing plural marriage could result in his death; but he was also courageous—he was determined to obey God's commandment, regardless of the consequence. During Joseph's last three years, he was successful in converting 27 men to enter into plural marriages. Included in this number were nine members of the Quorum of the Twelve (and the other three were supportive of plural marriage). While the number of Joseph's marriages was kept secret from most of the world for many years, nevertheless it is fully consistent with his stated purposes.

In examining the plural marriages of the Prophet Joseph Smith, I will here respond to two specific criticisms that have been made about Joseph Smith regarding plural marriage: His marriages to Helen Mar Kimball (age 14) and to Nancy Winchester (age 14 or 15); and his sealings to some women who were already married to other men.

## Marriage to a 14-Year-Old

Of Joseph Smith's 33 plural wives, records indicate that at the time of marriage, three of them were 17, two were 16, and one or two were 14. The remainder were all age 19 or older. Because a fourteen-year-old is very young, I will provide a little more historical information about Joseph's marriages to Nancy

Winchester (age 14 or 15) and to Helen Mar Kimball (at age 14 years, 9 months).

The marriage of a fourteen-year-old girl is much less common today than it was 175 years ago. One study I saw showed that in 1880 about one percent of marriages involved a 14-year-old. It is my understanding that in Illinois it was not illegal for a 14-year-old to marry in 1843 or 1844.

There is a lack of documentation on the date of Joseph's marriage to Nancy Winchester—it is not known whether it took place in 1843 or 1844. After Joseph's death Nancy was sealed to the Prophet Joseph Smith in 1846; she may not have even been married to Joseph before his death. Nancy then became a plural wife of Heber C. Kimball. There is no evidence that she and the Prophet ever had sexual relations.

With respect to Helen Mar Kimball we have more information. She was 14 years and 9 months old when she was "sealed" to Joseph Smith (in May of 1843). It has been referred to as a "marriage," but in her *Autobiography*, Helen wrote that her "sealing" to Joseph was "for eternity alone," and there is no evidence that Helen and Joseph ever had sexual relations.[63] Helen's parents (Heber C. and Vilate Kimball) consented to the sealing/marriage, and there is some evidence that they initiated the matter in order secure a link of their family with the Prophet's family into the eternities.[64] For a short period of time after her "marriage" to Joseph Smith, she felt that it interfered with the social life that she desired, including preventing her from attending parties at the Joseph Smith mansion house. But Helen's feelings changed shortly thereafter. Joseph died thirteen months after the "marriage." A year-and-a-half after the

---

[63] "Essay on Plural Marriage in Kirtland and Nauvoo," www.lds.org, footnote 27: Helen Mar Kimball Whitney, Autobiography, [2], Church History Library, Salt Lake City.

[64] *Id.*, footnote 31. See also J. Spencer Fluhman, "A Subject that Can Bear Investigation," in Robert L. Millet, ed., *No Weapon Shall Prosper—New Light on Sensitive issues* (Salt Lake City: Deseret Book Co., 2011) 110-11.

Prophet's death, Helen married Horace Whitney (on February 3, 1846). She and Horace then had eleven children. Helen said she received a witness that plural marriage was of God, and she became a strong advocate for it.[65] Her son, Orson F. Whitney, later became an Apostle, and he wrote the biography of Helen's father and his grandfather, Heber C. Kimball.

## Sealings to Women already Married

Records indicate that Joseph may have been sealed to eleven women who were then currently married.[66] These "sealings" raise additional questions, above and beyond those raised in other plural marriages. If those "sealings" led to marriages in the normal meaning of the word, then this would be bigamy. But those "sealings" were not treated as earthly marriages. And it does not appear that in those eleven cases there were any sexual relations between the women and Joseph. These sealings were regarded as being effective only in the next life. While they are sometimes referred to as "marriages," they were not marriages in this world—they were only for the life after death.

Witnesses report that most of these eleven women were sealed to Joseph Smith only "for eternity," but not to be his

---

[65] Id., footnote 28: "Helen Mar Kimball Whitney, *Plural Marriage as Taught by the Prophet Joseph: A Reply to Joseph Smith, Editor of the Lamoni (Iowa)* "Herald" (Salt Lake City: Juvenile Instructor Office, 1882); Helen Mar Kimball Whitney, *Why We Practice Plural* Marriage (Salt Lake City: Juvenile Instructor Office, 1884)."

[66] Brian C. Hales concludes that there were fourteen such sealings, but other sources support a smaller number. Brian C. Hales, "Joseph Smith's Practice of Plural Marriage" in Laura Harris Hales, ed., *A Reason for Faith* (Provo: Religious Studies Center, BYU and Salt Lake City: Deseret Book Co., 2016), 129-41. Regardless of the number, Hales' research and analysis is good. Hales discusses several reasons for "next life only" sealings to married women: (1) some women had experienced the equivalent of divorce; (2) some had unhappy marriages; (3) some had husbands who were not worthy (e.g., inactive or non-members); and (4) women have a right to choose their eternal companions. *Id.*, at 133-34.

wives on earth. "They were not to be his wives on earth, in mortality, but only after death in the eternities." (John A. Widtsoe, *Gospel Interpretations*, [Bookcraft, 1947], 151.) These sealings did not include intimate relations on earth. Some have disputed this, but there is no competent evidence to support such claims. An example of an "eternity only" marriage would be the one to Nancy Marinda Hyde. She was sealed to the Prophet for "eternity" when she was Orson Hyde's wife. Orson was aware of this. As I understand it there were no sexual relations between Joseph and Marinda.[67] I understand that Joseph's marriages to Elvira Cowles Holmes,[68] Ruth Vose Sayers, Sarah Kingsley Cleveland, and Elizabeth Davis Durfee were also of this same type.

With regard to some of these "eternity only" marriages, witnesses reported that the words used for some of the sealings were "for time and eternity." But it is my understanding that Joseph and those married women nevertheless regarded these sealings/marriages to be only for the next life, and that there were no sexual relations with these women. I understand

---

[67] The allegation has been made that two of Marinda's children, Orson Washington Hyde and Frank George Hyde could be children of Joseph Smith—their names are listed as alleged children in a *Wikipedia* article. But I do not know the source of such allegations. Apparently, it did not originate from Marinda. There doesn't appear to be anything to support this allegation other than speculation.

[68] Joseph's marriage to Elvira Cowles Holmes is interesting because her father, Austin Cowles, became an arch-enemy to the Prophet after he was made aware of the doctrine of plural marriage. At the time, Austin was a member of the Nauvoo Stake Presidency. In 1843, when Hyrum Smith presented the revelation to the Nauvoo Stake Presidency and High Council, Cowles rejected it and became closely aligned with William Law, a counselor in the First Presidency who also rejected the revelation. On April 18, 1844, William Law was excommunicated. Austin Cowles was excommunicated on May 18, 1844. Thereafter, Cowles and Law worked together to form a new church—declaring that the Prophet Joseph Smith was a fallen prophet; and the two also worked together to publish the *Nauvoo Expositor*, which strongly criticized Joseph Smith and which sought to establish their new church.

that Joseph's sealings to Patty Bartlett Sessions, Mary Elizabeth Rollins Lightner, Zina Huntington Jacobs, and Lucinda Morgan Harris are examples of this type of marriage.

Although allegations have been made that Joseph had sexual relations with some of the married women to whom he had been sealed, as previously discussed, there is no good evidence to support such assertions. For example, Richard L. Anderson concludes the evidence shows that there were no sexual relations.[69] Because of this, perhaps the issue does not even warrant discussion. But because of the seriousness of the charge, I have briefly addressed it above and I will discuss a little more about some of the major allegations being made, even though in my opinion the evidence is insufficient to support them.

Allegations have been made that Joseph had relations with five of the married women to whom he was sealed during the same time these women were living with the other husband.[70] These allegations surfaced years later in connection with claims that Joseph was the father of some of their children. Appendix D (at the end of this chapter) is a chart that shows the women listed in a *Wikipedia* article on nine alleged children of Joseph Smith from alleged plural wives. The chart also shows that recent DNA testing has refuted the claims as to six of these. The three remaining children are: (1) Orson Washington Hyde (born Nov. 9, 1843); (2) Frank Henry Hyde (born Jan. 23, 1845 or 1846); and (3) George Algernon Lightner (born March 22,

---

[69] Richard L. Anderson and Scott Faulring, "The Prophet Joseph Smith and His Plural Wives," Oct. 2, 1998—a review of Todd M. Compton, *In Sacred Loneliness: The Plural Wives of Joseph Smith* (Salt Lake City: Signature Books, 1997). See also, Hales, "Joseph Smith's Practice of Plural Marriage," 134.

[70] See, e.g., "Children of Joseph Smith," *Wikipedia* (August 24, 2017). There is no good evidence that Joseph Smith fathered any children from plural wives. With regard to the eleven married woman that were sealed to him, there is no good evidence that he ever had sexual relations with any of them. The above cited *Wikipedia* article lists Mary Frost Pratt (a wife of Parley P. Pratt) as a possible plural wife of Joseph Smith, despite the absence of any legitimate evidence in support of it. DNA evidence proved that Parley P. Pratt was the father of Mary's son Moroni.

1842).[71] I don't believe either of the mothers (Marinda Hyde for the first two, or Mary Elizabeth Rollins Lightner for the third) made such allegations.[72] Frankly, there is no good evidence that supports these three names being on the *Wikipedia* list. Mere speculation is no basis to support such a serious allegation.

It is not unexpected that there would be people who seek for themselves or for other reasons to assert that they were spouses, lovers or children of celebrities—and Joseph Smith was certainly a celebrity in Nauvoo and among Mormons. The honor of being a wife of the Prophet or having a child with the Prophet was something that could motivate false claims about such relationships. But there is no evidence to support the conclusion that Joseph Smith had relations with either Hyde or Lightner. And with respect to Lyon, the only evidence offered is an alleged hearsay statement made by Sylvia Lyon just before she died at 82 years of age, and the main part of the statement has been proven to be false. Just prior to Sylvia's death at the age of 82, Sylvia's daughter, Josephine Rosetta, said that at that time her mother told her that she was the daughter of Joseph.[73]

---

[71] Apparently, there is no DNA evidence for these three. There is no evidence that would support a conclusion that Joseph Smith is their father.

[72] Mary Elizabeth Rollins Lightner was a remarkable woman from an early age. It was she, at age 11 or 12, in late 1830, who read the Book of Mormon that she obtained from Isaac Morley, and which Isaac Morley obtained from missionaries Parley P. Pratt and Oliver Cowdery as they passed through Kirtland on that early missionary journey to Missouri. According to Mary, the Prophet told her as early as 1832 that he wanted her to be one of his plural wives. Nevertheless, in 1841, Mary married Adam Lightner, a good man, but a non-member. Thereafter, in February of 1842, she was sealed to the Prophet "for time and all eternity" by Brigham Young. Lightner recalls that the words of the sealing were "for time and for eternity," but the evidence supports this being a marriage that was for eternity only. There is no evidence of relations between the two. See also Mary E. Lightner, *Autobiography*.

[73] Sylvia's sealing to Joseph Smith was when she was 23. The statement to her daughter would have been made almost 60 years later, and this is apparently the only such statement by Sylvia. The following footnote cites DNA evidence that disproves this.

If true, this would mean that Joseph had sexual relations with Sylvia at the same time she was living with her husband, Windsor. However, a recent DNA test shows that Josephine is not the child of Joseph Smith.[74] This conclusion contradicts the statement that Josephine said her mother made only late in life, before her death at age 82; thus, Sylvia's hearsay statement is of questionable credibility, even if it could be admitted in a court of law, which it cannot be because of its hearsay nature.

During Joseph's lifetime only a few people knew about his plural marriages. It was not until after the Prophet's death that the number of such marriages was known. And then the participants and the Church kept this to themselves for many years. In 1945, Fawn Brodie published the book, *No Man Knows My History*, which publicized the marriage of Joseph Smith with over forty women (according to Brodie) in his lifetime. Ms. Brodie had legitimate documentation for many of her conclusions. This brought into public view the previously hidden facts of these many plural marriages. Subsequently, researchers found ample documentation to confirm some of Brodie's basic conclusions. Today, documentation from Church records and from the personal writings of dozens of contemporaries of Joseph Smith confirms that Joseph was married or sealed to between 29 and 37 different women during his lifetime. Members of the Church today are confronted by an issue that the saints did not face in 1844 and 1845. The extent of Joseph's marriages was not known by most of the saints at the time of his death.

---

[74] A recent DNA analysis concluded that Josephine was not the child of Joseph Smith. The citation for this test result was given in the *Wikipedia* article on the children of Joseph Smith, at footnotes 39 and 40: Perego, Ugo A (11 June 2016). "Supplemental online material for "Was Joseph Smith the biological father of Josephine Lyon? The evidence' presented at the 2016 Mormon History Association Conference in Snowbird, Utah."

## Appendix D Alleged Children of Joseph Smith of Married Women Sealed to Joseph Smith

| Woman (date of marriage) | Name of Child Alleged to Be Son of Joseph Smith | Results of DNA Test | Notes |
|---|---|---|---|
| Zina Huntington Jacobs (Oct. 1841) | Zebulon Jacobs | Neg. | --- |
| Presendia Huntington Buell (Dec. 1841) | Oliver Buell | Neg. | Brodie speculated Oliver was son of Joseph |
| Marinda Johnson Hyde (Apr. 1842) | Frank Henry Hyde | Not Avail. | No factual basis to even list this child |
|  | Orson Washington Hyde | Not Possible | No factual basis to even list this child |
| Mary Elizabeth Rollins Lightner (Jan. 1842) | George Algernon Lightner | Not Possible | No factual basis to even list this child |
| Sylvia Porter Sessions Lyon (Feb. 1842) | Josephine Rosetta Lyon | Neg. | Josephine said that her mother (Sylvia) told her (on her deathbed) that J.S. was her father |
| Mary Ann Frost Stearns Pratt (1843??) | Moroni Pratt | Neg. | No factual basis to list this child. Neither is there any factual basis for listing Mary as a plural wife of J. S. |

This information comes (except for the "Notes," which are mine) from "Children of Joseph Smith," *Wikipedia* (August 24, 2017). From this article, take the link, "Allegations of children born to alleged polygamous wives."

# Chapter 3

## OLIVER COWDERY AND SIDNEY RIGDON

It is interesting and insightful to consider how both Oliver Cowdery and Sidney Rigdon related and interacted with the Prophet Joseph Smith after they learned that he was teaching and practicing plural marriage. While each of them rejected the doctrine of plural marriage, both of them continued to believe that Joseph Smith was the Lord's anointed prophet. These two men had each shared separate, incredible heavenly visions with the Prophet—two of the greatest visions ever recorded in the annals of history. On February 16, 1832, Sidney and the Prophet together had a vision of the celestial kingdom of God, and together they saw God the Father and the resurrected Jesus Christ on the right hand of God. Together they heard the voice of God declaring that Jesus Christ is the Only Begotten Son of God, and that "by him, and through him, and of him the worlds are and were created," and that their inhabitants are the spirit children of God (D&C 76:22-24). Four years later, on April 3, 1836, in the newly dedicated Kirtland Temple, Oliver was with the Prophet when the Savior appeared to them and accepted the Temple. Together they "saw the Lord standing upon the breastwork of the pulpit, before us; and under his feet was a paved work of pure gold, in color like amber. His eyes were as a flame of fire; the hair of his head was white like the pure snow; his countenance shone above the brightness of the sun; and his voice was as the sound of the rushing of great waters, even the voice of Jehovah" (D&C 110:2-3). Then, a few moments later, Oliver was present when three great ancient prophets appeared and committed to them important priesthood keys; Moses, Elias and Elijah in turn appeared to Joseph and Oliver and delivered messages and powers to them.

All Latter-day Saints believe the accounts of these heavenly manifestations—but Sidney and Oliver were each privileged to be with the Prophet when they happened. Each of these great men was given great priesthood authority in the Church. And for a period of time each of them was a great and powerful leader in the Church. But both of them did not believe that the Prophet Joseph Smith was correct in teaching and practicing plural marriage—both rejected this teaching, this revelation. God did not come to them to reveal it, so they only learned of it through the Prophet. I think this shows that each of them came to regard himself a little bit too highly—that both of them began to think of themselves as equals with the Prophet in terms of receiving revelation for the Church. Each of them believed that he knew better than the Prophet with regard to plural marriage. Neither of them was able to humble himself sufficiently—neither of them was able to demonstrate the faith sufficient to receive the witness of the Holy Ghost that it was the will of God that Joseph restore and teach and practice plural marriage. Consequently, each of these two great men ultimately said and did things that attacked The Church of Jesus Christ of Latter-day Saints, and therefore each of them was excommunicated.

However, I find it instructive to consider how they each responded to Joseph's support of plural marriage before their excommunications. In the case of Oliver Cowdery, he was critical of this to a few people, but in his mind he did not attempt to make the case that Joseph Smith had been rejected as the Lord's prophet.[75] Oliver did not try to oust Joseph or to take over from

---

[75] While Oliver Cowdery was critical of Joseph's views on plural marriage, Oliver's biographer, Phillip R. Legg, concludes that Oliver continued to

Joseph. Rather, Oliver treated Joseph as if he was still the Lord's prophet, but that he was making a mistake in the matter of plural marriage. In other words, he gave Joseph limited support as the Prophet, but at the same time found fault with him in this one matter. In the case of Sidney Rigdon, the same combination of support and criticism was manifest; Sidney continued to sustain Joseph as the Prophet until his death, but he rejected the commandment of plural marriage. In other words, both Oliver and Sidney said they sustained Joseph as the Lord's prophet, but at the same time they asserted that he was in error in teaching and practicing plural marriage.

I find this intriguing because some of those who rejected plural marriage immediately began to call Joseph a fallen prophet. William and Wilson Law, Austin Cowles, Robert and Charles Foster, and Chauncy and Francis Higbee all took this latter approach, and thereafter openly fought to destroy Joseph Smith. But again, neither Oliver Cowdery nor Sidney Rigdon joined in these efforts. After the death of Joseph Smith, both Oliver and Sidney continued to believe that each was called of God and that each had a mission from God to do His work. Each took the position that it was just in the matter of plural marriage that Joseph was in error. Sidney Rigdon did not claim that Joseph Smith was a fallen prophet until after August 8, 1844—after the Church rejected his effort to become Joseph's successor. Eventually, in 1848, Oliver did return to the Church, and he was re-baptized by Orson Hyde. While Oliver had been critical of plural marriage before his re-baptism, he apparently was eventually willing to abandon that criticism and follow the brethren.[76] Sidney Rigdon, never did accept plural marriage

regard Joseph Smith as the Lord's prophet, even after his excommunication (Legg, 146-48). Joseph, on the other hand, stated on January 2, 1843, that he believed that Oliver considered Joseph a "fallen prophet," and that Oliver sought to rise above Joseph (HC 5:217).

[76] Based upon a letter from Oliver to David Whitmer, dated July 18, 1847 (Legg, 155-58). David Whitmer wrote that he does not believe that Oliver ever accepted the doctrine of plural marriage when he was re-baptized in

as divinely mandated, and he never did return to the Church. After his excommunication from the Church in 1844, he formed a church in Pittsburgh, but it never grew beyond a very few people. He remained aloof from any other organized church until his death in 1876.

In summary, until their expulsion from the Church, both Oliver and Sidney believed the Church was doing God's will, and both of them supported the Prophet Joseph Smith in most of what he was doing—except with respect to plural marriage. In other words, their message to others was that Joseph Smith was the Lord's prophet. And both of them were supportive of the Prophet in public—it was just in private that they found fault with Joseph's position on plural marriage. My point in focusing on this is not so much to criticize Oliver and Sidney, but rather is to point out that both of these men were supportive of most of what the Prophet was doing—it was just the one thing that they criticized. They did not regard Joseph as an evil man—rather they felt he was mistaken in this one matter. They continued to support Joseph as the Prophet of God, even though they were critical of him in one matter.

Not only did Oliver and Sidney consider themselves fully

---

November 1848 (Legg,155, citing an 1884 article published by the RLDS Church entitled: "S. W. Richards on O. Cowdery," The Saints Herald 6, no. 12 (Lamoni, Iowa: June 1884), 454). But Church leaders judged Cowdery otherwise. Richard Anderson wrote: "The High Council questioned him closely about his published letter (to David Whitmer) in which Oliver claimed that he retained the keys of priesthood leadership after Joseph Smith's death," and that Oliver acknowledged his error about this; Oliver said that the revelation in D&C 124:95 helped change his mind. Richard L. Anderson, "The Second Witness of Priesthood Restoration," Improvement Era, November 1968, p. 19. The High Council and Orson Hyde (who re-baptized Oliver) were convinced that Oliver's return to the Church was in full acceptance of all principles of the restored gospel. Richard Anderson also wrote this: "[I] n 1848 Cowdery said publicly and privately 'that Joseph Smith had fulfilled his mission faithfully before God until death' (Geo. A. Smith to Orson Pratt, MS 11 [Oct. 20, 1848]: 14), and 'that the priesthood was with this people, and the 'Twelve' were the only men that could lead the Church after the death of Joseph'" (Id., 18). See also, Brewster, 69-70.

supportive of the Church, but both of them were supportive of the character of Joseph Smith. On March 27, 1843, Sidney responded to a letter from Joseph wherein Joseph expressed his feeling that Sidney thought ill of him and was seeking to "destroy" him. Sidney responded to Joseph: "[T]here never was nor is there now existing anything privately or publicly to injure your character in any respect whatever." (HC 5:315; McKiernan, F. Mark, 123.) And when in 1844 William Law and his followers openly attacked the character of Joseph Smith and publicly accused Joseph of adultery, Rigdon had no part of their activities. In fact, after Law and his co-conspirators were publicly exposed for plotting to kill Joseph, Sidney Rigdon spoke in support of the Prophet in his April 6th address at General Conference. He defended the Prophet by ridiculing Law and the other apostates with these words:

> After the Church began to grow, it was favored with marvelously wise men. They had so much wisdom that they could dispute what God said. . . . [T]hey have had so much more wisdom, they knew all about the kingdom before God revealed it, and they know all things before they were heard; they understand more than God knows. . . . They would say they had revelations and visions, and were as certain that the Lord had given it as I was that the devil had. (HC 6:291-92)

On May 25, 1844, Sidney Rigdon resigned his office as postmaster of Nauvoo, and recommended Joseph Smith to be his successor (HC 6:407). The point is this: Sidney Ridgon knew that Joseph was teaching and practicing plural marriage, but he did not regard Joseph as an evil man or a fallen prophet.

Similarly, Oliver never rejected Joseph as the Lord's chosen prophet. Oliver felt that his excommunication was a mistake.

Oliver's biographer, Phillip R. Legg, said this: "Whether he erred or not, he [Oliver] felt betrayed [by the excommunication]. He waited for an apology which never came" (Legg, 135). Legg wrote: "At no time during his years of separation from the church did Oliver ever recant his testimony of the church or the Book of Mormon. Oliver's experiences in the early days of his association with Joseph and their divine encounters had left him devoted to the Restoration movement. His faith in God and a prophetic church had not wavered" (Legg, 147-48).

The point is that these two men, who were intimately acquainted with the Prophet Joseph Smith, and who had each shared spectacular divine manifestations with the Prophet, and each of whom knew of the Prophet's teaching and practicing of plural marriage, still regarded Joseph as the Lord's prophet, even though they respectfully disagreed with the commandment to practice plural marriage. Neither Oliver nor Sidney supported the accusations of men like William Law and his followers who declared Joseph to be an evil man and a fallen prophet.

I submit that it was the spiritual inadequacies (primarily pride) of Oliver and Sidney that prevented them from receiving (or recognizing) God's witness that the restoration of plural marriage was divinely mandated. All twelve members of the Quorum of the Twelve Apostles were supportive of plural marriage; nine of the twelve were practicing it before the Prophet's death, and the other three began to do so shortly thereafter. In addition, there were eighteen other faithful men who had entered into plural marriages before the Prophet's death, including Hyrum Smith, Isaac Morley, Theodore Turley, Erastus Snow, John Smith, William Clayton, and Ezra Taft Benson. (See appendix A, at page 53.) These men and their wives received the witness from God that plural marriage was commanded by God.

I think the same question must be answered for each of us today. Although we do not today have the same urgency to get

God's confirmation that plural marriage is a divine practice when God commands, it is nevertheless a part of God's gospel and a part of His order of things in the highest degree of glory in the celestial kingdom of heaven.

Construction of the Nauvoo Temple was completed about 18 months after the Prophet's death. Many endowments were performed there in January, 1846. Shortly thereafter, the temple was destroyed. It was rebuilt in 2002. The above photo was taken in 2017.

# Chapter 4

## THE CHARACTER OF JOSEPH SMITH

I have stated my unapologetic support for the doctrine of plural marriage because I believe that is the proper way to address the issue. I think a defensive, embarrassed discussion of plural marriage would misrepresent its divine, eternal role. I am not advocating its practice at this time at all. But its practice will exist with those who are exalted in the celestial kingdom. At that time its practice will bring glory and happiness to all participants, and the women participating will not find their happiness or personal fulfillment lessened by it, rather it will actually add to their eternal joy and glory.

Part of the significance of this discussion of plural marriage is what it says about the character of Prophet Joseph Smith. If the result of this examination had been to reveal deep character flaws in Joseph Smith, then this would undermine his witness that he was a prophet of God. But a thorough review of his words and actions does not support such a conclusion. Those who knew him best, including the Quorum of the Twelve Apostles and the women he took as plural wives did not criticize his character; rather they regarded him as a good and holy man—a true prophet of God. The statements, and many times the lack of statements, of the wives of Joseph Smith provides significant evidence about Joseph's character. If Joseph were a scoundrel or an evil man, then at least one of those thirty plus women who were "sealed" to him would have said something negative about him. But to my knowledge they never did. On the contrary, they regarded Joseph highly; they regarded their sealings to him as sacred and special; they were aware of his sealings to other women. These women regarded their sealings and marriages to Joseph as being in harmony with God's will and as great eternal blessings.

That Joseph Smith had multiple wives cannot be disputed, but this is not a character flaw in Joseph any more than it would be in Abraham, Moses or Jacob. If there were a character flaw in Joseph, it must be found in something other than his having plural wives. And in such a search I do not find any material character flaws.

Some of the accusations made against Joseph Smith cannot be proven. For other accusations there is conflicting evidence, and in many of those instances Joseph's accusers held deep grudges against him and/or were seriously lacking in credibility. Some of the troubling accusations against Joseph Smith pertain to Joseph's intentions and the quality of his character. For example, some of Joseph's enemies claim that he was evil, corrupt, hypocritical, abusive and a predator. But these attacks on his intentions and on his character are vehemently denied by many people who knew Joseph intimately, and those accusations cannot be established by convincing evidence. The criticisms that Joseph's character had serious flaws cannot be established by credible evidence. Today, 175 years after Joseph's death, there is no person alive who knew Joseph personally. Regardless of how we judge Joseph Smith today, we can only do it based upon what we read and hear and based upon personal revelation. What is indisputable is the fulfillment of Moroni's prophecy in 1823 that Joseph's name would be known for good and evil around the world.

I have personally conducted an extensive study into Joseph Smith's life and teachings. Of the many accusations that I have heard made against him, I have found most of them to be false, some of the minor accusations to be true, and some accusations to be unprovable. But on the other hand, I have found a wealth of evidence about his life and teachings that are pure and virtuous and inspiring. I conclude that Joseph Smith was God's chosen prophet, and that he was a courageous and dynamic man who feared God more than man. Joseph would not back down from doing God's will regardless of the threats against his life. He lived great, and he died great. His instituting of the practice of plural marriage led to his death at the hands of men who hated him and who had no legitimate cause for their murderous designs—his murderers were Satan's pawns. Joseph Smith was the greatest witness for the Lord Jesus Christ in all the world in the last two hundred years.

Joseph Smith was a friend to many, many people in Nauvoo. He was not the type of leader who was aloof from those he led. Joseph was approachable, and he shared personal things with many people. One example of this was with the two 17-year-old young men who advised Joseph in early 1844 of the plot to kill him. These young men, Dennison Harris and Robert Scott, had been invited to and attended some meetings of people who wanted to get rid of Joseph. These meetings resulted in a plot of about two hundred people to "destroy" Joseph Smith. The last of these meetings was held at the home of William Law. Dennison and Robert informed Joseph of the plot and conspiracy in late March, after which Joseph spoke to the saints on Sunday, March 24th and told the saints who the principal conspirators were—William Law, Robert Foster, Wilson Law, Joseph Jackson, and Chauncey Higbee. Announcing his awareness of the plot probably delayed violence upon Joseph, but it did not stop it. But one important insight that came from the Prophet's talking with the two young men was what Joseph told them about plural marriage. In the words of Dennison, the Prophet told them the following:

Before leaving Joseph put a seal upon our mouths, and told us to tell nobody, not even our fathers for twenty years. He cautioned us very seriously, and I did as he told me.

There was one thing which Joseph said which I have not related. He said: "They accuse me of polygamy, and of being a false prophet" and many other things which I do not now remember. "But," said he, "I am no false prophet; I am no imposter. I have had no dark revelations, I have had no revelations from the devil. I have made no revelations; I have not got anything up myself. The same God that has thus far dictated and directed me, and inspired me and strengthened me in this work, gave me this revelation and commandment on celestial and plural marriage, and the same God commanded me to obey it.

"He said to me that unless I accept it and introduce it and practice it, I together with my people should be damned and cut off from this time henceforth. And they say if I do so and so they will kill me. What shall I do! What shall I do! If I do not practice it I shall be damned with all my people. If I do teach it and practice it and urge it, they say they will kill me, and I know they will. But," said he, "we have got to observe that it [is] an eternal principle, and that it was given to [me] by way of commandment and not by way of instruction."[77]

---

[77] Dennison L. Harris, "Verbal Statement of Bishop Dennison L. Harris to President Joseph F. Smith in the Presence of Elder Franklin Spencer, at the house of Bishop Dorius of Ephraim, San Pete County, Utah, on Sunday Afternoon, May 15, 1881, and reported by George F. Gibbs," LDS Church

This is important because it confirms what many others have said about plural marriage. Joseph practiced it and taught it because God commanded it. Joseph knew that it would likely lead to his own death, but he knew God had commanded it, and therefore he practiced and taught it because the Lord told him to do so.

Joseph was one of the friendliest people to ever live. He had a magnetic personality. He made friends quickly, and he shared his personal feelings with many people. He was quick to accept new people and to open himself up to others and to recognize the unique skills and abilities of others. This led to his being betrayed a number of times (including betrayals by Oliver Cowdery, Sidney Rigdon, W. W. Phelps, John C. Bennett and William Law). But although some whom he trusted turned against him, most did not.

Joseph's ability to place trust in others was an important key in the rapid growth of the Church, and most of those in whom Joseph placed his trust developed into spiritual giants—men who themselves became powerful, dedicated, inspired disciples of Christ. The phenomenal growth of the Church, from six members in 1830, to over 25,000 people in 1844, was due to the witness of the Holy Ghost that attended the words and work of Joseph Smith and of those who joined him in this effort. Joseph Smith was authentic and pure and good. Those people who were looking for God's messengers in the latter-days were looking for gospel truth, and they were looking for messengers who were pure and holy men. They found this in Joseph Smith. The goodness of Joseph Smith was a key component of his appeal to good people.

Joseph Smith was a decisive man of unparalleled initiative and action. Perhaps there was never another man in the history of the world who asked God with real intent and faith for

---

Archives, Salt Lake City, Utah. Spelling and punctuation have been modernized; in Mark L. McConkie, *Remembering Joseph* (Salt Lake City: Deseret Book Co., 2003), 381.

answers to so many questions about life and about God's plan of happiness. Joseph courageously proclaimed the answers he received from God, and he was bold and decisive in dealing with those who crossed him and the Lord. This bold decisiveness caused many of them to accuse Joseph of unworthy motives and intents. Thus, to this day, Joseph's critics continue to malign him. But the basis for such accusations is primarily fiction in the mind of his enemies. Those who knew Joseph best regarded him as the purest and most noble of all men.

A thorough review of the practice of plural marriage by Joseph Smith does not disclose any serious defects in his character. Rather it supports the conclusion that Joseph Smith was a dedicated disciple of Jesus Christ who courageously obeyed the Lord and gave his life as a testimony of the truthfulness of his teachings. Joseph Smith was indeed the great prophet of the Lord foretold in multiple ancient scriptures, who presided over the restoration of all things in the last days, in preparation for the Second Coming of the Lord Jesus Christ.

Carthage Jail, in Carthage, Illinois, where Joseph Smith was killed on June 27, 1844.

# Part II—Succession in the Presidency

Statue of Joseph Smith and Brigham Young, looking west across the Mississippi River, where Joseph Smith prophesied that the Saints would go. Statue is the work of Kenneth R. Mays.

At the critical meeting of the Church membership in Nauvoo on August 8, 1844, the Quorum of the Twelve told the saints that the Prophet Joseph had conferred upon them all of the keys and authorities to enable them to lead the Church after the Prophet's death. When Brigham Young, as President of the Quorum of the Twelve Apostles made this presentation to the Church, many of the people there witnessed a spiritual manifestation of God's confirmation of this proposal: As President Brigham Young spoke to them, many of the saints saw and heard that he looked and sounded as if he were the Prophet Joseph Smith. When the matter was presented to the Church for a vote, the conference unanimously voted to sustain the Quorum of the Twelve, with Brigham Young as its President, to lead the Church.

With this important business completed, the Church continued moving forward, with near unanimous support for Brigham Young and the Twelve. The splinter groups that arose thereafter were few in number, and none of them developed any significant following. (See chart on page 104.) Almost all of them have ceased to have sufficient membership to function. Chapter 6 will discuss three of these groups. But first, in Chapter 5 we will review how the Prophet authorized the Twelve to lead the Church upon his death. We will also explore in more detail the key events that transpired with the Prophet Joseph and with the Quorum of the Twelve from the time shortly before the Prophet's death until the conference on August 8, 1844, when the Church sustained Brigham Young, as President of the Quorum of the Twelve Apostles, to lead the Church.

# Chapter 5

## ALL PRIESTHOOD KEYS WERE CONFERRED UPON THE TWELVE PRIOR TO THE PROPHET'S DEATH

In the five years preceding the Prophet's death, the Quorum of the Twelve assumed an increasingly greater role in the affairs of the Church.[78] Just prior to the Church's expulsion from Missouri, the Lord commanded the Twelve to go across the ocean to preach the gospel, and to leave for this mission from the Far West Temple Lot on a specified date in the future— April 26, 1839. This commandment had been given before Governor Boggs issued his Extermination Order on October 27, 1838. Thereafter the saints were driven out of Missouri, as the Prophet was wrongfully imprisoned in that state for six months. On January 16, 1839, from Liberty Jail, the Prophet directed the Twelve to lead the Church while the First Presidency was imprisoned, and he also directed the Twelve to return to Far West on April 26th to fulfill the Lord's commandment.[79]

---

[78] See, e.g., Ehat, 43, 69, 85-86.

[79] Orson F. Whitney, *The Life of Heber C. Kimball* (Salt Lake City: Bookcraft, 1888, Third Edition 1967), 237. The Prophet's directive to the Twelve was given in a letter signed by the First Presidency (Joseph and Hyrum and Sidney Rigdon). The letter specifically stated: "Inasmuch as we [The First

This they did. They were refugees in Illinois, struggling to build new homes and farms for their families. Despite the great inconvenience of travelling over 200 miles (one way), and despite the serious threats to their lives by daring to set foot in Missouri, they travelled to Far West on April 26th in order to fulfill the Lord's commandment. Then, despite their extreme difficulties—both economic and health—beginning in August, most of the Quorum began to leave for England—and there they did miraculous missionary work, converting a few thousand people in a year's time. They returned from this successful mission in the summer of 1841, after which the Prophet promptly expanded their role as a quorum in administering the affairs of the Church.[80]

The work of the Twelve in growing the Church at a time of great hardship and difficulty was recognized by the Prophet and the membership. This coincided with the time (1841-1842) when the Prophet began introducing the endowment and celestial marriage, including plural marriage; these ordinances and principles were shared with the Twelve and a few other of the faithful saints. The Prophet began to include the Twelve more often in his work and in his deliberations. At the same time, the work and influence of Sidney Rigdon (the First Counselor in the Presidency) began to wane. Sidney knew about plural marriage, but he did not support it. This was obviously a serious problem for the Prophet. Another counselor in the First Presidency, John C. Bennett, was excommunicated in May of

---

Presidency] are in prison, . . . the management of the affairs of the Church devolves on you, that is the Twelve." This incident was precedent for the succession that occurred on August 8, 1844, and it shows that the leading brethren all understood this important role of the Quorum of the Twelve.
[80] An excellent summary of the broadening powers of the Twelve that occurred from 1839-41 is found in Ronald K. Esplin, "Brigham Young and the Transformation of the "First" Quorum of the Twelve," *Lion of the Lord – Essays on the Life and Service of Brigham Young,* Susan Easton Black and Larry C. Porter, eds. (Salt Lake City: Deseret Book, 1995), 54-84. See also Milton V. Backman, Jr., "The Keys Are Right Here," also in *Lion of the Lord,* 108-9.

1842 for adultery, and shortly thereafter Bennett commenced a campaign intended to destroy the Prophet and the Church. Bennett knew some information about plural marriage,[81] but he apparently seduced some women and engaged in relations with them, telling them the Prophet said it was okay. But he lied; Joseph never authorized Bennett to enter into plural marriages nor to do any of his immoral acts. Bennett's actions exposed a sinful side of him, and he was promptly dismissed from the First Presidency and excommunicated. But this episode commenced an escalation of hostilities and attacks on Joseph and the Church that led to Joseph's assassination two years later.

## Sealing Keys Restored

On April 3, 1836, Moses, Elias and Elijah appeared and committed to Joseph and Oliver the keys of the gathering of Israel, the Abrahamic covenant, and the sealing powers of the priesthood. The conferral of these keys upon the Prophet and Oliver was of critical importance. There is no indication that these keys were bestowed upon Joseph by the laying on of hands. Although such is the normal method of conveying priesthood power and authority, God can certainly use whatever means he chooses to bestow authority on others. Building on the foundation of these keys and new revelation, beginning in 1842, the Prophet administered the holy ordinances of the Temple to the

---

[81] See, e.g., Ehat, 30-31 and 39. Bennett knew enough to cause problems for Joseph and the Church. But Bennett had never been included with the faithful few individuals to whom the Prophet introduced either the endowment, celestial marriage or plural marriage. For example, Bennett was not included in the group of nine men to whom the endowment was introduced on May 4, 1844. Consequently, after Bennett's excommunication, when he published his book, *History of the Saints,* in 1842 as an effort to hurt Joseph, his explana-tions and descriptions of the endowment and celestial marriage are filled with errors and misrepresentations. Joseph's famous biographer Fawn Brodie based some of her findings on Bennett's book, and accordingly Brodie also was mistaken in some of her conclusions.

Twelve, and he also conferred upon them the authority to hold and exercise all Priesthood keys upon his death.

## Temple Ordinances Restored

On January 19, 1841, the Lord revealed to Joseph Smith that He was about to "restore again" things pertaining to the temple and the "fulness of the priesthood" (D&C 124:28-30). These ordinances included baptisms for the dead (D&C 124:29-33) and other ordinances. The Lord said,

> [L]et this house be built unto my name, that I may reveal mine ordinances therein unto my people; For I deign to reveal unto my church things which have been kept hid from before the foundation of the world, things that pertain to the dispensation of the fullness of times. (D&C 124:40-41)

Following the Prophet's receipt of this revelation, the Lord did reveal to him various temple ordinances, including the endowment; the sealings of wives to husbands; the sealings of children to parents; and other blessings of the fullness of the priesthood. All these ordinances pertain to the temple; they were first performed outside the temple (prior to the temple's completion), but ultimately, they were to be performed only in temples. Joseph regarded these ordinances as necessary to bring the saints back to the presence of God and to becoming gods in eternity (Ehat, 47). These ordinances included all the crowning blessings of the gospel that God had prepared for mankind—so that the saints could become gods and goddesses. Joseph taught that these blessings were sublime and marvelous, and that they are only bestowed upon those who will obey all of God's commandments, sacrifice their all for Him and His work, and consecrate their lives to His service. The lengthy endowment ordinance[82] served to teach all this and to inspire and uplift those who would covenant with all their heart to live by every word that proceeded from the mouth of God. Joseph taught that these temple ordinances were the greatest eternal blessings and powers that can be bestowed upon man on the earth.[83]

## First Endowments Performed

When Joseph first administered the endowment ordinance on May 4, 1842, it was given to only nine brethren.[84] While the endowment is actually a separate ordinance from a marriage sealing, nevertheless it is preliminary to such a sealing. During the next year there were no endowments administered to anyone else. The John Bennett affairs came to light in May of 1842; this led to Bennett's excommunication, followed by his public campaign accusing Church leaders of adultery and polygamy. Also, during the last half of 1842, Joseph was in hiding much of the time, as he avoided the bogus extradition effort that was made to arrest him for an alleged assassination attempt on the Governor Boggs. These things and the fact that Joseph was waiting for Emma to accept plural marriage led to a delay of a year before the endowment was administered to additional

---

[82] The ordinance of the endowment includes a combination of instructions and covenants, and it takes a couple of hours to administer it. This and other temple ordinances were revealed to the Prophet over a period of time. Ehat, 22, 25.

[83] Andrew F. Ehat, *Joseph Smith's Introduction of Temple Ordinances and the 1844 Succession Question* (Master's Thesis, Dept. of History, BYU 1982), 47-48.

[84] Joseph's history only lists Hyrum Smith, Brigham Young, Heber C. Kimball, Willard Richards, James Adams, Newell K. Whitney and George Miller (HC 5:1-2), but Heber C. Kimball's Journal reports that William Law and William Marks were also among the group. See *Heber C. Kimball Journal 1840-1845*, cited in Lyndon W. Cook, "William Law, Nauvoo Dissenter," p. 54. See http://byustudies.byu.edu/file/2385/download?token=TAILt4N6. See also, Ehat, 17-20.

people.[85] Perhaps Joseph was waiting for Emma to accept plural marriage so that she could take a leadership role in administering part of the endowment to other women. Emma eventually accepted plural marriage by September of 1843.[86] On September 28, 1843, the endowment was administered to Emma and five additional brethren.[87] By the time of Joseph's death, the endowment had been administered to 36 men and 29 women.[88] While the endowment was ultimately to be a temple ordinance, Joseph introduced it to some of the faithful saints before the temple's completion because he had the premonition that he would not live to see the temple completed.[89] Those who had been privileged to receive the endowment beginning in 1842 frequently referred to themselves as the "Quorum."[90]

---

[85] Ehat, 37.

[86] Ehat, 45. Emma initially seemed to have accepted plural marriage in May of 1843, with the proviso, "if you will let me choose them" (Ehat, 37), whereupon she selected Emily and Eliza Partridge to be plural wives. These two women had already been sealed to Joseph two months earlier, but Emma didn't know it. But after this event, when Emma seemed to accept plural marriage, she then changed her mind for a while. It was not until August or September, after an evening discussion with Joseph and Hyrum that she seemed genuinely converted to the doctrine. Ehat, 53-54. Thereafter, Emma played a major role in administering the endowment to women in the mansion house. Ehat, 63-64.

[87] Ehat, 45 and 55. Thereafter the endowment began to be administered to other women. The five additional men endowed on September 28, 1843 were John Taylor, Amasa Lyman, John Smith, Josh Bernhisel and Lucien Woodworth.

[88] Ehat, 14 and 57.

[89] Ehat, 61.

[90] Ehat, 14.

Joseph and Emma moved into the Mansion House in 1843. Here Emma participated in presenting the Endowment to other women in 1843.

Joseph worked especially close with Brigham Young and Heber C. Kimball in administering the temple ordinances, such that these brethren learned them and helped administer them to others.[91] Sidney Rigdon was not initially included in the "Quorum." He eventually received his endowment on May 11, 1844 (two years after the first endowments were administered), but he did not receive a fullness of the Priesthood ordinances, whereas the Twelve did receive a fullness of all priesthood ordinances.[92] Those closest to the Prophet knew perfectly well that it was his intent that the Twelve should lead the Church upon his death.

## All Ordinances and Keys Conferred upon the Twelve

These temple ordinances and all the keys to administer them were conferred upon the Quorum of the Twelve by the Prophet. In late March 1844, Joseph told a majority of the Twelve

[91] See, e.g., Ehat, 65-67.
[92] Ehat, 103, 128.

who were assembled in Nauvoo that he had sealed upon their heads all of the keys of the kingdom.[93] Elder Wilford Woodruff said that at this meeting, the Prophet told them: "I have sealed upon your heads all the keys of the kingdom of God. I have sealed upon you every key, power, principle that the God of heaven has revealed to me." *The Discourses of Wilford Woodruff,* edited by G. Homer Durham (Bookcraft, Inc. 1946, 1990), 71-74. Brigham Young and Parley P. Pratt gave confirming accounts of this. (See, *History of the Church,* 7:230-35 and *Millennial Star,* October 1845, p. 151.[94]) But exactly how this conferral to the Twelve took place, the Church records are not clear. Whether or not an actual, physical ordination (or ordinations) upon individual members of the Quorum took place I do not know. Clearly the members of the Twelve had received actual, physical ordinations in connection with their endowments. But conferral of the sealing ordinances of the temple is not accomplished by laying hands upon one's head—the declaratory words of the one holding the authority is sufficient to seal individuals. So it would be futile for someone to attempt to dictate to the Prophet how he should have conferred such authority upon the Twelve. Nevertheless, Parley P. Pratt did state that at a meeting with the Twelve in March of 1844, the Prophet conferred on Brigham Young, President of the Quorum of the Twelve, all the sealing

---

[93] This meeting probably occurred on March 26, 1844. Joseph's records also identify a meeting occurring on March 22, 1844, about which he wrote: "In the afternoon, met with the Twelve in prayer at President Brigham Young's house" (HC 6:271). But Orson Hyde said that Joseph gave his charge to the Twelve in the presence of about sixty men. JD 13:180 (Oct. 6, 1869). Andrew F. Ehat believes that this meeting occurred on March 26th. Ehat, 93-94. Joseph's record for March 26th states: "From nine to twelve, noon, in council; also from two to five p.m." (HC 6:274). Joseph did not state specifically that he met with the Twelve on March 26th, but apparently the Twelve were present.

[94] Parley P. Pratt stated that at this March meeting, the Prophet "proceeded to confer on elder [Brigham] Young, the President of the Twelve, the keys of the sealing power. ...This last key of the priesthood is the most sacred of all, and pertains exclusively to the first presidency of the church" ("Proclamation," *Millennial Star,* March 1845, 151).

powers of the priesthood.[95] (I understand this conferral was accomplished by the laying on of hands, although Parley did not specifically so state.) Brigham Young, in turn, confirmed that the Prophet had conferred upon the Quorum of the Twelve the authority to exercise all priesthood keys that had ever been conferred upon Joseph himself (HC 7:230-35).

In 1889, President Wilford Woodruff spoke about the last meeting that the Twelve had with the Prophet (in March 1844), before they departed on their missions to the eastern states. Wilford Woodruff said this:

> The Prophet Joseph, I am now satisfied, had a thorough presentment that that was the last meeting we would hold together here in the flesh. We had had our endowments; we had had all the blessings sealed upon our heads that were ever given to the apostles or prophets on the face of the earth. On that occasion the Prophet Joseph rose up and said to us: "Brethren, I have desired to live to see this temple built. I shall never live to see it, but you will. I have sealed upon your heads all the keys of the kingdom of God. I have sealed upon you every key, power, principle that the God of heaven has revealed to me. Now, no matter where I may go or what I may do, the kingdom rests upon you." . . . "But," he said, after having done this, "ye apostles of the Lamb of God, my brethren, upon your shoulders this kingdom rests; now you have got to round up your shoulders and bear off the kingdom." And he also made this very strange remark, "If you do not do it you will be damned."

---

[95] *Millennial Star*, March 1845, 151.

I am the last man living who heard that declaration. He told the truth, too; for would not any
of the men who have held the keys of the kingdom of God or an apostleship in this Church
have been under condemnation, and would
not the wrath of God have rested upon them
if they had deserted these principles, or denied
and turned from them and undertaken to serve
themselves instead of the work of the Lord which
was committed to their hands? . . . . . . There [was]
a feeling—it was so in the days of Joseph Smith
—that he was not the man to lead the Church. . . .
Oliver Cowdery and others, considered him a
fallen prophet and thought they ought to lead the
Church. . . . There were other men who thought
they should be appointed to that office. But the
God of heaven manifested to you, and to me, and
to all men, who were in Nauvoo, upon whom
the mantle had fallen. Brigham Young took his
place, and led the Church and kingdom of God
up to the day of his death. (G. Homer Durham,
ed., *The Discourses of Wilford Woodruff* (Salt Lake
City: Bookcraft, Inc., 1946, 1990), 71-74)

Thus, by late March 1844, The Quorum of the Twelve held
all priesthood keys, such that upon the death of the Prophet
they would be able to exercise them and "bear off the kingdom," as the work continued going forward in preparation for
the coming of the Lord.[96]

---

[96] After March of 1844 the Quorum of the Twelve apparently prepared a
statement regarding the conferral of keys upon them, which confirms what
is described in these pages. However, that document is unsigned. The document is reported in Richard Neitzel Holzapfel and R. Q. Shupe, *My Servant
Brigham – Portrait of a Prophet* (Salt Lake City: Bookcraft, 1997), 66-67. That
document is identified as "Declaration of 12 Apostles, March 1844," Brigham
Young Papers, LDSCA.

While Joseph was preparing the Twelve to lead the kingdom, he was also moving forward with his campaign for the Presidency of the United States, to be undertaken as a part of a nationwide mission of many Elders. But Joseph did not have the needed support of either of his counselors in the First Presidency with respect to either plural marriage or introducing the temple ordinances. The temple endowment required one to commit to obey all of God's commandments, and those who would not obey the plural marriage commandment were not ready for the endowment. Neither Sidney Rigdon nor William Law would accept plural marriage. In January of 1844 William Law was dropped from the First Presidency, and he became bitter against the Prophet. William Law had received his endowment on May 4, 1844 (with the first few brethren). But the Prophet would not agree to seal Jane Law (his wife) to William. This rankled William. He was dropped from the First Presidency when he overtly made known his opposition to plural marriage, and when his hostilities became public. Shortly thereafter, Law became involved in a plot to destroy Joseph. When the plot and Law's involvement was exposed, he was excommunicated on April 18, 1844.[97] Within two weeks of his excommunication,

---

[97] William Law was one of the leaders of a conspiracy to overthrow the Prophet, including concrete plans to kill him. The knowledge of this conspiracy came to the attention of the Prophet in March of 1844, and the Prophet announced his awareness of it on March 24th, at which time he named some of the co-conspirators: William Law, Wilson Law, Joseph H. Jackson, Chauncey L. Higbee and Dr. Robert D. Foster (HC 6:272). The Prophet learned of this conspiracy from four different people. Joseph's history includes the affidavits he obtained about the conspiracy from Dr. Abiathar Williams and Marenus G. Eaton (HC 6:278-80). See also Ehat, 93, citing Joseph Smith diary, 24 March 1844. Joseph also learned of the plot from two, seventeen-year-old young men, Dennison L. Harris and Robert Scott. William E. Berrett gives a good rendition of this conspiracy and how Joseph learned of it through the courageous efforts of Harris and Scott. At least one of the meetings to overthrow the Prophet was held at the home of William Law. The effort to overthrow Joseph was initiated after the Prophet presented the revelation on Celestial (including plural) Marriage to the Nauvoo High Council. William Law (of the First Presidency), William Marks

Law formed a new church and stepped up his open opposition to Joseph Smith. He also severely criticized doctrines Joseph taught in the King Follett Discourse in April of 1844.[98] Thus neither of the Prophet's counselors in the First Presidency was fully supportive of him at this time. But all twelve members of the Quorum of the Twelve were supportive.

During the last six months of his life, the Prophet met with the Twelve a number of times, giving them ordinances and instructions. By the end of March, Brigham Young and the leading members of the Twelve had all received their endowments and were taught about celestial marriage, and nine of them had begun to practice plural marriage. Only Orson Pratt, Wilford Woodruff and George A. Smith had not taken plural wives before Joseph's death, but they each did so shortly thereafter. Thus, all of the Twelve fully accepted this commandment.

**Following the Martyrdom.** On June 27, 1844, Joseph and Hyrum were assassinated. Had Hyrum not been killed a few moments before the Prophet, he would have succeeded Joseph as the head of the Church. This result was provided in the revelation to the Prophet on January 19, 1841, when Hyrum was called to be assistant President of the Church (D&C 124:91-95). Brigham Young and the Twelve were united in this view.

Joseph and Hyrum were dead; Sidney Rigdon had left for Pittsburg just days before the martyrdom; and ten of the Twelve Apostles were away on missions in the eastern states. Thus, the leaders remaining in Nauvoo were Apostles John Taylor

---

(President of the Nauvoo Stake), Austin Cowles (a counselor to William Marks), Wilson Law, and Dr. Charles D. Foster rejected the doctrine of plural marriage, and immediately began efforts to not only oust the Prophet, but to assassinate him. The young men (Harris and Scott) reported that about two hundred people assembled at the home of William Law and took an oath to rid the Church of Joseph Smith, including plans to kill him. William E. Berrett, *The Restored Church* (Salt Lake City: Deseret Book, 1965), 168-71. These actions led to William Law and others being excommunicated on April 18, 1844, after which William Law promptly formed a new church, claiming that Joseph was a fallen prophet.

[98] See *Nauvoo Expositor* and Ehat, 101.

(seriously wounded), Willard Richards, and Nauvoo Stake President William Marks. The saints waited for the Twelve to return from their missions to deal with succession issues. But by the end of July, Emma was anxious for William Marks to take control over certain Church assets by virtue of his position as stake president. But Willard Richards and other of the brethren who were close to the Prophet objected to this.

On August 3, 1844, Sidney Rigdon returned to Nauvoo and immediately launched a plan to have himself established as "spokesman" or "guardian" to lead the Church. Working with William Marks, Sidney was able to address a body of the Saints on Sunday, August 4th, and he called a special meeting for the Church to be held Thursday, August 8th, at 10:00 a.m. in the Grove, where he proposed to have the Church sustain him as its guardian (HC 7:225). Some of the saints asked that he wait until the return of the Quorum of the Twelve, but he refused. He intended to secure his position of leadership before the Twelve could act. Despite Sidney's hasty maneuvers, his campaign was thwarted when a majority of the Twelve arrived in Nauvoo by August 6th.

On the evening of August 7th, eight members of the Quorum of the Twelve held a meeting in the Seventies Hall, and they requested Sidney Rigdon to meet with them. (Absent from the meeting were the three Apostles who had yet to return—Orson Hyde, William Smith and John E. Page; also absent was John Taylor, who was supportive of Brigham Young, but who was unable to attend because of his serious wounds.) The Twelve were unanimous in their view that they held the authority to lead the Church (HC 7:240 and Ehat, 109). Their position was in full compliance with Section 107 of the Doctrine and Covenants which requires that a majority of the Quorum be present to act, and that the actions of this majority must be unanimous in order for their actions to be equal in authority with those of the First Presidency when there is no First Presidency (D&C 107:21-24, 27-29). When Sidney arrived at the Seventies Hall on the evening of August 7th, Brigham Young asked Sidney what his intentions were for the next day's meeting. Sidney repeated his plan to have himself appointed guardian of the Church. Then Brigham advised him that the Prophet had empowered the Twelve to lead the Church, and that that was what they intended to do.[99] Sidney did not agree, so the meeting ended at an impasse.

On August 7, 1844, the Quorum of the Twelve met in the Seventies Hall.

---

[99] About the August 7th meeting of the Twelve with Sidney Rigdon, the *History of the Church* reports (volume 7, page 230) that Brigham Young stated the following:

> I do not care who leads the church, even though it were Ann Lee; but one thing I must know, and that is what God says about it. I have the keys and the means of obtaining the mind of God on the subject. . . .
>
> Joseph conferred upon our heads all the keys and powers belonging to the Apostleship which he himself held before he was taken away, and no man or set of men can get between Joseph and the Twelve in this world or in the world to come.
>
> How often has Joseph said to the Twelve, "I have laid the foundation and you must build thereon, for upon your shoulders the kingdom rests.

# Church Conference of August 8, 1844

The next day at 10:00 a.m., at Sidney's meeting, he addressed the saints for an hour-and-a-half, attempting to convince them that he should be appointed guardian over the Church. Perhaps Sidney could sense that he was not winning over the congregation. He never called for a vote of the Church on his proposal. After Sidney concluded, Brigham Young stood and addressed the saints—but only briefly; he told them to re-assemble there at 2:00 p.m., at which time he and the Twelve would address the Church. Thereupon, the meeting was concluded, and the saints anxiously anticipated what would transpire at the afternoon meeting. Brigham's announcement of the afternoon meeting turned the tables on Sidney Rigdon; his window of opportunity to seize control was effectively over.

In this Grove, west of the temple, thousands of Saints assembled in the shade on August 8, 1844, and unanimously sustained Brigham Young, as President of the Quorum of the Twelve Apostles, to succeed the Prophet Joseph Smith.

At 2:00 p.m. in the Grove, Brigham Young addressed the saints and told them that the Prophet had empowered the Twelve to lead the Church upon the Prophet's death. The Prophet had previously taught in 1836 that "where I am not, there is no First Presidency" (HC 2:347). None of the speakers referred to this quote on August 8th, but the Twelve were united in their understanding of that principle; the Prophet had made it clear to them in March of 1844 that it was they, the Twelve, who had the power and the duty to lead the Church upon his death. They knew that they had the authority—they just did not anticipate the Prophet's departure coming so soon. Thus, while there was some uncertainty and intrigue in Nauvoo in the first week of August—this was not because the Twelve was sending confusing signals—it was because of the rushed usurpation efforts of Sidney Rigdon that were intended to cut out the Twelve, ignore the revelations (D&C 107:22-24 and 27-30), and discard the Prophet's specific directions.

The *History of the Church* reports that seven of the Twelve[100] were present at the 2 p.m. meeting on August 8th, when the congregation unanimously sustained the Quorum of the Twelve, with Brigham Young as its President, to lead the Church. Apostles Hyde, Smith and Page still had not arrived. John Taylor was not present because he continued to be bed-ridden, recovering from the gunshot wounds he suffered in Carthage Jail. The records do not indicate that Lyman Wight was present at the August 8th meeting, although records state that he had been present at a meeting of the Twelve the day before.[101] But Lyman Wight

---

[100] Brigham Young, Heber C. Kimball, Parley P. Pratt, Orson Pratt, Wilford Woodruff, Willard Richards and George A. Smith.

[101] The *History of the Church* gives conflicting reports about Lyman Wight. In volume 7, page 228, it states that Wight was present at a meeting of the Twelve at the home of John Taylor on August 7th. That evening, at the meeting of the Twelve at the Seventies Hall, there is no specific listing of which members of the Twelve were present. In commenting upon whom of the Twelve attended the meeting on August 8th, the footnote on page 231 states that Wight "was still in the east." But Joseph Fielding Smith wrote in 1909 that Heber C. Kimball and George Miller went to Lyman's home specifically requesting him to attend the 2 p.m. meeting, but that Lyman refused to attend, "declaring that the Twelve were usurping authority." Joseph Fielding Smith, *Origin of the "Reorganized" Church and The Question of Succession* (Independence, MO: Press of Zion's Printing and Publishing Company, 1929, Third Edition), 65-66. Had Wight attended the meeting and voiced objections, he could have prevented the Twelve from acting

never made any overt objection or opposition to Brigham Young's leadership at this time. Nevertheless, with seven members of the Quorum present at the 2 p.m. meeting, they had a "quorum" to act, and they did so unanimously. Furthermore, to my knowledge, none of the Twelve ever voiced any opposition to such actions—certainly there was never any timely opposition made. Thus, the strict requirements of Section 107 were satisfied.

The moment of truth with respect to succession in the Church occurred while Brigham Young was addressing the saints:

> If the people want President Rigdon to lead them they may have him; but I say unto you that the Quorum of the Twelve have the keys of the kingdom of God in all the world. . . .

> I tell you in the name of the Lord that no man can put another between the Twelve and the Prophet Joseph. Why? Because Joseph was their file leader, and he has committed into their hands the keys of the kingdom in this last dispensation, for all the world. . . .

> We have a head, and that head is the Apostleship, the spirit and power of Joseph, and we can now begin to see the necessity of that Apostleship.

> Brother Rigdon was at his side—not above. No man has a right to counsel the Twelve but Joseph Smith. Think of these things. You cannot appoint a prophet; but if you let the Twelve remain and act in their place, the keys of the kingdom are

---

unanimously. But by declining to attend and declining to express his reservations, the requirements of section 107 were fully satisfied in sustaining the Twelve as the presiding authority of the Church at the 2 p.m. meeting.

with them and they can manage the affairs of the church and direct all things aright. (HC 7:233, 235)

As Brigham was speaking thousands of the saints gathered there witnessed the transfiguration of Brigham Young—he looked like and sounded like the Prophet Joseph Smith. About why this spiritual manifestation occurred, Wilford Woodruff answered as follows:

> Because there was Sidney Rigdon and other men rising up and claiming to be the leader of the Church, and men stood, as it were, on a pivot, not knowing which way to turn. But just as quick as Brigham Young rose in that assembly, his face was that of Joseph Smith's—the mantle of Joseph had fallen upon him, the power of God that was too upon Joseph Smith was upon him; he had the voice of Joseph and it was the voice of the Shepherd. There was not a person in that assembly, Rigdon, himself, not excepted, but was satisfied in his own mind that Brigham was the proper leader of the people, for he would not have his name presented, by his own consent, after that sermon was delivered. There was a reason for this in the mind of God: it convinced the people. (Wilford Woodruff's address, JD 15:81, as reported in Barrett, 524)

> At the end of that meeting, when Brigham Young called for a sustaining vote for the Quorum of the Twelve,[102] with him as its President, to lead

---

[102] Before calling for the sustaining vote, Brigham Young told the saints: "[D]on't make a covenant to support them [the Twelve] unless you intend to abide by their counsel; and if they do not counsel you as you please, don't turn round and oppose them." HC 7:239. Thus, the sustaining vote on that

the Church, the supporting vote was unanimous.
And when the congregation was asked if there
were any objections, there were none (HC 7:240).

By the end of August 8, 1844, the question of who was to
succeed the Prophet Joseph Smith was perfectly settled, and the
vast majority of the membership whole-heartedly sustained the
Quorum of the Twelve, with Brigham Young as its President, to
lead the Church. (See also Ehat, 113-19.)

The overwhelming majority of the Church sustained this
action and continued to follow Brigham Young and the Twelve
to the valley of the Great Salt Lake. And despite many severe
trials through which the saints had to pass during the next few
years, the work of taking the gospel to all the world continued
without interruption under the leadership of Brigham Young.
The chart below shows the growth of the Church from 1829 to
1850, which shows that its growth was not stopped or hindered
by the death of Joseph Smith. That the Church continued to
grow despite the Prophet's death is a witness that it is God's
work and not just Joseph Smith's personal project.

| Year | Membership | Number Change | Percentage Growth |
|------|-----------|---------------|-------------------|
| 1829 | 6 | 6 | 0 |
| 1830 | 280 | 274 | 4566.67% |
| 1831 | 680 | 400 | 142.86% |
| 1832 | 2,661 | 1,981 | 291.32% |
| 1833 | 3,140 | 479 | 18.00% |
| 1834 | 4,372 | 1,232 | 39.24% |
| 1835 | 8,835 | 4,463 | 102.08% |
| 1836 | 13,293 | 4,458 | 50.46% |
| 1837 | 16,282 | 2,989 | 22.49% |
| 1838 | 17,881 | 1,599 | 9.82% |
| 1839 | 16,460 | -1,421 | -7.95% |
| 1840 | 16,865 | 405 | 2.46% |

occasion was not just a casual vote of little significance; it was accompanied
by the saints covenanting to support, defend and follow the Twelve.

| 1841 | 19,856 | 2,991 | 17.73% |
|------|--------|-------|--------|
| 1842 | 23,564 | 3,708 | 18.67% |
| 1843 | 25,980 | 2,416 | 10.25% |
| 1844 | 26,146 | 166 | 0.64% |
| 1845 | 30,332 | 4,186 | 16.01% |
| 1846 | 33,993 | 3,661 | 12.07% |
| 1847 | 34,694 | 701 | 2.06% |
| 1848 | 40,477 | 5,783 | 16.67% |
| 1849 | 48,160 | 7,683 | 18.98% |
| 1850 | 51,839 | 3,679 | 7.64% |

Figures from *Wikipedia*, "The Church of Jesus Christ of Latter-day Saints Membership History," and from two web sites: http://www.census.gov/ipc/www/idb/worldpop.html and http://www.census.gov/population/international/data/worldpop/table_population.php

While the Church as a whole continued to move forward, there were nevertheless a number of brethren (including three members of the Quorum of the Twelve) who apostatized in the first few years following the Prophet's death. In October of 1845, William Smith was excommunicated for apostasy. William sought to lead the entire Church by virtue of his ordination in 1844 as Patriarch "over" the Church. Stubborn William would not concede on this point, and therefore he was excommunicated for insubordination and apostasy. John E. Page was excommunicated on June 27, 1846, for refusing to move west with the Church. John Page was also a man who would not take counsel. Just as he refused to go with Orson Hyde on the mission to dedicate Palestine for the return of the Jews, so Page's insubordination eventually led to his excommunication. Lyman Wight was equally insubordinate as Smith and Page, only in his case he was subtle about it for several years. Wight had spoken of building up a branch of the Church in Texas for a long period of time. In August of 1844, Brigham Young specifically approved of Wight's doing this. Wight set up a branch of the Church in Wisconsin beginning by 1845; later he led his branch to Texas. Wight was insubordinate for a long time, but it was a couple of years before the Twelve had sufficient evidence of Wight's apostasy. Eventually, Wight was excommunicated in February 1849. Later that year Lyman Wight joined with William Smith to start a new church. William Law also affiliated with them. But this effort disintegrated in 1851.[103]

The chart on the following page lists the splinter churches that were supported by fifteen men who at one time held the priesthood in the Church before separating from the Church. The next chapter discusses three of the principal early splinter churches.

---

[103] The pride and insubordination of Apostles Smith, Page and Wight existed for some time prior to each being excommunicated. William Smith had a reputation for being uncooperative and unavailable to work with the Quorum. Neither Smith, Page nor Wight would obey the Lord's revelation (D&C section 118) to go across the ocean with the Twelve to preach the gospel. These three were mostly absent when In early 1844, the Prophet met regularly with the Twelve and gave them instructions regarding priesthood keys to lead the Church upon his absence. See e.g., Esplin, 67 & 69; and Backman, 111 & 115.

## Early LDS Apostates Who Formed Splinter Churches

| Name | 1844 | 1845 | 1846 | 1847 | 1848 | 1849 | 1850 | 1851 | 1852 | 1853 | 1854 | 1855 | 1856 | 1857 | 1858 | 1859 | 1860 | 1861 | 1862 | 1863 | Later |
|---|---|---|---|---|---|---|---|---|---|---|---|---|---|---|---|---|---|---|---|---|---|
| Sidney B. Rigdon | xRRRRRR | | | | | | | | | | | | | | | | | | | | |
| William B. Smith | | x | STRANG | | | BBBBBBBB | | | | | RLDS | RLDS | RLDS | RLDS | RLDS | RLDS | RLDS | RLDS | RLDS | RLDS | HHHHHH |
| John E. Page | | x | iiii | STRANG | | | | | | PPPP | | | | | | | | | | | iiiiiiiiiiiiiiiiii* |
| Lyman Wight | | | WightWight | | x | BBBBBB | | | | | | | | | | | | | | | |
| David Whitmer-x | | | | | iiii | | | | | | | | | | | | | | | | |
| Wm E. McLellin-x | | | RRSTRANG | iiii | | | | | | | | | | | | | | | | | |
| William Law | | xLL | | | | | BBBBBB | | | | | | | | | | | | | | |
| John C. Bennett -x | | | | | | | | | | | | | | | | | | | | | |
| William Marks | | | STRANGST | | x STRANGSTRANGST | | | | | TTTTTTTTT | | | | | | | | | | | RLDSRLDSRLDSRLDS |
| Austin Cowles | | x LL | RRRSTRANGST JJJJ | | | | | | | | | | | | | | | | | | RLDSRLDSRLDSRLDS |
| James J. Strang | | | x STRANGSTRANGSTRANGSTRANGSTRANGSTRANTSTRANGST | | | | | | | | | | | | | | | | | | |
| Jason W. Briggs | | | a STRANGSTRANG | | | BBBBB | | | | | RLDS | RLDS | RLDS | RLDS | RLDS | RLDS | RLDS | RLDS | RLDS | RLDS | R |
| Zenos H. Gurley | | | | a STRANGSTRANG | | | | | | | RLDS | RLDS | RLDS | RLDS | RLDS | RLDS | RLDS | RLDS | RLDS | RLD | |
| Glanville Hedrick | | | | | | | | | | | | | | | | | | HHHHHHHHHHH | | | |
| Charles B. Thompson | | | a STRANGSTRANG | | | | | | a | TTTTTTTTTTTTTTTTTTTTTTTTTTTTTT | | | | | | | | | | | |
| Joseph Smith, III | | | | | | | | | | | | | | | | | | | | | RLDSRLDSRLDSRLDS |

x = date excommunicated; a = date apostatized (never officially excommunicated)

* By the 1870s David Whitmer's church was again functioning. By 1925 most of his church combined with the Church of Christ—Temple Lot

### Shade of Color Indicates Which Splinter Church

| Code | Description |
|---|---|
| RRRRR | Church of Christ (formed by Sidney Rigdon) |
| STRANG | "Church of Jesus Christ of Latter Day Saints" formed by James J. Strang (Strangites) |
| BBBB | Church formed by William B. Smith—declared himself president of LDS Church |
| iiiii | Church of Christ (formed by David Whitmer and John E. Page) |
| PPPP | Church formed by John E. Page |
| Wight | Church that Lyman Wight led into apostasy in Wisconsin, and then moved to Texas |
| LL | "True Church of Jesus Christ of Latter Day Saints," formed by William Law after his excommunication |
| TTTTT | "Congregation of Jehovah's Presbytery of Zion" ("Baneemyites) formed by Charles B. Thompson |
| HHHH | Church of Christ—Temple Lot (formed by Granville Hedrick - also called "Hedrickites") |
| RLDS | Reorganized Church of Jesus Christ of Latter Day Saints (now, Community of Christ) |
| JJJJJ | Church of Christ (formed by James C. Brewster) |

# Chapter 6

# THREE LDS SPLINTER CHURCHES

In the 189 years since the Church was organized there have been many off-shoot churches formed by those who have apostatized from the Church. Most of them were short-lived, and none of them have had a significant following. By far the largest splinter group that I am aware of is the Community of Christ (formerly the Reorganized Church of Jesus Christ of Latter Day Saints [RLDS Church]) with about 250,000 people world-wide. This chapter will briefly discuss the Community of Christ and two other splinter groups whose presence has had some significance to The Church of Jesus Christ of Latter-day Saints. The three groups that I will discuss are, in the order of their treatment:

1.  True Church of Jesus Christ of Latter Day Saints (formed in 1844 by William Law);
2.  The Reorganized Church of Jesus Christ of Latter Day Saints (formed between 1852-1860, with Joseph Smith, III as its leader beginning in 1860) (now called "Community of Christ"); and
3.  Church of Christ – Temple Lot (also called "Hedrickites") (formed in 1863 by Granville Hedrick).

Before proceeding with this discussion, I draw your

attention to the chart on page 104 which lists fifteen men who apostatized from the LDS Church (1838-49), which identifies the various splinter churches they later formed or joined, and which shows the approximate dates of such involvement.

# I. True Church of Jesus Christ of Latter Day Saints

Immediately after his excommunication from the Church in April of 1844, William Law proceeded to form his own church, which he denominated, the "True Church of Jesus Christ of Latter Day Saints." The church was also referred to as the "Reformed Mormon Church" or just "Reformed Church."[104] This church was of very short duration—I don't believe it lasted even a year. But because of its connection with the martyrdom of Joseph Smith, it is worth knowing a little about it.

William Law was a counselor to Joseph Smith in the First Presidency from 1841 until January 8, 1844. On April 18, 1844, a Church council excommunicated him, Jane Law (his wife), Robert D. Foster, Wilson Law, William Law and Howard Smith for "unchristianlike conduct" (HC 6:341).

William Law would have learned about plural marriage by the latter half of 1843, after Section 132 was written (Ehat, 38). On August 12, 1843, Hyrum Smith presented the doctrine to the Nauvoo Stake High Council.[105] Most of the High Council accepted the doctrine, but stake president William Marks and his counselor, Austin Cowles, did not. Law was not present at this meeting, but thereafter he certainly had conversations with Marks and Cowles about it. Law did not accept plural marriage, and he began working with other opponents of Joseph Smith to take over the church, charging Joseph with being a fallen prophet. This conspiracy escalated into plans to kill Joseph,

---

[104] Ehat, 76; "William Law," *Wikipedia*; and *Nauvoo Expositor*.
[105] Ehat, 53.

which were exposed publicly on March 24, 1844.[106] Joseph specifically named William Law, Wilson Law, Joseph Jackson, Robert D. Foster and Chauncey Higbee as being involved in a plot to kill him (HC 6:272, 278-80). Less than a month later, William Law was excommunicated.

That plot was interrupted, but Joseph's enemies were not subdued. William Law insisted that Joseph was a fallen prophet, and to fix things he proceeded to form his own church. Law's church subscribed to most of the original doctrines of Mormonism, but not plural marriage. He accused Joseph of serious transgressions and crimes. Law made himself "President" of his new church. Other prominent members of his church were Austin Cowles, Wilson Law, Robert D. Foster, Charles A. Foster, Chauncey L. Higbee, and Francis M. Higbee. These men also joined with Law in publishing a newspaper, the *Nauvoo Expositor*, whose one and only edition was published on June 7, 1844. The paper consisted of four pages and announced that it was the "organ" of the newly formed "Reformed Mormon Church." Most of the paper was devoted to criticizing and denigrating Joseph Smith. The publishers presented themselves as exposing the true and evil Joseph Smith.

The *Nauvoo Expositor* accused Joseph Smith of many things, including adultery, polygamy, and secretly teaching polygamy to Mormons. It also accused Joseph Smith of wielding too much power in civic matters, and it complained that the charges of adultery and perjury brought against Joseph Smith by Law and Foster could not be fairly adjudicated in Nauvoo because of Joseph Smith's excessive influence. The paper denounced Joseph Smith for the excommunication of the Laws and the Fosters, contending they were not given notice of their church trials. The paper accused Joseph and church leaders of teaching false and damnable doctrines, including doctrines of exaltation

---

[106] HC 6:272, 278-80; Ehat, 93; and Berrett, 169-71.

and that men can become like God.[107] The paper accused Joseph of preaching a hasty gathering of saints from around the world, to the detriment of his followers. The paper also accused Joseph of personally profiting from the monies that members contributed to the Church, and it called for repeal of the Nauvoo Charter, which they said was working to combine church and state in an improper manner. In summary, most of the publishers were recently excommunicated members, who had openly apostatized and who had a strong and emotional vendetta against Joseph Smith.

The publishers of the *Nauvoo Expositor* were partly venting, partly acting in revenge, and partly seeking to establish their own new church. The Nauvoo area was experiencing a lot of anti-Mormon and anti-Joseph Smith sentiment in the spring of 1844, and publication of the *Nauvoo Expositor* was clearly going to put gas on this raging fire. On Monday, June 10, the Mayor and City Council met and determined that the *Nauvoo Expositor* was libelous and was a nuisance, and they voted to abate the nuisance by destroying the newspapers and the press. The Sheriff carried out this order that same evening.

Not all false statements are libelous. Did the newspaper contain libelous material? Here is the definition of libel: a written false statement, published to a third party, which defames another and causes damage to the one defamed. Not all false statements are defamatory. But defamatory statements include those that: (i) disparage a person in his/her office, profession or business; (ii) accuse someone of unchastity; (iii) accuse someone of having a loathsome disease or illness; or (iv) accuse someone of a crime.

Normally, in U.S. constitutional jurisprudence, prior censorship is not legal. But the law in this regard was not well

---

[107] On April 7, 1844, Joseph delivered his famous King Follett Discourse, in which he taught that God was once as we are now, and that we can become like Him. Law was quick to pounce on this doctrine and to use this as one of his bases for concluding that Joseph was a fallen prophet.

developed in 1844. It does appear that the newspaper did include libelous material because Joseph was accused of the crimes of adultery, perjury, and theft. In addition, his character was maligned because of allegations of immoral conduct and of being a vile character. And while there was no judicial finding that these accusations were either true or false, under libel laws the perpetrator can be found liable for libel if he cannot prove that the accusations are true. Thus, in defamation cases, the burden can shift such that he who accuses another can be held liable for defamation if he cannot prove his accusations to be true. Thus, it is quite possible that it could be proven that the publishers of the *Nauvoo Expositor* were guilty of libel.

Nevertheless, in 2019, I don't believe any court in America would have justified destruction of the newspapers and press. The remedy today would be a civil remedy for monetary damages. I am not aware of any criminal statute today that provides for censorship of libelous material. In any event, while the destruction of the press would not be acceptable today, such an action was not necessarily without legal merit in 1844.

The publishers of the *Nauvoo Expositor* made so many different accusations about Joseph Smith that it actually cast them in the light of just being sour complainers; most of Nauvoo disagreed with most of their criticisms. The publication of the *Nauvoo Expositor* exposed the intense animosity of Joseph's accusers. Remember, all the publishers were in apostasy, and were seeking vindication for their being excluded from the Church. So, when they criticized (a) the gathering of saints, (b) the doctrine of the potential exaltation of man, (c) eternal marriage, and (d) accusing the prophet of personally aggrandizing himself with monies from members—these accusations cast the publishers in a bad light. The publishers complained that Joseph was a vile person, and they criticized the Nauvoo Charter—but most citizens of Nauvoo strongly disagreed with them. The one accusation for which we know there was evidence was Joseph's secret practice of polygamy. To many people, polygamy was synonymous with adultery. So, it is understandable that the accusation about adultery would exist and cause problems.

Finally, I would just note that the assassination of Joseph Smith served to draw attention away from the polygamy issues. The thirst for the blood of Joseph Smith was far greater than could possibly be warranted for either adultery or destruction of a printing press. The public outcry against Joseph Smith ended with his death, but that did not stop either the Church or plural marriage. In fact, Joseph's death bought the Church some time to get away and to move west, where the revelation on plural marriage could be publicly announced, and where, for a short time, it could be practiced in a way that served the Lord's purposes in establishing the kingdom of God and in accelerating the gathering of Israel through missionary work.

As for the history of William Law's church—it disappeared as quickly as it appeared. I found no record that it continued after the year 1844. It is worth noting that in 1849 William Law joined with William B. Smith, the Prophet's brother (and an apostle), who was excommunicated in 1845) in forming a church with William Smith as Prophet. That church lasted about two years, after which William Smith became affiliated with the RLDS Church.

## II. The Reorganized Church of Jesus Christ of Latter Day Saints

The "Reorganized Church of Jesus Christ of Latter Day Saints" ("RLDS Church") is the second largest church stemming from the one founded by the Prophet Joseph Smith in 1830.[108] The headquarters of the RLDS Church is in Independence, Missouri, with an estimated 250,000 members world-wide. In 2001, the church changed its name to "Community of Christ."

---

[108] The largest is The Church of Jesus Christ of Latter-day Saints (the LDS Church), with 16 million members.

In 1852 Brigham Young publicly acknowledged that the Church was practicing plural marriage. Once this became known, some members (who had not moved to Utah with the majority of the church) who were living in Illinois and Wisconsin began to meet together occasionally with the purpose of uniting as a church, but without Brigham Young and without polygamy. To them, Brigham Young had apostatized and had introduced polygamy into the Church. In what they considered an effort to set things right, some of these members first met in 1852, and then continued meeting from time to time in an effort that they called a process of "reorganization."[109] Between 1852 and 1860, the movement gained support from a number of disgruntled Mormons, as well as from a number of men who had been excommunicated from the Church, including many who had been followers of James J. Strang, William Smith and William Marks. (Some of the followers of Strang included Jason W. Briggs and Zenos H. Gurley, Sr., the latter of whom became the *de facto* leader of the "reorganization" until Joseph Smith, III, agreed to join them in 1860.)

The Reorganization movement insisted that the "Utah" Church had gone astray, and that they, the Reorganized Church, were faithful to the true doctrines and that they were the lawful successor to the church founded by Joseph Smith. Nevertheless, they had to organize a new church, with a different name. They chose: "The Reorganized Church of Jesus Christ of Latter Day Saints." However, rather than adhering to the doctrines taught by Joseph Smith, they actually rejected several of those key doctrines that he restored, and they began to add some of their own new doctrines, such as their doctrine that the church head must be a lineal descendant of Joseph Smith.[110] In 1856,

---

[109] Aleah G. Koury, *The Truth and the Evidence* (Independence, MO: Herald Publishing House, 1965), 14.

[110] The origin of the RLDS doctrine of lineal descent apparently came from a purported revelation to Jason W. Briggs in 1851 (Samuel R. Carpenter, *Facts about differences that persist* (Deseret News Press, 1958), 7-8). As the

the "Reorganization" began inviting Joseph Smith, III to become their prophet-leader. Initially he declined their requests, but eventually he agreed to be their prophet. On April 6, 1860, Joseph Smith, III (at the age of 28) took the helm of the RLDS Church and became their prophet.

Although the RLDS Church initially contended that its

---

"Reorganization" movement progressed, they adopted a resolution in 1852 that "the successor of Joseph Smith, Jr., as the Presiding High Priest . . . must of necessity be the seed of Joseph Smith, Jr" (Arthur M. Smith, 9). Later, the RLDS Church began to claim that the Prophet "ordained" his son to be his successor in 1843, and that John Taylor and Willard Richards witnessed this (Carpenter, 8). But neither John Taylor nor Willard Richards ever confirmed this; on the contrary, they always asserted that the Quorum of the Twelve were the successors. The RLDS Church also claimed that Lyman Wight stated that the Prophet blessed his son to be his successor while in Liberty Jail in 1839 (Carpenter, 9), but Wight's statement is not corroborated by any others who were at the jail (i.e., Hyrum Smith, Sidney Rigdon, Alexander McRae and Caleb Baldwin). Furthermore, Wight's statement is contradicted by his and Sidney Rigdon's actions: (1) Neither Wight nor Rigdon ever raised this issue at the critical meetings with the Twelve where the succession matter was discussed on August 7th and 8th, 1844; (2) Neither Wight nor Rigdon ever raised this issue before being excommunicated (Rigdon in 1844; Wight in 1849); and (3) Both Wight and Rigdon each formed his own church in which there was no such lineal descent policy. None of the accounts that Joseph Smith III was blessed or ordained by the Prophet to succeed him are credible—it was clearly an afterthought.

At the Independence Temple Lot trial, James Whitehead testified that Joseph "ordained" his son to succeed him, and that John Taylor, Willard Richards, W. W. Phelps were present. But all three disputed this, and Whitehead contradicted himself so much that he was widely known to be an unreliable perjurer (see Joseph Fielding Smith, *The Origin of the Reorganized Church*, 64-71). Joseph, III, said that his father blessed him to be his successor, but never "ordained" him to such (Koury, 78).

In 1981, Mark W. Hoffmann sold a forged document to the LDS Church that purported to be written by Thomas Bullock (the Prophet's scribe) and purporting to report a blessing given by the Prophet to his son Joseph III on January 17, 1844, blessing him to be the Prophet's successor. By 1982 the RLDS Church had acquired this document from the LDS Church, and in that year they canonized it and put it in the Appendix of their *Doctrine and Covenants*. This, of course, backfired on them when the document was exposed in 1986 to be one of Hoffmann's many forgeries.

leader needed to be a lineal descendant of Joseph Smith, that tenet was abandoned in 1995. The RLDS Church has some beliefs in common with the LDS Church, but it has several that are significantly different. The RLDS Church accepts the Book of Mormon as scripture. It owns the Kirtland Temple, in Ohio, and it owns other historic properties in Nauvoo that are important to it and to the LDS Church. Members of the RLDS Church do not refer to themselves as "Mormons"; neither do they use the terms "Reorganized" or "RLDS" any more. Notwithstanding this, and without intending to speak disparagingly of them, I use the name "Reorganized" Church because historically that is how the church self-identified, and it is a compact way to refer to it.[111]

Those individuals who formed the RLDS Church contended that the LDS Church had apostatized and was rejected by God. They objected to the LDS Church's practice of polygamy, to Brigham Young's leadership as prophet, to the doctrine of eternal marriage, and to the doctrine that man can progress to become like God. But the RLDS Church erred on all of these points. There are significant flaws in several RLDS doctrines and practices. They do not have God's Priesthood—they claim their authority from people who had been excommunicated and/or apostatized from the LDS Church. They have abandoned the belief in God taught by the Prophet Joseph Smith, and in its place they have embraced the belief in the Trinity that is commonly accepted in many other Christian churches. They recently gave the priesthood to women. They recently embraced same-sex marriage. They do not believe that marriage can be for eternity. They do not believe in baptism for the dead or in other temple ordinances.

Historically, as they have sought to distinguish themselves

---

[111] Gurley, a Seventy, had been a supporter of Brigham Young and the Quorum of the Twelve until the Church moved west in 1846, but he would not move west with them. Shortly thereafter, he joined with the Strang group (Carpenter, 6).

from the LDS Church, they have referred to two court cases, which they state produced a judicial finding that their church is the lawful successor to the church established by Joseph Smith. However, those cases do not make any such finding.

We will first review the historical leadership of the RLDS Church. Second, we will review some of their doctrines. Third, we will review some of particular facts of interest about the RLDS Church. Finally, we will review the two court cases that the RLDS Church has incorrectly characterized as holding that they are the true successor to the church organized by Joseph Smith in 1830.

One of the original tenets of the RLDS Church—at least a tenet that they could use once Joseph Smith, III, agreed to join and lead them—was their doctrine that the leader of their church should be a descendant of Joseph Smith, Jr. That seemed to work pretty well for a while. The following two charts show the lineal descendants of Joseph Smith, Jr., and the leaders of the RLDS Church from 1860 to present. As the charts indicate, the RLDS Church abandoned its lineal descent doctrine when Wallace B. Smith retired as church president in 1995. Apparently, there was no descendant left to carry on this leadership tradition.

## Descendants of Joseph Smith, Jr. who presided over RLDS Church

Joseph Smith, III (1832-1914)

| * | * | * |
|---|---|---|
| Frederick M. Smith (1874-1946) (no sons) | Israel A. Smith (1876-1958) (no sons) | W. Wallace Smith (1900-1989) * |
| | | Wallace B. Smith (1929-) (no sons) |

**Leaders of the Reorganized Church (1860-present)**

Joseph Smith, III (1860-1914)
Frederick M. Smith (1914-1946)
Israel A. Smith (1946-1958)
W. Wallace Smith (1958-1989)
Wallace B. Smith (1989-1995)         retired & named
                                     McMurray his succes-
                                     sor—this ended the
                                     Church's practice of hav-
                                     ing for as its president
                                     a direct descendant of
                                     Joseph Smith
W. Grant McMurray (1995-2004)        resigned & named no
                                     successor (He resigned
                                     due to health & family
                                     issues and "inappropri-
                                     ate choices" in his per-
                                     sonal life.)
Stephen A. Veazey (2004-present)

Despite the fact that the RLDS Church claims to have started with the same doctrinal base as the LDS Church, the RLDS Church has incrementally drifted further and further away from some of the teachings of the Prophet Joseph Smith—not only doctrines about plural marriage and the potential of mankind to become like God, but also other doctrines set forth in the *Book of Mormon* and the *Doctrine and Covenants*. I respectfully acknowledge that the RLDS Church will dispute this, but it is not within the scope of this book to fully discuss these matters. Here is a list of some doctrines and some facts of interest about the RLDS Church.

**Doctrines**

1. <u>They believe the traditional Christian doctrine of the Trinity</u>. Their current pamphlet, *Basic Beliefs*, states the following about their belief in God:

   > We believe in one living God who meets us in the testimony of Israel, is revealed in Jesus Christ, and moves through all creation as the Holy Spirit. We affirm the Trinity—God who is a community of three persons. All things that exist owe their being to God: mystery beyond understanding and love beyond imagination. This God alone is worthy of our worship.

While the RLDS Church had previously endorsed and widely used Joseph Smith's 1838 account of the First Vision (Joseph Smith—History, in the *Pearl of Great Price*), in recent years they have acted embarrassed by that account, which states that two distinct beings, God the Father and his Son, Jesus Christ, appeared at the same time to Joseph in 1820. They do not seem to believe that God the Father and Jesus Christ both have resurrected, immortal bodies of flesh and bones. RLDS leader Steven L. Shields explained in 1986: "We refer to God as 'our Father' because our relationship with him is not unlike that of a child and a parent." But he quickly added, "This is not to imply that the RLDS church believes God has a physical form like a human . . . ."[112] Thus, the RLDS Church focuses on their belief in the traditional "Trinity," with all of its attendant confusion and ambiguities.

2. <u>They believe in the Book of Mormon, but . . . .</u> The *Wikipedia* article "Community of Christ" includes the

---

[112] Steven L. Shields, *Latter Day Saint Beliefs – A Comparison of the RLDS and the LDS Church* (Independence, MO: Herald Publishing House, 1986), 13.

following statement about the RLDS belief in the Book of Mormon:

At the 2007 Community of Christ World Conference, church president Stephen M. Veazey ruled as out of order a resolution to "reaffirm the Book of Mormon as a divinely inspired record". In so doing he stated that "while the Church affirms the Book of Mormon as scripture, and makes it available for study and use in various languages, we do not attempt to mandate the degree of belief or use. This position is in keeping with our longstanding tradition that belief in the Book of Mormon is not to be used as a test of fellowship or membership in the church."

Community of Christ leaders have concerns about the historicity of the Book of Mormon. Apparently, they do not wish to limit the range of beliefs that one has in the Book of Mormon or in doctrines that may be addressed in that book.

3. They believe in continuing revelation—new revelations have been added to their *Doctrine and Covenants*, which now has at least 165 sections.
4. They began to ordain women to the priesthood in 1984. See section 156 of the RLDS *Doctrine and Covenants*.
5. They now accept same-sex marriage (2014). Previous to this, Pres. McMurray had allowed the ordination of practicing homosexuals. The church later renounced this, but then in 2014 they changed back to what President McMurray had started, and they now accept same-sex marriages.
6. They believe marriages are only for mortal life.

7.  <u>They do not believe in plural marriage</u>. For over a hundred years they denied that Joseph Smith either taught it or practiced plural marriage.
8.  <u>They do not believe the practice of baptism for the dead</u>.
9.  <u>They do not believe that there is an "only true church."</u>

**Other Facts of Interest**

--They received a revelation to build a temple in 1984 (Sec. 156).

--An effort to rescind sec. 156 (ordaining women to the priesthood) failed in 1986.

--Their temple in Independence, MO, was dedicated in 1994.

--The first two women apostles were ordained in 1998—Gail E. Mengel and Linda L. Booth.

--They changed their name to "Community of Christ" in 2001.

--In 2007 Becky L. Savage became the first woman in their First Presidency.

--In 2013 Linda L. Booth was their first woman President of the Council of the Twelve Apostles.

--They use the New Revised Standard Version of the Bible.

--They have revised some language in the Book of Mormon to make it more consistent with current language usages.

One interesting part of the history of the RLDS Church is its involvement in two court cases regarding title to and possession of temple lots. They lost both cases, and yet for over a hundred years they have argued that these cases held that the RLDS Church is the lawful successor to the church organized by Joseph Smith in 1830. As will be shown below, this is a misrepresentation of the result of those cases.

## A. The Kirtland Temple Case

In 1873 Joseph Smith, III, and Mark Foscutt acquired the Kirtland Temple property with a quitclaim deed—meaning that the grantor did not guarantee that he had good title to the property. In addition to this recently acquired interest, Joseph Smith, III, also had a claim to an interest in that property as the heir/ successor to Joseph Smith, Jr., as trustee of the property for the LDS Church (the beneficiary of the trust). (See Reimann, 49-59 [especially 52-54].) This created an ethical conflict for him because his duty to the LDS Church conflicted with the interests of the RLDS Church. But Joseph Smith, III, was not interested in securing the property for the LDS Church—the church to whom he owed a fiduciary duty. His dilemma was that he wanted the Kirtland Temple for the RLDS Church, and he was attempting to secure the property for the RLDS Church in spite of his duty to secure it for the LDS Church. By 1879, Joseph Smith, III, knew that the RLDS Church had or would have a good claim to ownership of the property by adverse possession; filing of

the law suit was not necessary to achieve that.[113] The purpose
of the law suit appeared to be primarily to get a court ruling
that the RLDS Church was the lawful successor of the "original"
Church. He felt this would bolster the claims of legitimacy of
the RLDS Church.

In 1879 Joseph Smith, III, as President of the RLDS Church,
filed a law suit in Lake County, Ohio, suing himself and several
others, including "The Church in Utah" and "John Taylor."[114]
The ostensible purpose of the suit was for the RLDS Church to
get full legal title to and possession of the Kirtland Temple.[115]
(I.e., Joseph Smith, III (on behalf of the RLDS Church) sued
Joseph Smith, III (individually).) The RLDS Church regarded
this as a suit to quiet title, even though there was no existing
legal dispute; their purpose for filing the suit was to obtain a
court order that it was the "legitimate successor of the original
Church" founded by Joseph Smith. But the Petition had some
fatal flaws in what it alleged: The RLDS Church did not allege
possession; it did not allege that Joseph Smith, III, kept Plaintiff
out of possession; it did not allege it held legal title; and it did
not ask for ejectment. Consequently, in February 1880, the court
dismissed the Petition for not stating a valid cause of action
upon which any relief can be granted. The Plaintiff (the RLDS
Church) lost the case (Reimann, 83-88). This case does not establish any holding that is beneficial to the RLDS Church. The
specific ruling of the Court is as follows: "The Plaintiff is not in
possession thereof. And thereupon the Court finds as a matter

---

[113] Tolling of the time requirement for adverse possession was achieved by
1901. "Kirtland Temple Suit," *Wikipedia*.

[114] The full names given for these defendants are: "The Church in Utah
of which John Taylor is President and commonly known as the Mormon
Church" and "John Taylor, President of said Utah Church." The RLDS
Church intentionally declined to use the full and proper name of the LDS
Church.

[115] My source for this report and analysis of the two temple lot cases is primarily the exceptional book written by Paul E. Reimann, *The Reorganized
Church and the Civil Courts* (Salt Lake City: Utah Printing Company, 1961).

of law that the Plaintiff is not entitled to the judgment or relief prayed for in its petition."[116]

Joseph Smith, III, did not use the correct name of the LDS Church when he listed it as a defendant in the case, even though he knew very well the correct name. The names of both churches were extremely important to him. Then, Joseph Smith, III, never served either the LDS Church or President John Taylor with process in this case. This shows that the RLDS Church was never serious about obtaining a legitimate legal resolution of the claims they were pursing. The litigation was for a different purpose.

Normally a case such as this would hardly be worthy of any mention. But what makes this case unusual is how the RLDS Church has misrepresented the holding in this case. The case was dismissed; the case changed nothing; all parties were left exactly as they were before the case was filed. Yet leaders of the RLDS Church have repeatedly mischaracterized the case. Joseph Smith, III, said the following about this, the Kirtland Temple lot case: "It resulted, as is well known, in the title being found to belong to the Reorganized Church as the lawful successor to the one organized April 6, 1830." (*The Saints Herald*, January 9, 1943, page 10 [Reimann, 83].) The problem is that this is a false statement. A subsequent president of the RLDS Church, Israel A. Smith, repeated the same falsehood about the Kirtland Temple lot case (in 1943): "The Reorganized Church today has legal title to and is in possession of the Kirtland Temple at Kirtland, Ohio, because a court there held that it is the true church in succession to the original church that built and owned it at the death of Joseph Smith." (*The Saints' Herald*, September 22, 1945, page 12 [Reimann, 83].) But these statements of Joseph Smith, III, and of Israel A. Smith are false. It is true that there are written statements in the Court's order of dismissal that states that the RLDS Church is the lawful

---

[116] Book "T", Common Pleas Record, Lake County, Ohio, page 488, Lake County Courthouse, Painesville, Ohio - reported in Reimann, 84.

successor to the church founded by Joseph Smith, Jr. But those statements have no legal consequence; in fact, those statements misrepresent what the court did. The following explanation will help in understanding this matter.

The RLDS leaders based their position on a statement of findings by the court written in the sentences preceding the order dismissing the case. Non-lawyers might not grasp the irregularity of what I am about to explain, but lawyers will immediately recognize the impropriety. When the court dismisses a case for not stating a valid cause of action, then there can be no findings of fact by the court; the two are inconsistent. The Ohio court never should have signed that part of the dismissal order that mentioned any findings of fact. We now know that it was E. L. Kelley, the attorney for the RLDS Church, who drafted the Order for Judge Sherman to sign.[117] Judge Sherman should have deleted the lengthy findings before signing the Order because those findings made no legal sense and because they were not true.[118] But now that the statement of findings remains in the Order, that Order now stands as a monument to the disingenuousness of the RLDS Church for using that statement as support for its being the lawful successor to the church founded by Joseph Smith, Jr. The case does not support this position, and they know it. But by contending that it does, the RLDS Church merely shows how it, through its attorney, misused the legal system in a way that misrepresents the truth. As the *Wikipedia* article states, an attorney for the RLDS Church advised them in 1942 that for them to use the factual findings part of the dismissal order can "make us look ridiculous."[119]

Despite the problems discussed above, the RLDS Church has continued to make these misrepresentations about the

---

[117] "Kirtland Temple Suit," *Wikipedia*.

[118] The text of the findings of fact are published in the book by Aleah G. Koury (an Apostle of the RLDS Church), *The Truth and the Evidence* (Independence, MO: Herald Publishing House, 1965) pp. 106-7.

[119] "Kirtland Temple Suit," *Wikipedia*.

Kirtland Temple lot case for many years. I heard it myself from a tour guide at the Kirtland Temple in the 1980s. The simple truth is that the Kirtland Temple case of 1879 established nothing for the RLDS Church; the court dismissed the case and did not give the RLDS Church any relief.

The Church of Christ temple lot in Independence, Missouri is a lot just across the road from the RLDS Temple (shown above) and from the RLDS Tabernacle (just to the right of what is shown in the photo).

## B. The Independence Temple Lot Case

In 1891, eleven years after the Kirtland Temple case in Ohio, the RLDS Church filed another law suit to obtain possession of property—this time to attempt to obtain title and possession of the Independence, Missouri temple site—which lot was dedicated in 1831 to be the location of the main, central latter-day temple in the New Jerusalem.[120] The 2 1/2 acre temple site was

---

[120] In 1831 Edward Partridge acquired 63 acres of land, which included the 2 ½ acre plot for the future temple. In the intervening years, the RLDS Church has acquired 33 acres of this original tract; the LDS Church has acquired

owned by the Church of Christ, who had acquired it in 1869. The RLDS Church did not own the temple lot, but they wanted it. At some point they acquired a bogus deed that they thought could get the property for them. The person responsible for the forged document has not been determined, but there were multiple defects in the deed. The deed purported to be signed in Ohio by Edward Partridge on March 25, 1839, giving the property to three, non-existent children of Oliver Cowdery—John, Jane and Joseph Smith Cowdery. The deed purported to be witnessed by Elias Higbee. The bogus deed was not recorded until 1870—31 years after its purported execution date. Then, twenty-one years after the deed was recorded, the RLDS Church brought its law suit. By the time the case was litigated, the deed's fraudulent nature was proven several times over. The grantees were not real people—neither John Cowdery, Jane Cowdery nor Joseph Smith Cowdery was a child of Oliver Cowdery. Thus, the grantees were not real people, making the deed a nullity, even if it had been properly executed. But the execution was also a fraud: The deed said it was executed in Ohio on March 25, 1839, but on that date Partridge was in Illinois and Higbee was in Missouri (Reimann, 123-125). Notwithstanding these defects in the bogus deed, in 1891 the RLDS Church brought a suit in the United States District Court in Missouri to attempt to divest the temple lot from the Church of Christ. Included in the relief requested by the RLDS Church was a request that the court declare it to be the lawful successor of the church organized by the Prophet Joseph Smith in 1830.

In this law suit, the RLDS Church was the Complainant (plaintiff), and the Church of Christ was the primary Respondent (defendant), plus a few other respondents who were connected with the Church of Christ. The LDS Church was not named as a party. The Complaint alleged the following:

---

23 acres; and the Church of Christ acquired the 2 ½ acre temple lot parcel (in about 1869).

a. That the LDS Church became disorganized and separated into factions or parties;

b. That the Church of Christ denies the ordinance of Baptism for the Dead;

c. That the RLDS Church is entitled to title and possession of the property by adverse possession; and

d. That the RLDS Church is the lawful successor to the church organized by Joseph Smith.

At the trial, there was no proof given that the LDS Church ever became disorganized. The RLDS Church correctly alleged that the Church of Christ denied the ordinance of Baptism for the Dead. (This is interesting because the RLDS Church also denies the ordinance.) The RLDS Church provided the bogus deed to support its claim for title. In summary, the case presented by the RLDS Church was insufficient to prove its claims.

Notwithstanding the overwhelming evidence in favor of the Church of Christ, the trial court Judge, John F. Philips, ruled in favor of the RLDS Church on virtually everything it asked for, including the substantial dicta that the RLDS Church was the lawful successor of the Church founded by Joseph Smith. The Church of Christ appealed to the United States Circuit Court of Appeals for the Eighth Circuit, and on September 30, 1895, that Court reversed the ruling of the trial court (in a unanimous decision), and the case was dismissed.[121] The United States Circuit Court of Appeals for the Eighth Circuit ruled against the RLDS Church on two technical grounds, without even getting to the dubious merits of the trial court ruling. The Court said that as a matter of law the RLDS Church could not win its suit unless it

---

[121] The final Order of the Eighth Circuit Court of Appeals that ended this case stated this: "In accordance with the views herein expressed, the decree of the circuit court will be reversed, and the cause will be remanded, with directions to dismiss the bill of complaint" (from 70 Federal 189, reported in Reimann, 149).

either held legal title or was in possession of the property—and the RLDS Church had neither. In addition, the Court denied the RLDS Church's claim because of "laches"—meaning that the RLDS Church has delayed too long in asserting the right that they sought to enforce, and that while the RLDS Church had been neglecting to enforce its alleged rights for a period of 30 years or more, that many other people had obtained deeds to property that is now under question and that they had erected homes and buildings on these properties.

For a hundred years after this case was decided in 1896, the RLDS Church has erroneously cited this case as holding that it is the lawful successor of the church founded by Joseph Smith in 1830. When confronted with the fact that the church lost this case on appeal, they would counter by saying that they only lost on appeal on a technicality, and that the appellate court did not disturb the lower court finding that the RLDS Church was the lawful successor to the original church. This argument is nonsense; it is false. With dismissal of the case, the finding of Judge Philips is vacated—it means nothing. There is no basis whatsoever for the RLDS Church to say that this case determined it to be the lawful successor to the original church. Furthermore, even if civil courts could decide such an ecclesiastical matter, the LDS Church was never a party to this adjudication, and therefore no lawful determination could be made against it. Further, the chain of title that the RLDS Church claimed through the alleged 1839 deed to the purported children of Oliver Cowdery was a blatant forgery. And further still, the LDS Church never became disorganized, as the RLDS complaint alleged.

The flaws in the RLDS Church's law suit were many and were extensive and were fatal to their case, just as they were fatal to the Kirtland Temple lot case. Neither of these cases can honestly be used as a basis for saying anything positive about the RLDS Church. Rather, any reference to them for such a conclusion could be done only out of ignorance or dishonesty.

## A Visit to Nauvoo – RLDS Church Properties

To illustrate and amplify some of the differences between the LDS and RLDS beliefs, let me tell you about a recent visit we had at the RLDS Nauvoo Visitors Center in 2017. We visited the Community of Christ Visitors Center shortly after 9 a.m. on a Wednesday morning in May. We looked through their book store a little bit. They have a lot of LDS books and some of their own publications. I was interested, for example, to see that they continue to sell the book, *Joseph Smith Fought Polygamy*.[122] (For 150 years the RLDS Church steadfastly denied that Joseph ever practiced or taught polygamy.) I bought that book from them a number of years ago. It is interesting to see that they continue to sell it because some of the RLDS publications now acknowledge that Joseph both taught and practiced plural marriage during his lifetime. Today some of the RLDS materials contend that he repented of this during the last two years of his life.

While in the RLDS bookstore we bought the latest edition of their version of the *Book of Mormon*. It cost $25.00—about ten times as much as an LDS hardback edition. The chapter divisions and verses are totally different from the book we use. That is because they do not use the divisions made by Orson Pratt in 1879. According to *Wikipedia*, the RLDS Church made its own chapter and verse divisions in 1874. There are no footnotes and cross-references in the RLDS Book of Mormon, whereas the LDS Book of Mormon has extensive cross-references and footnotes.

As I reviewed some of the current beliefs of the RLDS Church, it became apparent that they do not necessarily believe in the truthfulness of the Book of Mormon. Here is what their former President Grant McMurray said in 2001 about belief in the Book of Mormon (according to *Wikipedia*):

---

[122] Richard and Pamela Price, *Joseph Smith Fought Polygamy*, vol. 1 (Independence, MO: Price Publishing Co., 2000).

In 2001, church president W. Grant McMurray reflected on increasing questions about the Book of Mormon: "The proper use of the Book of Mormon as sacred scripture has been under wide discussion in the 1970s and beyond, in part because of long-standing questions about its historicity and in part because of perceived theological inadequacies, including matters of race and ethnicity." . . . I cannot speak for each person within our community, but perhaps I can say some words on behalf of our community."

In summary, this means that it's fine to believe all, part or none of the Book of Mormon. Of course, the RLDS Church does not believe that there is any one, true church, so they don't think they have anything critical to offer that other churches do not have.

It is interesting to note that Grant McMurray was the first President of the RLDS Church who was not a direct descendant of Joseph Smith. He was appointed President by Wallace B. Smith in 1995, when Wallace B. Smith resigned/retired and became "President Emeritus." (At the time of writing [2019], Wallace is still alive.) Initially it was a requirement that the leader of their church must be a descendant of Joseph Smith. There is no scriptural basis for this contention, and this is one of the reasons that the Hedrickites (Church of Christ – Temple Lot) would not combine with the RLDS Church in the 1850s (Arthur M. Smith, 8-9). But now, over 150 years after the RLDS Church was founded, they have abandoned the doctrine that they once said was critical. Grant McMurray served as President of the RLDS Church from 1995-2004, when he resigned for health and family issues and for "inappropriate choices." He did not appoint a successor, and so the RLDS Council of the Twelve Apostles appointed and ordained Stephen A. Veazey to be President.

Now, getting back to the RLDS Visitors Center—After checking out their book store, we saw their 12-minute video presentation on the origin of their church. Admittedly, twelve minutes is not enough time to cover a lot of material, but they certainly could have given more than 10 seconds to tell about Joseph's First Vision. All they said was that Joseph "had an experience with the divine." They did not say that Joseph saw God the Father and the Son Jesus Christ. Why? They didn't say why, but the reason can be inferred from their doctrinal beliefs: They don't believe that God the Father and His Son Jesus Christ have immortal bodies of flesh and bones; they don't believe that they are separate and distinct beings; and they do not believe that Jesus is literally the only begotten son of God. Had they believed this they would have said it because this truth that Joseph Smith learned in his first vision is the most magnificent and significant truth that was restored to the earth—the simple, but profound knowledge about the nature of God—that we were literally created in the image of God; that God the Father and His Son Jesus Christ both have glorious, immortal bodies of flesh and bones; that they are two separate and distinct beings; and that Jesus is literally the only begotten son of God. If the RLDS Church believed this, they would state it. But instead their presentation is evidence that they neither believe nor understand this most fundamental of all truths restored by the Prophet Joseph Smith. What they do believe is the traditional, widely accepted doctrine of the Trinity—three indistinguishable beings in one. Thus, declining to believe in the true nature of God, they also reject the doctrine that man can become like God; they reject the doctrine of celestial, eternal marriage; and they reject the doctrine of baptism for the dead and the other temple ordinances for the living and the dead.

The RLDS Temple, built in 1994, across the street from the Independence Temple lot, which still stands vacant.

Another indication of how the RLDS doctrines departed from those taught by Joseph Smith is their rejection of the temple ordinances for which the Nauvoo Temple was built. Completing the building of the Nauvoo Temple was a very high priority for the Prophet Joseph Smith. He spoke often of baptisms for the dead and other ordinances for the living and the dead. Joseph taught those closest to him of the temple endowment and of celestial marriage. But the RLDS Church has no use for temple ordinances, and when they did build their temple at Independence (in 1994—see photo) it was not built for the performance of ordinances.

When the video ended, we proceeded with a tour of the Homestead, the Mansion House and the Red Brick Store. Our tour guide was Lachlan Mackay, who we later learned is the newest member of the RLDS Quorum of the Twelve (and a great-great-great grandson of the Prophet Joseph Smith). On the tour with us were about six RLDS tour guides in training. One of those was the young lady who was our tour guide through the Kirtland Temple the year before. Brother Mackay knew a lot of historical facts and details, so we enjoyed our tour very much.

It was interesting to visit the Red Brick Store. (This building was entirely rebuilt on its original foundation about 40 years ago.) Joseph used the upstairs of this building as Church headquarters, for completing the translation of the Book of Abraham, and for organizing the Relief Society. It was here that the Prophet administered the Endowment beginning May 4, 1842, and where some celestial marriages were performed. The RLDS guides did not get into these things.

## III. The Church of Christ – Temple Lot

The Church of Christ which owns the Independence Temple Site was formally organized in 1863 by Granville Hedrick and Jedediah Owens. Hedrick had been a member of the LDS Church, but he did not go west with the pioneers. He and some other remained in Illinois, and according to their church Apostle, Arthur Smith, "continued to function in their local capacity till 1852."[123] Apostle Smith then describes their history as follows:

> About this time (1852), the church in Utah, un-
> der the leadership of Brigham Young, came out
> in open and proclaimed polygamy to be a tenet

---

[123] Arthur M. Smith, *A Brief History of The Church of Christ (Temple Lot)* (Fourth edition, August 1971), 8. Most of my information about The Church of Christ comes from this pamphlet, which I obtained from that church on one of my visits to the Temple Lot in Independence, Missouri. Arthur M. Smith was one of their Apostles.

of the Gospel and an ordinance of the church. Along with this doctrine, which had long been secretly taught and practiced among many of the divisions of the church, came the teaching of other doctrines such as the Exaltation of Man, Adam God, Celestial Marriage, and other doctrines just as unscriptural as these. This open teaching and practicing of these false doctrines, seemed to arouse the more sober-minded men throughout the Restoration to a new interest in the welfare of this Church which had been established "by the will and commandment of God."

In the fall of 1857, a little group of Saints in Illinois sent two of their elders, Jedediah Owens and Granville Hedrick, to meet with a group of Saints who were meeting in conference at Blanchardville, or Zarahemla, Wisconsin, October 6, 1857. This group was known as the New Organization, and consisted of men from the various groups, mostly from the Strang and William B. Smith movement. That this effort to unite with this group of Saints was a failure was due to a resolution that this "New Organization" had adopted in 1852 in a conference held at Beloit, Wisconsin, from which we quote the following: "Resolved, that the successor of Joseph Smith, Jr., as a Presiding High Priest in the Melchisedec Priesthood, must of necessity be the seed of Joseph Smith, Jr., in fulfillment of the law and promises of God." (Arthur Smith, 8-9)

In addition to the above, the founders of the Church of Christ also objected to there being a First Presidency for the church, and they rejected the name given to the church at Far

West (i.e., The Church of Jesus Christ of Latter-day Saints); they believed that "The Church of Christ" was the proper name. Arthur Smith goes on to give the following account of this church:

> In 1864, this group of Saints in Woodford County, Illinois, received a revelation directing them to dispose of their properties and go to Independence, Missouri, and the way would be opened up for them to purchase the property that had been dedicated as the place where the Temple was to stand. These Saints were obedient to this command, and in 1867 they came to Independence, Missouri. In March, 1867, they held their first conference in Independence. Two years later, 1869, they made the first purchase of that property known as the Temple Lot.... (Arthur Smith, 11)

Today, 2019, the Church of Christ continues to own the 2 ½ acre temple site at Independence, Missouri, and they have a small chapel on the land. According to *Wikipedia*, they have about 7,000 members worldwide. Their success in defending against the effort by the RLDS Church to take the temple lot from them was detailed in the previous section of this chapter.

# Part III—Doctrines and Prophecies

Statue in Harmony, Pennsylvania depicts Jesus' Apostles Peter, James and John conferring the Melchizedek Priesthood on Joseph Smith in 1829. Oliver Cowdery is shown next to Joseph. Statue is the work of Avard T. Fairbanks.

Joseph Smith brought to the world hundreds of pages of new scripture, which introduced dozens of doctrinal clarifications and expansions. Part III addresses some of these.

None of the new scriptures provided more profound implications than Joseph Smith's Book of Abraham. Chapter 7 will address and refute the claims of some critics that Joseph Smith's "translation" of the Book of Abraham is a fraud.

Chapter 8 discusses statements of Joseph Smith concerning the ancient scriptural practice of withholding the priesthood of God from descendants of Cain. This chapter discusses historical, scriptural examples of God's limiting priesthood opportunities until it was right in His timetable. The chapter also gives a review of recent history that confirms the timeliness of Official Declaration 2 in 1978, which announced that the priesthood is now available to all worthy males.

Chapter 9 presents an interesting discussion of six prophecies by Joseph Smith that some critics contend are false prophecies. But a close review of each of them demonstrates how each has been or will be fulfilled and that they are evidence that Joseph Smith was indeed a prophet of God.

Above is a photo of the papyrus that was found in the 1967 in the Metropolitan Museum of Art in New York City, which includes the drawing that is Facsimile 1 in the Book of Abraham. This portion of papyrus is designated Joseph Smith Papyrus XI (left) and I (right). Photo courtesy of Intellectual Reserve, Inc.

# Chapter 7

# THE BOOK OF ABRAHAM

Critics have challenged the authenticity of the Book of Abraham for over 175 years. With the discovery in 1967 of some of the fragments of the original papyrus that had been in Joseph Smith's possession, this sparked a new wave of criticisms about the Book of Abraham.[124] Recently some of these critics have produced writings and videos that present Joseph Smith as a fraud. But these hit pieces are based upon several errors and flaws—flaws which are not readily apparent from a superficial review. I will discuss some of these flaws in the following pages.

---

[124] It was thought for many years that most of the original papyrus scrolls had been lost or destroyed. It was thought that they may have been destroyed in a great Chicago fire. However, in 1967, some of the papyrus scrolls were found in the Metropolitan Museum of Art in New York City. The Church acquired them in 1967, after which the Church published an extensive article about them in the January and February 1968 issues of the *Improvement ERA*. However, most of the papyrus scrolls remain lost or destroyed. Those scrolls that do exist include a portion of Facsimile No. 1. But *The Book of Abraham* is not a translation of Facsimile No. 1. With each of the three facsimiles that was published with the Book of Abraham text, there is an explanation written with it (see pages at end of chapter), which gives a brief description of what various figures represent. Hugh Nibley points out that the Egyptians would often include illustrations with their writings, and sometimes the illustrations would be separated from the text that described them.

These flaws undermine the validity of the major conclusions of these critics.

Some of the discussion in this chapter is a little technical, but for those who may be inclined to be persuaded by the conclusions of these critics, they should be grateful for the thorough discussion that follows. I will first discuss the origin and background of the Book of Abraham. Then I will discuss and refute some specific criticisms of the Book of Abraham. Finally, I will discuss some recent evidence supportive of the authenticity of the Book of Abraham.

Printing Office in Nauvoo, where the Book of Abraham was published in two March editions of *The Times and Seasons* in 1842. The home of John Taylor (who worked closely with Joseph in publishing) is adjacent to the Printing Office.

## I. Background of the Book of Abraham

The Book of Abraham consists of eleven pages in *The Pearl of Great Price*. Joseph published this in two editions of the *Times and Seasons*, on March 1 and 15, 1842 (HC 5:524). Joseph said that this was a translation of writings of the ancient prophet Abraham.

He said that it was translated from some papyrus scrolls that he acquired in 1835, which scrolls had been found with some mummies in Egypt.[125] Most experts today date the writing of the existing papyrus to be between the third and first centuries B.C.[126] After Joseph Smith's death (in 1844), the translation was next included in a publication made by Apostle Franklin D. Richards in 1851 called "The Pearl of Great Price." That publication also included three "facsimiles" or copies of drawings of certain portions of the papyrus manuscripts that Joseph Smith had. With each facsimile there was a written explanation of various figures in each facsimile. (See pages at the end of this chapter.) The facsimiles evoke some interest because they include drawings of people doing things. For example, Facsimile No. 1 includes the explanation that it depicts "Abraham fastened upon an altar" and a "priest of Elkenah attempting to offer up Abraham as a sacrifice." The "Book of Abraham" translation relates to, but was not taken from those facsimiles. The "Book of Abraham" was canonized by the Church as scripture in 1880 (as a part of *The Pearl of Great Price*). The three facsimiles and their "explanations" have continued to be published with the translated text ever since then.

Since the Book of Abraham was not presented to the Church to be canonized until over 35 years after Joseph's death, Joseph did not have the opportunity to include additional explanations about what portions of the papyrus he translated, about the role of revelation in the translation process, and about the content and relevance of the facsimiles. Nevertheless, for over 175 years

---

[125] The papyrus consisted of "two rolls of papyrus" and "[t]wo or three other small pieces of papyrus" (HC 2:349). At the time the papyrus was acquired in July of 1835, Joseph wrote that "much to our joy [we] found that one of the rolls contained the writings of Abraham, another has the writings of Joseph of Egypt" (HC 2: 236). In December of 1835 Joseph stated: "The record of Abraham and Joseph, found with the m[u]mmies, is beautifully written on papyrus, with black, and a small part of red, ink or paint, in perfect preservation" (HC 2:348).

[126] See footnote 146, below.

members of the Church have found these eleven pages to be insightful, inspiring and enlightening.

I have read and studied the Book of Abraham many times throughout my life, and I have been repeatedly inspired by the messages found in those eleven pages. The Spirit has witnessed to me the truthfulness of these messages, and this has been a great source of enlightenment and uplift for me. Hereafter I will identify some criticisms that have been leveled at the Book of Abraham. But first, consider a list of some of the valuable contributions of this book of scripture:

1.  Importance of <u>seeking</u> the blessings of the Priesthood;
2.  Incident where an angel of the Lord saved Abraham from being sacrificed;
3.  Priesthood was denied to the descendants of Ham;
4.  Explanation of the Abrahamic Covenant;
5.  Abraham had a Urim and Thummim;
6.  About the Universe—Kolob is the star nearest to God;
7.  Intelligences are eternal essences—each is different;
8.  Foreordination;
9.  Purpose of Life—to obey God and to be "added upon";
10. War in Heaven;
11. In the pre-earth existence, Jesus Christ was selected by God to be our Redeemer; and
12. Gods went "down" and organized the earth.

Before introducing specific criticisms, you should know that I am not an Egyptologist, and I don't intend to weigh in on all of the various interpretations of the remaining papyrus fragments. But I am an attorney, and as you will see, the primary point of dispute regarding the Book of Abraham is not a question of interpreting Egyptian, but rather relates to an assertion made by Joseph Smith's critics that he pretended to make his translation from the Hôr papyrus. Addressing this issue does not require expertise in Egyptology; it requires experience in the legal areas of the authenticity of documents, burdens of proof, and evaluating evidence. I will share some critical analysis about these issues. I would also point out that The Church of Jesus Christ of Latter-day Saints has an essay on its website, "lds.org," which gives an excellent, concise statement about many of the criticisms leveled at the Book of Abraham. The essay is entitled: "Translation and Historicity of the Book of Abraham."[127] That would be a good starting point for those interested in learning more about these issues. However, because I was interested in delving a little deeper into some of those issues, I have prepared this discussion.

A. Meaning of "translation." Regarding his translation of the golden plates into the Book of Mormon, Joseph said that he translated them "by the gift and power of God" and that he used the Urim and Thummim to do it. Similarly, Joseph's translation of the Bible was a labor of inspiration and revelation. And while it is my understanding that the translation of the Book of Abraham was also done by the gift and power of God, Joseph Smith did not describe his translation that way when he introduced his translation in the *Times and Seasons* in March of 1842. Joseph's introduction merely states that it was "translated from the papyrus, by Joseph Smith." Because the introduction does not explicitly state that the translated text was the product of divine revelation, some contend that it was merely a scholastic exercise by Joseph. However, it was always the understanding of those who were close to Joseph Smith that the translated text was an inspired translation, and that Joseph represented it to be such. (See section II, E, below.) We don't know Joseph's translation process, and we do not have 83% of the original papyri. All we have is Facsimile 1 and perhaps 17% of the papyri, and we also have some manuscripts prepared by Joseph's scribes early in the translation process. Despite the absence of key information, for 175 years some scholars and speculators

---

[127] Historicity means "historical authenticity."

have been more than willing to offer opinions on the validity of Joseph's translation. The current generation of critics continues to eagerly condemn Joseph Smith, all the while they ignore or deny that they lack sufficient evidence to prove their opinions. As will be shown in the following discussion, these critics never do overcome this lack of critical data.

It is important to recognize that Joseph's use of the term "translation" has a technical meaning to him that is different from a traditional, academic translation. His translation of the gold plates was more by revelation than by traditional methods of translation, even though the word "translation" is used.[128] It was God who translated the gold plates into the Book of Mormon. Joseph Smith was merely the prophet through whom God did this work. Similarly, Joseph's work in doing an "inspired translation" of the Bible was primarily a revelatory exercise. Joseph did not actually translate anything in making his inspired corrections to texts in the Bible. Similarly, Joseph's "translation" that resulted in publication of the Book of Abraham in 1842 was also a revelatory work—the last of Joseph's "translation" works.

B. Setting when the Book of Abraham was published. To help give some understanding of the significance of the Book of Abraham, it is helpful to recognize what other revelations the Prophet was bringing to light at this same time—early 1842. During this same period of time Joseph was introducing the temple endowment ordinance that was administered for the first time on May 4, 1842. This is significant because Facsimile 2 has a reference to information pertaining to the temple. The point is that the temple ordinances and teachings were made known to the Prophet Joseph Smith at this same time period. The Church does not have an official statement of which I am aware which attributes these temple ordinances and teachings to the papyri. But the proximity in time to the publication of

---

[128] See, e.g., Draper, Brown & Rhodes, 242.

the Book of Abraham gives the implication that there may have been some relationship.[129] My impression is that all of them are the product of revelation from God to the Prophet Joseph Smith. Whether or not the temple ordinances or the Book of Abraham is found word for word in any of the papyri, it appears that the papyri were a tool that helped lead Joseph to receive revelation on both of them.

Hugh Nibley has written extensively on Joseph Smith's translation of the Book of Abraham and his explanations of the facsimiles.[130] Nibley points out that the discovery and publication of other ancient texts about Abraham lend support to the legitimacy of Joseph Smith's Book of Abraham.[131] Recently, E. Douglas Clark, Kerry Muhlestein and John Gee authored publications which refer to dozens of documents and sources

---

[129] Another thing that was going on in the spring of 1842 was that Joseph was introducing the doctrine of plural marriage to some of the faithful saints. And it was also in May of 1842 when the John Bennett scandal erupted, in which he was excommunicated for sexual improprieties after which he began his campaign to accuse Joseph and the Mormons of practicing polygamy. I am not trying to connect these things directly to the Book of Abraham questions, but it is worth noting that these were all taking place at the same time.

[130] See, e.g., Hugh Nibley, *Abraham in Egypt* (Salt Lake City: Deseret Book and Foundation for Ancient Research and Mormon Studies [FARMS], 2000); Hugh Nibley, *An Approach to the Book of Abraham - The Collected Works of Hugh Nibley: Volume 18* (Salt Lake City: Deseret Book and FARMS, 2009); and Hugh Nibley, *The Message of the Joseph Smith Papyri, An Egyptian Endowment* [hereafter, *Message of the Joseph Smith Papyri*] (Deseret Book and Foundation for Ancient Research and Mormon Studies, 2005). It is worthy to note that the explanation of some of the figures in Facsimile No. 2 include things that are not to be revealed at the present time and/or things that may be made known in the Holy Temple of God. This implies that perhaps information about the Temple Endowment is referenced in Facsimile No. 2 and perhaps in other of the papyri. This is a theme that Hugh Nibley develops in his book.

[131] Hugh Nibley, *Abraham in Egypt*, pp. 11-73—especially see pp. 11 and 26. Two of the texts cited by Nibley are the pseudepigraphic writings, *Apocalypse of Abraham* (1897) and the *Testament of Abraham* (1892).

which support many details that Joseph Smith included in his Book of Abraham.[132]

C. The papyri. It is thought that we now have only about one-sixth of the original papyri manuscripts.[133] Because of this, and because Joseph's "translation" process was more revelatory than academic, it is impossible to academically either confirm or refute the correctness of Joseph's translation of the Book of Abraham. I would also point out that Kerry Muhlestein, a professor of Ancient Scriptures at BYU (Ph.D. in Egyptology, UCLA, 2003) has produced several informative YouTube videos that provide support for the authenticity of the Book of Abraham.

Hugh Nibley and other scholars concur that some of the papyrus fragments that we do have appear to be what has been called the *Book of Breathings*.[134] Some experts initially contended that the papyri could be an ancient Egyptian text called the *Book of the Dead*, but scholars agree that the papyrus containing Facsimile 1 is not.[135]

When the Prophet Joseph Smith published the Book of Abraham in two editions of the *Times and Seasons* in 1842, he never identified the particular parts of the papyri from which

---

[132] E. Douglas Clark, *The Blessings of Abraham—Becoming a Zion People* (Covenant Press, 2005) pp. 45-59. See footnote 176, below, for a listing of some of those sources. See also John Gee, *An Introduction to the Book of Abraham* (Salt Lake City: Religious Studies Center, BYU and Deseret Book Co., 2017), p. 51-54; and Kerry Muhlestein, "Egyptian Papyri and the Book of Abraham," in Robert L. Millet, ed., *No Weapon Shall Prosper*, 226-27.

[133] Egyptologist John Gee, who has studied and written about these papyri has concluded that we have less than 13% of the original manuscripts that were in the possession of Joseph Smith. See John Gee, "A Guide to the Joseph Smith Papyri" (Provo: Foundation for Ancient Research and Mormon Studies, 2000) at p. 23. Kerry Muhlestein suggests that may have only 5% of the originals. Muhlestein, 226-27.

[134] Nibley, *The Message of the Joseph Smith Papyri* is devoted to extensive analysis and discussion about this.

[135] *Id.*, 22-23 and 62.

the translation was taken.[136] You cannot begin to evaluate the correctness of a particular translation without first specifically identifying the text that is being translated. As will be pointed out below, some critics contend that they do know the papyrus from which Joseph Smith claimed to translate—they call it the "Hôr papyrus"—and that Joseph's translation is false. But, as will be pointed out below, this conclusion is based upon unproven assumptions and is therefore speculation. There is insufficient basis to conclude that Joseph Smith's translation is false. We don't know what particular parts of papyri were the subject of Joseph's translation, and we don't have all the pieces of papyri that Joseph had. Joseph described some of the papyrus to be written "with black, and a small part red, ink or paint" (HC 2:348). But the Hôr papyrus has no writing in red ink.[137] Further, even the pieces that Joseph did have were only part of the original parchments. Also, through revelation Joseph may have had access to Abraham's original writings and drawings, which could be different from what is on the papyri.[138] Thus, the most any critics could legitimately say would be that based upon the pieces that they examined, in their opinion the Book of Abraham was not translated from them. But there is no sound

---

[136] See, e.g., Nibley, *The Message of the Joseph Smith Papyri*, at p. 2, where Nibley writes: "The facsimiles were published, along with explanations of what they depicted, but at no time was any Egyptian text put forward as the original of the Book of Abraham."

Several critics contends that Joseph pretended to translate from certain symbols on the papyrus. This criticism is based on assumptions that are not authenticated. (See, e.g., Charles H. Larson, *By His Own Hand on Papyrus* (1985, 1992). See also the discussion below in the section, "**First Assumption**."

[137] Michael D. Rhodes, "Why doesn't the translation of the Egyptian papyri found in 1967 match the text of the Book of Abraham in the Pearl of Great Price?" *Ensign*, July 1988, 51-53.

[138] This was how Joseph translated a record of the Apostle John in 1829 (D&C 7). See also, Richard D. Draper, Kent S. Brown & Michael D. Rhodes, *The PEARL of GREAT PRICE, A Verse-by-Verse Commentary* (Salt Lake City: Deseret Book Co., 2005), 242.

basis to conclude that the translation is false since we don't know the text from which it was translated.

D. Joseph was not an Egyptologist. Joseph never explained exactly how he translated the parchments. And while he spent some time studying Egyptian writing, he was not an Egyptologist with expert understanding of the Egyptian writings.[139] The placement of the three facsimiles (drawings) at pages 28, 36 and 41 of *The Pearl of Great Price* (copies of which are shown at the end of this chapter) is interesting, but it may also be misleading to a casual reader who might assume that the text was translated from the facsimiles. However, from the explanations provided with each of the facsimiles, it is clear that the translation or interpretation of those facsimiles/drawings includes a number of things different from what is covered in the Book of Abraham. The facsimiles are mostly drawings— they are not the texts that were translated. Verses 12 and 14 in the first chapter of Abraham specifically refer to the drawing in Facsimile No. 1 as a drawing that is different from the translation of the text.[140]

Joseph did not leave a statement or explanation connecting the revealed text of the Book of Abraham with particular pieces of parchment. Despite Joseph's acquiring some understanding

---

[139] It is true that Joseph and his associates began to construct an "Egyptian Alphabet and Grammar" (A&G) while they studied the papyri, but that project was never completed nor published, nor ever presented by Joseph Smith to be reliable or even valid. See, e.g., H. Donl Peterson, "Book of Abraham," *Encyclopedia of Mormonism,* (New York: Macmillan Publishing Company, 1992); see also, Nibley, *An Approach to the Book of Abraham,* 516-525, 528, 529. Nibley gives a thorough discussion of the A&Gs and states that there is no evidence that an A&G was ever used in the creation of the Book of Abraham text. Nibley said there were at least two sets of A&G documents, most of which were written by Oliver Cowdery and W. W. Phelps, and that they contain a number of inconsistencies. Further, John Gee concludes that "[t]he grammar seems to have been produced from the Book of Abraham and not the other way around." Gee, *An Introduction ... Book of Abraham,* 37.

[140] "[T]hat you may have a knowledge of this altar, I will refer you to the representation at the commencement of this record." Abraham 1:12.

of Egyptian writing, he represented the Book of Abraham to be the result of revelation from God. (See discussion below in section II, E.)

## II. Addressing Five Criticisms of the Book of Abraham

A. Allegation that the papyrus writings are not the actual writings of Abraham. The short introduction to the Book of Abraham in *The Pearl of Great Price* includes a statement that can be interpreted to mean that Abraham actually wrote on the papyrus that was in Joseph Smith's possession. I don't think this to be the case, and I don't think that Joseph Smith claimed this to be the case. However, I do think the issue is worthy of examination because the language of the introduction could certainly be interpreted to mean that.

To begin, the introductory words that for many years have been placed immediately before the translated text of the Book of Abraham in *The Pearl of Great Price* (1979 edition), are these:

> A Translation of some ancient Records that have fallen into our hands from the catacombs of Egypt.—The writings of Abraham while he was in Egypt, called the Book of Abraham, written by his own hand, upon papyrus. *See History of the Church, vol. 2, pp. 235, 236, 348-351.*

It is interesting to note that this wording continues to exist in the Church's 2013 edition, except that the reference citation at the end is omitted. This change is good, because that citation does not address the issue of whether the papyrus was actually "written by his [Abraham's] own hand." The source of that phrase is the introduction written by Joseph Smith above the translation of the Book of Abraham when it was first published

in the *Times and Season* on March 5, 1842.[141] But the current introduction omits some key words from Joseph Smith's statement.
Joseph's introduction in 1842 included the words: "purporting
to be the writings of Abraham, . . . written by his own hand."[142]
The meaning that is added by the use of the words "purporting
to be" is very important, and the omission of those words in
the current version creates an ambiguity that is responsible for
the interpretation that Joseph claimed that Abraham actually
wrote on the papyrus in his possession. However, a close look
at the original introduction makes it clear that Joseph was not
making such a contention, rather he was stating that the writing
"purports" to be that of Abraham.

The text of the Book of Abraham clearly purports to be
the writings of Abraham. It is written in the First Person,
and Abraham states in several places: "I, Abraham, saw," "I,
Abraham, took," "I left," "I, Abraham, departed," etc.[143] Thus,
the Book of Abraham itself clearly "purports" to be written by
Abraham himself—not by someone else telling about Abraham.
I submit that this was the meaning that Joseph Smith was intending to convey when he used the words "purporting to be"
in his 1842 introduction. It makes no sense to interpret "purported" in a way that would be expressing doubt as to who the
ultimate author was, for Joseph represented the text to be the
words of Abraham.[144]

But by adding the word "purporting" to his introduction,
Joseph was expressing uncertainty as to whether the papyrus

---

[141] The exact wording of the introduction is this: "A TRANSLATION of some
ancient Records that have fallen into our hands, from the Catecombs [sic] of
Egypt, purporting to be the writings of Abraham, while he was in Egypt,
called the Book of Abraham, written by his own hand, upon papyrus."

[142] See, e.g., Hugh Nibley, *Abraham in Egypt*, 4.

[143] Abraham 1:1, 2: 2, 4 and 14.

[144] It should be noted that in the initial publication of the Book of Abraham
in the *Times and Seasons* on March 1, 1842 that some of the references to
Abraham were written as "Abram": Abraham 1:16 & 17 and 2:3, 6, 14 & 17.
These original designations as "Abram" were consistent with the time before his name was changed to "Abraham."

in his possession was actually the writing of Abraham. That would be an astute observation by him, and Joseph's using of the word "purporting" in the initial introduction provides a helpful insight.

Why the phrasing with the word "purporting" was removed from the introduction to the Book of Abraham, I do not know. Perhaps it was thought that the word would be interpreted to express doubt as to whether the Book of Abraham was actually a true, scriptural account. This is just speculation on my part. But clearly, Joseph did not intend to discredit the translation that he asserted to be divinely inspired. Frankly, I would suspect that in the past, 99% of the readers of the Book of Abraham have not even been aware of this issue. However, now that attacks on Joseph Smith's translation of the papyrus have become more aggressive and more readily available today, it is helpful to understand the history and evolution of the introductory statement that is currently in place. And from that original statement with his use of the word "purporting," it is clear that Joseph's introductory statement in 1842 was not an affirmative statement by him that Abraham actually wrote on the papyrus that Joseph translated.[145]

Experts have estimated that those papyrus fragments still in existence date back to perhaps the second century B. C.[146] Abraham lived about 2050 - 1875 B.C. Thus, these papyrus scrolls would not have been personally written by Abraham.

---

[145] See also, Draper, Brown & Rhodes, 242.

[146] "Joseph Smith Papyri," *Wikipedia*, see footnotes 22 and 23, and associated text. Baer estimated the scrolls to have been written around the time of Christ. In 2005, Rhodes estimated their time of writing to be in the second century B. C. See also, Marc Coenen, "The Dating of the Papyri Joseph Smith I, X and XI and Min Who Massacres His Enemies," in *Egyptian Religion: The Last Thousand Years* (Leuven: Peters, 1998) 2:1103-15, which is cited in Hugh Nibley, *The Message of the Joseph Smith Papyri*, at xxii. John Gee reported that currently experts date the existing papyri to either the first centuries B.C. or A.D., or to the second or third centuries B.C. John Gee, "A Guide to the Joseph Smith Papyri" (Provo, Foundation for Ancient Research and Mormon Studies 2000). See also Gee, *An Introduction to the Book of Abraham*, 180.

But ancient records are often transmitted as copies or copies of copies.[147] This is the case with ancient documents that have been recovered for the Book of Enoch. It is also true with respect to some of the Dead Sea scrolls and some of the Nag Hammadi ancient scrolls. Thus, the scrolls that were delivered to Joseph Smith could have been copies of ancient writings of Abraham—and they still would be authentic ancient texts. But it is not likely that Abraham actually wrote on the papyrus in Joseph Smith's possession. Thus, the account could be characterized as being "written by his own hand," but it would be a copy (or a copy of a copy) of what Abraham personally wrote.

What does all of this mean? To me, the inclusion of the words, "written by his own hand" in the introduction to the Book of Abraham can be misleading. The use of this phrase without adding the words "purporting to be," that Joseph Smith added, makes a representation that the papyrus from which Joseph translated the Book of Abraham was actually written by Abraham's own hand. But based upon the original sources for this introduction, it appears that Joseph himself expressed reservations about whether it was actually "written by [Abraham's] own hand." Thus, the current introduction appears to alter the words and meaning of what Joseph had previously written.[148]

Whether or not Abraham actually penned some of the writing on the scrolls does not affect my appreciation of the Book of Abraham. Hugh Nibley points out that ancient texts are typically identified by the original author, whether or not a particular document is the original text, a copy of the original, or a

---

[147] See, e.g., lds.org, "Translation and Historicity of the Book of Abraham" [hereafter "Historicity"](2016), especially footnotes 28, 29 and 30 and associated text. See also, Hugh Nibley, *Enoch the Prophet* (Salt Lake City: Deseret Book Company, 1986); and Charles Francis Potter, *Did Jesus Write This Book?* (Fawcett Publications, Inc., 1965).

[148] This conclusion is based upon the original sources that I have found. If there are other sources or explanations for omitting the word "purported," they are not known to me.

copy of a copy.[149] Such a mistake (even if it were a mistake) does not affect the inspiration and validity of The Book of Abraham.

B. Allegation that the plural renditions of "Gods" is wrong. In the account of the creation that is found in chapters 4 and 5 of The Book of Abraham, Joseph Smith's translation repeatedly states that "the Gods" said "Let there be light," and "the Gods" did the other acts of creation. Some critics complain that this plural reference to God is wrong. This is a curious and uninformed argument. Joseph Smith learned in his study of Hebrew that the reference to God in connection with the creation of the world in Genesis was a plural form of the word. Even in the King James Version of the Bible, the plural form of God manifests in several key places—most importantly in Genesis 1:26-27, where it states that God said, "Let us make man, in our own image, . . . male and female created he them." The plural rendition of "Gods" that is used in the Book of Abraham is consistent with the Bible, and it provides an inspiring insight into the nature of God and the divine destiny of mankind. Abraham certainly understood the truth about the plurality of God, and Abraham's account of the creation would have certainly reflected this.

C. Allegation that the missing portions of Facsimile No. 1 were wrongly completed—that the person standing should have a black, jackal head, but not knife; that there should be a second bird; and that the prone person should be lying on his arms. There are other ancient Egyptian drawings similar to Facsimile No. 1, that depict a man on a bed-altar and with a black priest, with a jackal head and not holding a knife. But this does not prove that Facsimile No. 1 is not a genuine drawing, and it does not prove that the drawing does not depict Abraham. We do not have the entire parchment that shows the complete drawing. The photo that precedes this chapter shows what remains today of the papyrus from which Facsimile No. 1

---

[149] Nibley, *Abraham in Egypt*, 5-10.

was taken. Each of the facsimiles in *The Pearl of Great Price* and
in the original publication in the *Times and Seasons* was printed
from a craftsman's engraving, attempting to duplicate what was
on the papyrus. It appears to me that the craftsman made an
assumption that the individual standing had a white, human
head and that he was holding a knife. I don't know if the completed drawing of Facsimile No. 1 in the Book of Abraham is a
correct depiction of what was originally drawn on the papyrus
that Joseph had. But the possibility that Facsimile 1 *might* show
a minor drawing error is of insignificant consequence because
The Book of Abraham is not a translation of Facsimile No. 1.

What is interesting to me is that Joseph Smith's critics are
so obsessed with discrediting him that they go too far in their
speculation about what they think this drawing should look
like, and what it shouldn't look like. In addition to the criticisms
mentioned in the paragraph above, the critics also insist that
those are not two hands being raised by the person on the altar,
but that rather they should be the wings of a second bird. Based
upon what I see with my own eyes, this is not only speculation,
but it conflicts with what I see. Then the critics insist that the
prone person would be lying on his arms. That is not consistent
with the drawing, and it certainly would be a most unnatural
position.

D. Allegation that Joseph's "Explanations" for the three
facsimiles are mistranslations. Included with the three facsimiles that Joseph published with his translation of the Book
of Abraham are three separate "explanations" of key figures
in each of the facsimiles—one for each of the facsimiles. (See
the end of this chapter.) The inclusion of these "explanations"
makes it clear that the Book of Abraham does not pretend to
be a translation of these facsimiles. This is an important point.
Some critics have argued that his "explanations" are not consistent with interpretations of those facsimiles by Egyptologists
today, and therefore some argue that this proves that Joseph
Smith's translation (his "Explanations") are false, and that this

proves that he is a fraud. I don't believe the evidence supports such a conclusion, but I will briefly discuss this criticism.

There is no unanimity of opinion among Egyptologists as to the translation and meaning of Facsimiles 1, 2 and 3. And some Egyptologists reject the contention that evidence proves Joseph Smith's translation of the three Facsimiles to be false. There is a difference between interpreting text and interpreting drawings. I am suspicious of those who are too quick to turn assumptions and conjecture into fact. There is virtually no text with Facsimile 1, while there is a mixture of text and images in Facsimiles 2 and 3.

Hugh Nibley and Egyptologists Michael D. Rhodes, John Gee, and Kerry Muhlestein have written extensively, analyzing the Joseph Smith facsimiles and comparing them with other ancient Egyptian writings.[150] Nibley, Gee and Muhlestein establish a credible case for Joseph Smith's translation being authentic, credible and consistent with other ancient Egyptian texts.[151]

I will not include specific analysis of all of the various

---

[150] *Id.* See Hugh W. Nibley, "The Three Facsimiles from the Book of Abraham" (1980), [hereafter, "The Three Facsimiles"], http://www.boap. org/LDS/HughNibley/TrFac.html; Hugh Nibley, *Abraham in Egypt* (Deseret Book and Foundation for Ancient Research and Mormon Studies, 2000); Hugh Nibley, *The Message of the Joseph Smith Papyri, An Egyptian Endowment* (Deseret Book and Foundation for Ancient Research and Mormon Studies, 1975 and 2005); and Draper, Brown & Rhodes, 284-287. Draper, Brown and Rhodes suggest that the explanations given by Joseph Smith for the three facsimiles "match the original drawings done by Abraham," not the modified drawings in the papyrus. Nevertheless, they note other support for Joseph Smith's explanations (*Id.*).

[151] As will be discussed below, some critics insist that Joseph's translations of the Facsimiles are all false. But other experts disagree and argue that the numerous specific identifications made by Joseph Smith "leave us with an abundance of examples that Joseph Smith had to have had help from a Power above his own to make such accurate restorations of missing signs and such sound and appropriate interpretations." (H. Donl Peterson, Ph.D., *The Pearl of Great Price: A History and Commentary* (Salt Lake City: Deseret Book, 1987), 54.) Peterson lists a number of identifications made by Joseph Smith with respect to the three facsimiles which he says support this conclusion. *Id.*, 47-55.

figures in each of the Facsimiles.[152] But I will point out that the main parts of Facsimiles 1, 2 and 3 are pictures—depictions of events with various people and things. Depictions are not texts—they're just pictures. And pictures can have multiple meanings as well as indecipherable meanings. They are also susceptible to people ascribing meanings to them that were never intended by the artist/drawer. Some critics complain that Joseph Smith's Facsimile No. 1 was not rendered properly because it is different from other, similar drawings from that era. This is a poor argument. Hugh Nibley points out that while there are many similar drawings from that era, most of them have differences.[153] It is an erroneous assumption to think that all drawings that accompany an Egyptian text must be stock drawings, without variation. It is also an erroneous assumption to think that if the name of Abraham is not specifically written on Facsimile No. 1, then the individual on the altar could not be Abraham. This is a baseless conclusion. It is true that there are a number of known ancient, Egyptian drawings similar to Facsimile No. 1. But this does not prove that Facsimile No. 1 does not refer to Abraham on an altar. All it proves is that drawings like this were not unique. There is no basis to conclude that this could not refer to Abraham.

While some Egyptologists have ascribed specific proper nouns to some of the individuals depicted in these facsimiles,

---

[152] "Critical appraisal of the Book of Abraham," *Wikipedia*, includes a comparison of Joseph Smith's explanations of various figures with that of Theodule Deveria (1860). That article has some value because it is a relatively concise article on the subject, even though the writers of that article dismiss Nibley, Gee and Rhodes as apologists for Joseph Smith. However, if the reader also consults the sources identified in footnotes 150 and 151, this will provide a more thorough analysis of the matter.

[153] Nibley, "The Three Facsimiles," 2, and Nibley, *The Collected Works of Hugh Nibley: Volume 5, The Book of Mormon* (Salt Lake City: Deseret Book Co., 1988), 336-40. Nibley points out that the drawings in Facsimiles 1 and 3 have conventional Egyptian figures in an "unconventional scene" (*Id.*, 338). Nibley says these drawings are consistent with the historic Egyptian culture and with Joseph Smith's "explanations" and his Book of Abraham text.

based upon other ancient texts, this does not prove that those proper nouns must also exclusively apply to the drawings in facsimiles 1, 2 and 3.[154] The best conclusion one can make is that those proper names "might" apply to certain individuals in the facsimiles.

According to John Gee, Egyptologists do not agree on what Facsimile 1 depicts.[155] But one interpretation is that Facsimile 1 resembles a number of ancient Egyptian drawings about the mythological Egyptian god Osiris, who had been murdered by his brother Set. Osiris' wife Isis restored Osiris to life, allowing him to posthumously conceive a son with her. That son was Horus. Some of the ancient drawings have been interpreted to depict Isis bringing Osiris back to life as he is lying on a lion bed. This apparently is the basis for Theodule Deveria's interpretation of various figures on Facsimile 1. (See chart at the end of this chapter.) But there are multiple variations of the Osiris myth, which is thought to date back to about 2000 BC,[156] and some of these versions conflict.[157] At best these drawings are of "myths," and there are different versions of the myths. And this does not exclude the possibility that some of these drawings could relate to an episode where Abraham's life was threatened, and where he was ultimately saved by an angel. Dr. Muhlestein points out one aspect of Facsimile 1 that confirms that the drawing does not depict the Osiris myth—that is that the papyrus drawing shows that the black priest is standing in

---

[154] "Book of Abraham," *Wikipedia*. There is a section in this article where Joseph Smith's "explanations" are compared with those of Theodule Deveria (1860). But the fact that Deveria gives different names to certain figures does not mean that the names given by Joseph are wrong. The figures could have additional names, and the figures could have multiple meanings. But, again, I don't believe there is a unanimity among Egyptologists that Deveria's interpretation is the one and only true interpretation of the three facsimiles.

[155] John Gee, *An Introduction to the Book of Abraham*, 149-51 and 183-84.

[156] "Osiris myth." *Wikipedia*. For reference, note that some think that the great flood took place about 2304-2344 B.C., and that Abraham lived about 2050 B.C. to 1875 B.C.

[157] *Id.*

front of and not behind the lion bed. This shows that the person in the horizontal position is resisting the priest's attack and that his feet are not on the lion bed. Compare the photo of the actual papyrus (at the end of this chapter) with Facsimile 1 shown in *The Pearl of Great Price* (which is also shown at the end of this chapter (Muhlestein, "Egyptian Papyri," 234).

Facsimile 3 is interesting because Joseph's "explanation" states that Abraham is seated upon the Pharaoh's throne, with the full approval of Pharaoh, who is standing behind Abraham. The text of the Book of Abraham does not cover this particular scene,[158] but the incident depicted is clearly most unusual: it depicts Pharaoh giving honor and respect to Abraham as "Abraham is reasoning the principles of astronomy, in the king's court." Joseph Smith did not know of any scholarly support for such a scene in 1842. But what sounded preposterous then is now supported by other ancient documents. John Gee, Kerry Muhlestein and Douglas Clark refer to several sources that now support the historicity of this scene in their books.[159] Thus, this particular Facsimile is evidence that Joseph Smith was a prophet, for Joseph had no other way of knowing that any evidence existed that Abraham ever sat on the Pharaoh's throne with his full approbation.

Also, with regard to Facsimile No. 3, some critics point out that Joseph's explanations identified two women as men. But whatever this is, it does not appear to be a translation issue.

---

[158] But it does state that God was revealing things to Abraham about Kolob and the stars before Abraham went into Egypt so that Abraham could "declare all these words"—presumably, to declare them to the Egyptians (Abraham 2:15).

[159] Gee, *An Introduction to the Book of Abraham*, 51-54 & 153-56; and Clark, 114, 118-22. Two of Clark's sources are "Pseudo-Eupolemus" and Josephus, *Antiquities*, 1.viii.2. See also, Muhlestein, "Egyptian Papyri," 220-24; and E. Douglas Clark, "Abraham," *Encyclopedia of Mormonism*. Other sources cited by Clark that support this include: *Genesis Apochryphon* (one of the Dead Sea scrolls, discovered in 1947), *Apocalypse of Abraham* (1897), and *Testament of Abraham* (1892). See also footnote 176, below for additional sources.

Gee and Nibley point out that for certain ritual purposes there were times when Egyptian men did wear women's clothing.[160]

Some scholars think that the translation of figure number 5 in Facsimile No. 3 is "Horus," not "Shulem," as Joseph Smith translated it. I understand that this is a difference. But the difference does not prove Joseph's translation to be incorrect. Again, we know that some drawings like this were based upon an earlier incident or myth. But while some may not agree with Joseph Smith's "explanations," this does not prove that Joseph's explanations are not correct. In fact, there is evidence that supports Joseph Smith's explanation of Facsimile 3.

In conclusion, a review of the differences between Joseph Smith's explanations and those of Deveria does not prove Joseph's to be false. There is no one, true interpretation that all Egyptologists accept with respect to the three facsimiles. Many of the differences in Joseph's explanations with those of Deveria are inconsequential. The Egyptologists who condemn Joseph Smith's explanations of Facsimiles 1, 2 and 3 base their conclusions on unproven assumptions. They have not proven that their interpretations are right or that Joseph's are wrong.

E. Allegation that Joseph Smith's translation of the Book of Abraham is a fraud. Dr. Robert K. Ritner translated the papyrus that was re-discovered in 1967 and which includes Facsimile 1 and the Egyptian text around it. (See footnote 162, below.) He calls this the "Hôr papyrus." Dr. Ritner said that his examination of this papyrus indicates that we have substantially all of the material parts of that document, and that we have more than enough parts of that papyrus to test for the authenticity of the Joseph Smith translation. Dr. Ritner says that his translation of this is a funerary text that is totally different from Joseph Smith's Book of Abraham. He said that Joseph fabricated his text of the Book of Abraham to appear to be a translation of

---

[160] Gee, "Book of Abraham Facsimile 3: The throne scene," p. 2; and Nibley, *Collected Works*, Vol. 5, 337. See also, Gee, *An Introduction to the Book of Abraham*, 63.

the Hôr papyrus.[161] Dr. Ritner says that Joseph's translation is so different from a true translation of the Hôr papyrus that it proves that Joseph's is clearly a fraud.[162] Egyptologists Rhodes, Gee and Muhlestein agree that the Book of Abraham is not a translation of the Hôr papyrus, but they do not agree that Dr. Ritner has proven that Joseph's Book of Abraham is a fraud. I agree with them, and the following discussion will show why the evidence does not support Dr. Ritner's accusation of fraud.

It is one thing to say that the Book of Abraham is not a translation of the Hôr papyrus. But it is something altogether different to state that the Book of Abraham is a false translation. Dr. Ritner attempts to confuse the two. In his effort to try to disprove Joseph Smith, Dr. Ritner offers into evidence the statement by Warren Parrish that Joseph stated that his rendition of the Book of Abraham was given to him by "inspiration from heaven." By including this reference, Dr. Ritner acknowledges

---

[161] This is the same mistaken assertion that was made fifty years ago by Grant Heyward and Jerald Tanner in "The Source of the Book of Abraham Identified," *Dialogue* 3.2 (summer 1968): 93. Hugh Nibley refuted this in 1975 in *The Message of the Joseph Smith Papyri: An Egyptian Endowment* (Salt Lake City: Deseret Book Co.), 1-3. Reprinted in Robert L. Millet and Kent P. Jackson, eds., *Studies in Scripture, Volume Two: The Pearl of Great Price* (Salt Lake City: Randall Book Co., 1985), 187-93.

[162] Dr. Robert K. Ritner, Professor Egyptology at the University of Chicago, published the results of his translation of the papyrus that was re-discovered in 1967 and which is associated with Facsimiles 1 and 3 ("Hor" papyrus). His results are found in *The Joseph Smith Papyri: A Complete Edition* (Salt Lake City: Signature Books, 2013). Subsequently, Dr. Ritner also published *A Response to "Translation and Historicity of the Book of Abraham"* (Signature Books, 2017). This was written in response to the essay that the LDS Church put on its website in 2014. The on-going debate has now become personal to Dr. Ritner, such that he now has a bias to defend himself. Dr. Ritner has stated that "except for the willfully blind, the case is closed." This statement is an attempt by him to discourage scrutiny of his own reasoning, but my review of the bases for his conclusions show that he is willfully ignoring substantial evidence and reasons that dispute his conclusions. There is indeed some blindness here on the part of Dr. Ritner. See the remaining discussion in this chapter.

that Joseph claimed that his translation was revealed to him by God. Instead, Dr. Ritner denies that Joseph made such a claim, and then he asserts that Joseph claimed to have translated it by his own scholastic abilities from the Hôr papyrus. Dr. Ritner succeeded only in exposing his own biases and flawed reasoning. Joseph never identified the particular papyrus from which his translation was taken. Dr. Ritner does not give legitimate evidence to support his conclusion—he only offers speculation and assumptions. Dr. Ritner's analysis includes five major false assumptions and one major omission; together they invalidate his conclusion that the Book of Abraham is a fraud.

**Omission.** Dr. Ritner wrongly concluded that there is no significant historical evidence supporting the story of Abraham found in Joseph Smith's Book of Abraham. Dr. Ritner's denial of the substantial historical evidence supportive of the Book of Abraham narrative is unacceptable. In his 2017 *Response*, Dr. Ritner presents himself as being the ultimate authority on matters of Egyptian and Mesopotamian history, such that he seems quite comfortable failing to even acknowledge the evidence from dozens of sources that does support the historicity of the Book of Abraham story. Dr. Ritner's *Response* takes issue with three historical interpretations of Dr. Gee, but this is hardly a sufficient rebuttal to the mountain of evidence that now exists that is contrary to Dr. Ritner's view. Maybe such a cavalier approach will be sufficient to convince those who do not dare to scrutinize Dr. Ritner's analysis, but it is not sufficient for a legitimate scholarly review. To repeat what I have set forth above—dozens of reliable historical sources now support many elements of the stories contained in the first three chapters of Joseph's Book of Abraham—matters for which there did not exist independent corroboration for Joseph Smith in 1842, but which now supports his work.[163] Research by John Gee, Kerry

---

[163] See e.g., Kerry Muhlestein, "The Explanation-Defying Book of Abraham," in Laura Harris Hales, ed., *A Reason for Faith* (Provo: Religious Studies Center, BYU and Salt Lake City: Deseret Book Co., 2016) at 86, especially

Muhlestein and E. Douglas Clark gives dozens of sources that support Joseph Smith's account of Abraham. It would be scholastic negligence to ignore Gee's, Muhlestein's and Clark's books and those multiple sources and to conclude that there is no historical support for Joseph's accounts. Dr. Ritner's failure to address this evidence is unacceptable. Dr. Ritner cannot deny or ignore this great body of evidence and then have any credibility when he concludes that Joseph Smith's stories about Abraham are without historical support.

Furthermore, other Egyptologists dispute Ritner's conclusions, and they point out that Ritner's conclusion outpace the evidence. Larry E. Morris said that Dr. Ritner fails to acknowledge similarities between Joseph Smith's texts about Abraham and the other existing texts about Abraham.[164] Dr. Ritner is entitled to his opinion, but the evidence does not support him on this point. Dr. Ritner dismisses those Egyptologists who disagree with him, and he labels them as "apologists" for Joseph Smith. This is a lame dismissal, at best.

**First Assumption**. Dr. Ritner said: "No lost papyrus was used in the composition of the Book of Abraham," and that Joseph "fabricated" his translation from the Hôr papyrus. This is an enormous assumption; it is contradicted by some of his own findings; and it is riddled with so many errors that it is fatal to the validity of Dr. Ritner's conclusion. To begin with, it must be observed that without positively identifying the original text it is impossible to determine the correctness of a translation. Dr. Ritner bases his assumption mostly on some 1835 manuscripts, some of which had Egyptian symbols placed in their

footnotes 16, 17 & 18. See also prior text and footnotes and footnote 176 below for a list of additional sources.

[164] Larry E. Morris, "The Book of Abraham: Ask the Right Questions and Keep on Looking (Review of: "'The Breathing Permit of Hôr' Thirty-four Years Later." *Dialogue* 33/4 (2000): 97-119)," *FARMS Review* 16/2 (2004): 355-80. See especially, the section "A Pastiche of Genesis." Below is the web location for this review of Dr. Ritner's work: (https://publications.maxwellinstitute.byu.edu/fullscreen/?pub=1459&index=18).

margins. But these documents have not been authenticated (as will be discussed below), and some pages had no symbols, and some had symbols that were not taken from the Hôr papyrus (which Dr. Ritner acknowledged). This directly contradicts his statement that "no lost papyrus" could have been a basis for the Book of Abraham. There could have been other papyrus, plus Joseph could have had access through revelation to Abraham's original writings.

I understand that it might be frustrating for critics when the original text has not been identified, and when a man says that God revealed the translation to him. But in such circumstances, all an Egyptologist can do is wait until the original text is produced before he can check its translation.

Notwithstanding the inability to identify the source for the Book of Abraham, Dr. Ritner concluded that some 1835 manuscripts prove that Joseph Smith fabricated a false translation that he intended to tie to the Hôr papyrus. Those manuscripts are an early draft, written by someone other than Joseph Smith. At various spots on the left-hand margin of some of those manuscripts someone has drawn certain Egyptian symbols. On the following page is a copy of a hand-written page covering Abraham 1:13-18.

The 1835 manuscript is not an initial, working draft. The cursive manuscript has only a few corrective markings. It has every appearance of a near-final draft, with Egyptian symbols placed at various places on the left-hand margin. Only 18 symbols were placed on a few pages, and no symbols were placed on two-thirds of the pages.[165] Nibley said that the text of those particular manuscripts have the appearance of "copying down an already completed text." "No 'working papers' of a difficult

---

[165] Nibley, *An Approach to the Book of Abraham*, 544. At pages 516-68 Nibley gives a thorough refutation of the allegation that Joseph pretended to translate the Book of Abraham from the Hôr papyrus. See also, Nibley, *Message of the Joseph Smith Papyri*, 1-3.

translation look like this."[166] Dr. Ritner concludes that all of this means that Joseph Smith was representing the text to be a translation of those symbols. But the evidence does not support this. Dr. Ritner has to speculate to arrive at this conclusion. Joseph Smith never stated that the associated text was a translation of those symbols, and we do not know who put the symbols there or when or why. Further Joseph Smith made revisions to his work in the next seven years—before he presented the final text in 1842.

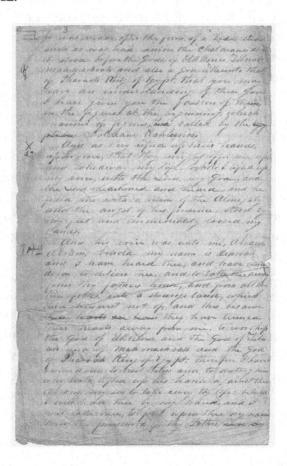

Warren Parrish Copy of Manuscript, Fall 1835 [Abraham 1:4 -2:2]," p. 3. Photo courtesy of Intellectual Reserve, Inc.

[166] Id., 527 and 543. See also Gee, *An Introduction to the Book of Abraham*, 32-33.

Notwithstanding all of this, Dr. Ritner asserts that draft manuscripts from 1835 show that Joseph pretended to make a translation from certain specific Egyptian symbols from the Hôr papyrus. He calls these manuscripts the "smoking gun" that proves Joseph is a fraud. But he jumps the gun in concluding this. Dr. Ritner clearly is overly anxious to prove Joseph to be a fraud. His so-called "smoking gun" evidence would never be admitted in a court of law because it cannot be authenticated—meaning that it cannot be determined who wrote it. We don't know who put the symbols there, or when or why. Dr. Ritner attempts to dismiss this authentication requirement as unnecessary; he said it does not matter in whose handwriting the 1835 manuscripts were written, "since Smith alone controlled the translation process." But Dr. Rinter is dead wrong. Further, he used his pre-determined conclusion as proof for one of the essential elements of that proof. This is merely circular reasoning that even a first-year law student would recognize. You can't do that. There must first be proof that Joseph Smith was responsible for placement of the symbols, and then that Joseph Smith did this with the intent to misrepresent. There is no such proof, and therefore the manuscripts from 1835 do not prove what Dr. Ritner wishes they proved. Dr. Ritner's conclusions are based upon unproven assumptions.[167]

In court I have often faced such very attempts by people to use unauthenticated documents to prove a point. You just can't do it because it is unreliable and because it runs the risk of using unsubstantiated assumptions to prove facts. I find it quite telling to see how Dr. Ritner is willing to dispense with fundamental principles of proper authentication in order to prove Joseph Smith to be a fraud. If it cannot be proven who wrote the symbols and if he cannot prove that Joseph explicitly represented the text to be a translation of those symbols, Dr. Ritner has no case. The mere fact that some manuscripts from

---

[167] See, e.g., Gee, *An Introduction to the Book of Abraham*, 177.

1835 were found does not magically mean that Joseph Smith used them to make a misrepresentation.

Furthermore, no reasonable person could think that that text was a translation of those symbols. Nibley labels this speculation an "absurdity."[168] There is no way that anyone could believe that those symbols could be translated into the associated text shown next to those symbols. Look at it. (See, for example, the document shown two pages above.) It is totally unreasonable for anyone to conclude that those symbols on the left margin could be translated into the 60+, 70+ or 130+ words next to them. It is not rational to think that Joseph Smith could have derived multiple proper names, multiple verbs in various tenses, sequences and ideas just from a small, sketchy symbol.[169] There had to be another source for the translated material. Whatever the placement of those symbols was intended to do, and regardless of who put them there—it is not credible that anyone could believe that the English text was a translation of them. There had to be a source other than those symbols for the Book of Abraham text.

Dr. Ritner is aware of, but dismisses the explanation that revelation played a major role in the Book of Abraham. Dr. Ritner acknowledges that Joseph Smith told his scribe, Warren Parrish, that the text of the Book of Abraham was given to Joseph by "inspiration from heaven."[170] Warren Parrish published his statement in 1838—four years before Joseph published the finished

---

[168] Nibley, *Message of the Joseph Smith Papyri,* cited by Millet and Brown, 192.
[169] Nibley points out that "one needs no knowledge of Egyptian to point out that a dot and three strokes can hardly contain the full message of an English paragraph of a hundred words or more." *Id.,* 534.
[170] On November 14, 1835, a revelation to Joseph Smith called Warren Parrish to be a scribe for Joseph in connection with the papyrus (HC 2:311). Part of that revelation says that Warren "shall see much of my ancient records, and shall know of hidden things, and shall be endowed with a knowledge of hidden languages; and if he desire and shall seek it at my hands, he shall be privileged with writing much of my word, as a scribe." According to Joseph's records, Warren was still acting as a scribe for him in connection with the translation three months later, on February 22, 1836 (HC 2:398).

text. Despite his knowledge that Joseph claimed that "inspiration from heaven" was responsible for his Book of Abraham, Dr. Ritner disingenuously concluded that Joseph denied any revelatory input in his translation. Thus, by concluding that Joseph Smith based his translation solely on the Hôr papyrus, Dr. Ritner misrepresents Joseph Smith. His analysis is flawed.

I believe that God can and does reveal things to prophets—including ancient texts—therefore I do consider what role God played in the final text that was produced. And while I recognize that claims of revelation may not be verifiable by Egyptologists today, that does not give Egyptologists the license to assert falsehoods and to ignore evidence to reach flawed conclusions—at least I have the right to point out such flaws when they do.

**Second Assumption.** Dr. Ritner's insistence that Facsimile No. 1 was drawn incorrectly is without any factual support. It does appear that the head of the priest and a knife in the priest's hand were drawn in after the original drawing was made. He calls this a "forgery," but then he proceeds to speculate about how the drawing should have been completed. It is purely speculation by Dr. Ritner to state how he thinks the drawing should have been made.

**Third Assumption.** Dr. Ritner insists that the original meaning of Facsimile 1 had to comport with the meaning of the traditional myth that goes with other ancient drawings similar to Facsimile 1. This is also an unsupported assumption. It is unreasonable speculation to assume that all ancient drawings and texts must be identical—totally consistent with one particular myth and one particular interpretation of that myth. Dr. Ritner assumes that there is only one true interpretation of a myth, even though by definition we do not know the exact origin and meaning of the myth that we seek to interpret 4,000 years after it originated. On the contrary, Dr. Ritner denies that Facsimile 1 could have multiple interpretations or different meanings from the one he endorses.

**Fourth Assumption.** As was mentioned above, Dr. Ritner denies that Joseph received any revelation from God in connection with his translation, and he assumes that Joseph's translation was made exclusively from the remnants of the Hôr papyrus that he (Dr. Ritner) examined; Dr. Ritner does not acknowledge that through revelation Joseph could have had access to the original writings and drawings and to the original meanings of Abraham before changes and alterations that may have occurred in subsequent transcribing and copying. Joseph's translation process was more revelatory than scholarly. If God revealed to Joseph the words of Abraham's original text, it might be difficult even for Joseph to identify the specific papyrus sections that pertain to the ultimate translation text. I understand that Joseph's intent was to bring to light the original scripture—just as was his purpose in his inspired translation of the Bible. Consequently, it is certainly possible that the ultimate text produced by Joseph Smith would have differences from the papyrus.

Dr. Ritner made a significant error in how he reported and used the quote from Warren Parrish that we previously discussed. Dr. Ritner quoted Parrish as stating that he (Warren) "penned down the Egyptian hieroglyphicks [sic] as he claimed to receive it by direct inspiration from heaven." But Dr. Ritner omitted three important words, which change the meaning; here is the correct quote, with the three omitted words in bold print: Warren Parrish stated that he "penned down the **translation of the** Egyptian hieroglyphicks (sic) as he [Joseph Smith] claimed to receive it by direct inspiration from heaven." The correct quote says that the "translation" was revealed to Joseph, rather than that the "Egyptian hieroglyphicks" were revealed to him. Clearly this mistake by Dr. Ritner came from his reliance on the Fawn Brodie reference that he cited. The problem is that Fawn Brodie misquoted Parrish, and then Dr. Ritner repeated Brodie's error. A review of the original source, *Painesville Republican*, February 16, 1838, exposes the error. Brodie is a notorious anti-Mormon writer with an acknowledged bias against Joseph Smith.

Dr. Ritner misconstrues Joseph Smith's statement in the introduction to the Book of Abraham, that he (Joseph Smith) "translated" the Book of Abraham. Dr. Ritner insists that this means that Joseph Smith was representing that the translation was <u>not</u> done by heavenly inspiration and was only done by Joseph Smith's personal knowledge and abilities. Dr. Ritner errs in this conclusion. This misrepresents Joseph Smith.[171] While the introduction to the Book of Abraham indicates that it was Joseph who translated the text, this does not preclude the participation of God in the endeavor. The title page to the Book of Mormon also states that it was translated by Joseph Smith, but this has never been intended to deny that the translation was wrought by the "gift and power of God." Thus, it is not proper to conclude that those words introducing the Book of Abraham were intended to mean that Joseph Smith did the translation without the assistance from God.

Joseph Smith always regarded the production of the Abrahamic text to be one of his prophetic missions. For example, on June 18, 1840, Joseph wrote that it was important for him to attend to matters pertaining to "the spiritualities of the Church, and commence the work of translating the Egyptian records" (HC 4:137). On September 1, 1842, Joseph referred to the recently published Book of Abraham as "present revelation" (*Times and Seasons*, 902). And we previously discussed the

---

[171] *History of the Church* includes 39 references to Joseph's working on a translation of the writings of Abraham that he said was in the papyrus. (See "Abraham," *Encyclopedia of Joseph Smith's Teachings*, Larry E. Dahl and Donald Q. Cannon, eds. (Salt Lake City: Bookcraft, Inc., 1997), 4-11.) Rarely did he describe his work as a revelatory process. But such a description would have been redundant because he and those around him knew that inspiration was a major part of this translation, just as it was with the Book of Mormon and with the inspired translation of the Bible. Thus, the lack of such additional descriptive words should not be taken to mean that Joseph did not represent his final text to be an inspired translation.

statement of Warren Parrish that Joseph claimed that the translation was "inspiration from heaven." Dr. Ritner characterizes
Joseph Smith's translation project as one that was divorced from
revelatory input—but this is just plain false.

Those closest to the Prophet understood that Joseph represented his translation of the Book of Abraham text to be an
inspired translation. For example, "[b]oth Wilford Woodruff
(in his journal) and Parley P. Pratt (in the July 1842 *Millennial
Star*) maintained that the translation was done by means of
the Urim and Thummim, although Joseph Smith himself does
not mention using this instrument anywhere in the translation." (Michael D. Rhodes, "Book of Abraham," sub-heading:
"Facsimiles from the Book of Abraham," *Encyclopedia of
Mormonism.*) Similarly, from 1842 until today, the Church leaders have always believed that "it was principally divine inspiration rather than [Joseph's] knowledge of languages that
produced the English text of the book of Abraham. His precise
methodology remains unknown" (H. Donl Peterson, "Book of
Abraham," *Encyclopedia of Mormonism,* (Macmillan Publishing
Company, 1992)). Dr. Ritner, however, wishes to challenge this
by changing the facts; he denies that divine revelation was a
part of the source for his Book of Abraham text, even though
he cites evidence that Joseph said just the opposite. It is one
thing for Dr. Ritner to say he doesn't believe Joseph Smith, but
it would be wrong to say that Joseph never said that heavenly
inspiration revealed translated text to him.

**Fifth Assumption.** Dr. Ritner's evidence does not meet the
required standard of proof for his fraud conclusion. The standard of proof he applied was merely a "probability" or "probable cause" standard—that it seems only reasonable to him
that the Joseph Smith translation may be false—even though
he cannot prove that he even has the text from which the Book
of Abraham was translated. The "probable cause" standard requires only a minimal amount of evidence, and it is used in the
law to determine whether a matter is even worth prosecuting.

But that standard is considerably less stringent than any of the three other standards which must then be applied in a court proceeding to reach a legal determination. Those standards are: (1) a preponderance of the evidence, (2) clear and convincing evidence, or (3) proof beyond reasonable doubt.[172] Thus, Dr. Ritner might reasonably believe that Joseph Smith's translation is "probably" not true, but the evidence is insufficient to prove those allegations under either the "beyond reasonable doubt" or the "clear and convincing evidence" or the "preponderance of evidence" standards. In any event, the "clear and convincing" standard must be applied to make a finding of fraud; and Dr. Ritner's evidence falls woefully short of meeting this standard.

**Final Comments on Dr. Ritner's Conclusions.** I have addressed a number of comments about the work of Dr. Ritner because he has assumed the position of being the chief critic of Joseph Smith's Book of Abraham, and Dr. Ritner's conclusions have been troubling for some Mormons. The effectiveness of Dr. Ritner's criticisms warrants a response, and I believe the response I have made here is sufficient to expose the significant flaws in Dr. Ritner's analysis and conclusions. In 2017, Dr. Ritner published his *Response* to the Church's website essay about the Book of Abraham. Although the Church's essay does not direct itself at Dr. Ritner, and while he is not even specifically mentioned in the essay or in any of its sources, nevertheless Dr. Ritner felt the need to specifically respond to the essay. This is understandable, because Dr. Ritner's conclusions (including calling Joseph Smith's Book of Abraham a fraud) have made him the foremost critic of the authenticity of the Book of Abraham. In his 2017 *Response*, Dr. Ritner reiterated his conclusions from

---

[172] A preponderance of evidence is the lowest of the three standards; it merely means it is more probable than not that a certain thing happened. Proof beyond reasonable doubt is the highest standard—it applies in criminal cases. Clear and Convincing evidence is somewhere in between the other two. This standard applies to accusations for fraud; it is insufficient to conclude that one has committed fraud based on a mere preponderance of the evidence.

his 2013 book. He says that Joseph's Book of Abraham is a total fraud, and he cites reasons for his conclusions. This is primarily a repetition of his 2013 book. He did not seem to alter any of his opinions after reading the 2014 LDS essay. But neither did he rectify either the major omission or any of the false assumptions that he had made in his 2013 book. His continued reliance on those mistaken assumptions undermines his conclusions. He clings to his traditional interpretation of a 4,000-year-old myth. He will not acknowledge the substantial sources that corroborate the historicity of Joseph's rendition of the attempted sacrifice of Abraham by the idolatrous priest. He continues to insist that some unauthenticated manuscripts from 1835 are proof that Joseph's "translation" was false. But Dr. Ritner fails to address the other evidence that gives support to Joseph Smith's version of Abraham's history. And, of course, because Dr. Ritner has been so bold as to call the Book of Abraham a fraud—he is now in the position where this argument is personal for him.[173] He is now a biased witness. He got into this predicament when he announced conclusions that exceeded what was warranted from his evidence. Again, he refuses to admit that we don't have the ultimate text from which the Book of Abraham is translated. His string of false assumptions undermine his opinions. Dr. Ritner's ultimate conclusion that the Book of Abraham is a fraud is itself flawed because of the material omissions and erroneous assumptions he makes.

---

[173] See Larry E. Morris (at footnote 164, above). Morris' excellent critique of Dr. Robert K. Ritner points out that not only does Dr. Ritner fail to address key evidence that corroborates Joseph Smith's Book of Abraham, but Dr. Ritner also allowed himself to depart from objective scholarship and to make repeated personal, disparaging attacks (ad hominem attacks) against those with whom he disagrees. Dr. Ritner ridiculed Joseph Smith, the Church, Nibley, Gee and other LDS scholars. In addition to the flaws in Dr. Ritner's scholarship, this personal bias further taints his work as unreliable.

# III. Other Evidence Supportive of the Book of Abraham

Since the time when Joseph Smith translated the Book of Abraham (1835-42) evidence has surfaced that lends support to the authenticity of Joseph's translation. Here is some of it.

1.  Scholars have found instances of human sacrifice in Abraham's time.[174] Furthermore, an Egyptian text discovered in the 20th century recounts a similar story of someone trying to sacrifice Abraham.[175] This text recounts a Pharaoh's attempt to sacrifice Abraham that was prevented by the intercession of an angel.

2.  There now exist dozens of sources supportive of Joseph Smith's account that Abraham's life was threatened in Ur, and that an idolatrous priest tried to kill Abraham as a sacrifice, and that an angel of God saved Abraham.[176]

---

[174] "Historicity," at footnotes 35 & 36, and associated text. (See John Gee, "An Egyptian View of Abraham," in Andrew C. Skinner, D. Morgan Davis, and Carl Griffin, eds., Bountiful Harvest: Essays in Honor of S. Kent Brown, (Provo, UT: Maxwell Institute, 2011), 137-56.) See also, Muhlestein, "Egyptian Papyri," 220-21.

[175] "Historicity," at footnote 45, and associated text.

[176] See e.g., E. Douglas Clark, *The Blessings of Abraham—Becoming a Zion People* (Covenant Press, 2005), 45-59, which gives a number of sources that together support the historicity of Joseph Smith's Book of Abraham. Clark cites the following sources for various aspects of the sacrifice incident: Jubilees 12:7, in VanderKam, *Book of Jubilees*, 69-70; Apocalypse of Abraham 4:6, in Charlesworth, *Old Testament Pseudepigrapha*, 1:690; Qur'an 19:44-47, in Asad, *Qur'an*, 462; Maaseh Avraham Avinu 5:37-65 & 6:41-63, in Levy, *A Faithful Heart*, 51-61; Nachmanides on Genesis 11:28, in Chavel, *Ramban*, 1:159; Rabbi Joseph, *Sha'are Orah*, 277; Pirke de Rabbi Eliezer 26 & 52, in Friedlander, *Pirke de Rabbi Eliezer*, 188 & 420; Klinghoffer, *Discovery of God*, 21; Ginzberg, *Legends of the Jews*, 1:198-201; Baring-Gould, *Legends of the Patriarchs*, 158; Knappert, *Islamic Legends*, 1:74; Jasher 12:7-8, in Noah, *Book of Yashar*, 32; Wainwright, *Sky-Religion in Ancient Egypt*, 26-27, 32, 38, 47-53, 60 & 64-66; Nibley, *Abraham in Egypt*, 80-82; Gorion, *Mimekor Yisrael*, 1:45; Brinner,

3. Recent discovery of the ancient town of "Ulisum,"in northwestern Syria seems to correspond with Joseph Smith's inclusion of "the plain of Olishem" in Abraham 1:11.[177] The words "Ulisum" or "Olishem" would not have been known to Joseph Smith.

4. The idolatrous god "Elkenah," mentioned in Abraham 1:17 is now confirmed to be a god worshipped by ancient Mesopotamians.[178] No mention is made of "Elkenah" in the Bible. Joseph had no way to know of such a god. His inclusion of this reference to "Elkenah" supports Joseph's claim that his translation is true.

5. Other ancient texts now confirm that Abraham taught the Egyptians about the heavens and astronomy.[179]

6. "The discovery of other texts, including *Testament of Abraham* (1892) and *Apocalypse of Abraham* (1897), may provide some support for the historicity of Joseph Smith's *Book of Abraham*."[180]

---

*History of al-Tabari*, 59; Al Rabghuzi, *Stories of the Prophets*, 2:104; and Pseudo Philo 6:17, in Jacobson, *Liber Antiquitatum Biblicarum*, 1:100.

Of the numerous corroborating sources, one reported by Maaseh Abraham Avinu is especially interesting. Avinu reported that Abraham took an axe and damaged a number of the king's idols. Some he pushed over and broke. He lopped off the hands of one, cut off the head of another, broke the eyes of another, and broke the legs of yet another—until all of them were broken. Then Abraham placed the axe into the hand of the largest idol. Later, when Abraham was confronted with having damaged the idols, Abraham responded to the king and his ministers: "I didn't break them, no. Rather, the large one of them smashed them. Don't you see that the axe is in his hand? And if you won't believe it, ask him and he will tell" (Clark, 47). This would have been an event leading up to the time when the priest was about to kill Abraham on the altar.

[177] "Historicity," at footnote 37, and associated text. See also, Muhlestein, "Egyptian Papyri," 222-23.

[178] "Historicity," at footnote 39, and associated text.

[179] "Historicity," at footnotes 42, 43 and 45, and associated text.

[180] See Hugh Nibley, *Abraham in Egypt*, 11-33. See also footnote 176, above.

# Conclusion

Joseph Smith's translation of the Book of Abraham is an inspiring text that makes many valuable contributions to one's understanding of the purpose of life, the nature of God, and the divine nature and potential of mankind. It is impossible to either confirm or reject the veracity of Joseph Smith's translation by reference to original ancient texts. This is so because we do not have the original text, and because the "translation" was given to Joseph Smith by revelation. While there continue to be critics who assert that Joseph Smith's translation is a fraud, facts and reason do not support such a conclusion.

Facsimile No. 1

## EXPLANATION

Fig. 1. The Angel of the Lord.

Fig. 2. Abraham fastened upon an altar.

Fig. 3. The idolatrous priest of Elkenah attempting to offer up Abraham as a sacrifice.

Fig. 4. The altar for sacrifice by the idolatrous priests, standing before the gods of Elkenah, Libnah, Mahmackrah, Korash, and Pharaoh.

Fig. 5. The idolatrous god of Elkenah.

Fig. 6. The idolatrous god of Libnah.

Fig. 7. The idolatrous god of Mahmackrah.

Fig. 8. The idolatrous god of Korash.

Fig. 9. The idolatrous god of Pharaoh.

Fig. 10. Abraham in Egypt.

Fig. 11. Designed to represent the pillars of heaven, as understood by the Egyptians.

Fig. 12. Raukeeyang, signifying expanse, or the firmament over our heads; but in this case, in relation to this subject, the Egyptians meant it to signify Shaumau, to be high, or the heavens, answering to the Hebrew word, Shaumahyeem.

Facsimile No. 2

EXPLANATION

Fig. 1. Kolob, signifying the first creation, nearest to the celestial, or the residence of God. First in government, the last pertaining to the measurement of time. The measurement according to celestial time, which celestial time signifies one day to cubit. One day in Kolob is equal to a thousand years according to the measurement of this earth, which is called by the Egyptians Jah-oh-eh.

Fig. 2. Stands next to Kolob, called by the Egyptians Oliblish, which is the next grand governing creation near to the celestial or the place where God resides; holding the key of power also, pertaining to other planets; as revealed from God to Abraham, as he offered sacrifice upon an altar, which he had built unto the Lord.

Fig. 3. Is made to represent God, sitting upon his throne, clothed with power and authority; with a crown of eternal light upon his head; representing also the grand Key-words of the Holy Priesthood, as revealed to Adam in the Garden of Eden, as also to Seth, Noah, Melchizedek, Abraham, and all to whom the Priesthood was revealed.

Fig. 4. Answers to the Hebrew word Raukeeyang, signifying expanse, or the firmament of the heavens; also a numerical figure, in Egyptian signifying one thousand; answering to the measuring of the time of Oliblish, which is equal with Kolob in its revolution and in its measuring of time.

Fig. 5. Is called in Egyptian Enish-go-on-dosh; this is one of the governing planets also, and is said by the Egyptians to be the Sun, and to borrow its light from Kolob through the medium of Kae-e-vanrash, which is the grand Key, or, in other words, the governing power, which governs fifteen other fixed planets or stars, as also Floeese or the Moon, the Earth and the Sun in their annual revolutions. This planet receives its power through the medium of Kli-flos-is-es, or Hah-ko-kau-beam, the stars represented by the numbers 22 and 23, receiving light from the revolutions of Kolob.

Fig. 6. Represents this earth in its four quarters.

Fig. 7. Represents God sitting upon his throne, revealing through the heavens the grand Key-words of the Priesthood; as, also, the sign of the Holy Ghost unto Abraham, in the form of a dove.

Fig. 8. Contains writings that cannot be revealed unto the world; but is to be had in the Holy Temple of God.

Fig. 9. Ought not to be revealed at the present time.

Fig. 10. Also.

Fig. 11. Also. If the world can find out these numbers, so let it be. Amen.

Figures 12, 13, 14, 15, 16, 17, 18, 19, 20, and 21 will be given in the own due time of the Lord.

The above translation is given as far as we have any right to give at the present time.

## Facsimile No. 3

## EXPLANATION

Fig. 1. Abraham sitting upon Pharaoh's throne, by the politeness of the king, with a crown upon his head, representing the Priesthood, as emblematical of the grand Presidency in Heaven; with the scepter of justice and judgment in his hand.

Fig. 2. King Pharaoh, whose name is given in the characters above his head.

Fig. 3. Signifies Abraham in Egypt as given also in Figure 10 of Facsimile No. 1.

Fig. 4. Prince of Pharaoh, King of Egypt, as written above the hand.

Fig. 5. Shulem, one of the king's principal waiters, as represented by the characters above his hand.

Fig. 6. Olimlah, a slave belonging to the prince.

Abraham is reasoning upon the principles of Astronomy, in the king's court.

## Facsimile No. 1: A Comparison of Joseph Smith's Explanations with Those of Theodule Deveria (1860)

This portion of papyrus is designated Joseph Smith Papyrus I. Photo courtesy of Intellectual Reserve, Inc.

**Figure 1**     Joseph wrote: "The     Deveria wrote: "The soul Osiris
                 angel of the Lord."     (which should have a human head)"

The comment by Deveria is quite presumptuous. It may be true that other, similar drawings may have a human head on the bird, but Deveria is just speculating. Egyptologists believe this scene is one related to the mythical Osiris, but I don't believe the name "Osiris" is written in Facsimile No. 1.

**Figure 2**     Joseph          wrote:     Deveria wrote: "Osiris coming to life
                 "Abraham fastened     on his couch, which is in the shape
                 upon an altar."     of a lion."

Joseph Smith did not assert that the name of Abraham was found on Facsimile No. 1. Deveria's interpretation is based on various assumptions. Whether the drawing depicts a "couch" or an "altar," is of little significance.

The result of comparing several of the explanations shows that the explanations are different, but not that they are necessarily contradictory.

In other words, even if Deveria were correct, there is no basis from which one can conclude that Joseph Smith's explanation is wrong or false. For example, consider explanations for figures 4, 5, 6, 7 & 8 in Facsimile No. 1:

**Figure 4**   Joseph wrote: "The al- Deveria wrote: "The funeral bed tar for sacrifice by the of Osiris" idolatrous priests"

## The following explanations are not necessarily contradictory.

**Figure 5**   Joseph wrote: "The idol- Deveria wrote: "Canopic jar por- atrous god of Elkenah" traying Qebehsenuf with a fal- con's head – one of the four sons of Horus"

**Figure 6**   Joseph wrote: "The idol- Deveria wrote: "Canopic jar por- atrous god of Libnah" traying Duamutef with a jackal's head – one of the four sons of Horus"

**Figure 7**   Joseph   wrote:   "The Deveria wrote: "Canopic jar por- idolatrous   god   of traying Hapy with an ape's head – Mahmackrah" one of the four sons of Horus"

**Figure 8**   Joseph wrote: "The idol- Deveria wrote: "Canopic jar por- atrous god of Korash" traying Imsety with a human head – one of the four sons of Horus"

With regard to these four figures, the explanations are different, but they are not necessarily contradictory. It is my understanding that Deveria is assuming that the four jars refer to Qebehsenuf, Duamutef, Hapy and Imsety. But I would also point out that figure 7 does not look like an ape's head and figure 8 does not look like a human head.

Note: The explanations of Theodule Deveria (from 1860) are taken from "Book of Abraham," *Wikipedia* (retrieved June 3, 2016). Subsequently, the *Wikipedia* article has been revised, and the specific comparison of Smith's and Deveria's explanations has been removed. By taking the link to "Critical appraisal of the Book of Abraham," there is a new chart that compares Joseph Smith's explanations with those of "Egyptologists" (but not a comparison with only Deveria's explanations). Since the Deveria interpretations are now not readily available, the above comparison chart becomes even more valuable.

# Chapter 8

## Blacks and the Priesthood— God Controls When the Priesthood Is Bestowed

Throughout the ages, in God's church and kingdom, His priesthood has been extended to only a relatively few people. For example, God limited it to only some of the seed of Abraham. Nevertheless, in this day and time—the last days and the dispensation of the fullness of times—God is now making His priesthood available to all righteous males. Historically this is a new and marvelous development; through it, God's choicest blessings are being poured out on faithful and virtuous people around the world. This marvelous work is helping to prepare the entire world for the imminent coming of the Lord Jesus Christ, who will soon rule and reign on earth.

Despite this great blessing for the world in the latter-days, some people go out of their way to accuse The Church of Jesus Christ of Latter-day Saints of being a racist church because prior to 1978 it did not give God's priesthood to blacks of African descent. Historically, God has limited the holding of His priesthood to only a select, few individuals, and His priesthood was not extended to blacks of African descent until 1978. But God's greatest eternal rewards have always been equally available to every human being who has ever lived on the earth, even though dating back to biblical times God's priesthood had been bestowed upon only a few of God's children.

Since the Church now extends the priesthood to men of all races and ethnicities, the accusations of racism have mostly become moot. A good discussion of this is found on the Church's website (lds.org): an essay entitled "Race and the Priesthood." But that essay does not address the ancient scriptures that discuss this matter. This essay will discuss those scriptures and additional historical information that pertains to the prior restriction. First, we will discuss how all of God's children have an equal opportunity for exaltation. Second, we will discuss how God chooses those who receive His priesthood. Third, we will review a history of racial relations in America in terms of its effect on preaching the gospel. Fourth, we will review how Jesus declined to participate in political activism. Fifth, we will review statements and scriptures from the Prophet Joseph Smith on slavery, blacks and the priesthood. A thorough review of the scriptures and history shows that while God has sometimes restricted who holds His priesthood, He nevertheless makes His greatest eternal blessing of exaltation available equally to all of His children.

Introduction. Race relations continues to be one of the biggest societal issues in 2019.[181] According to Chris Rice, co-author of *More Than Equals: Racial Healing for the Sake of the Gospel*, "Ninety percent of African-American Christians worship in all-black churches. Ninety percent of white American Christians worship in all-white churches."[182] Sociologist Michael O. Emerson reported that churches in America are twenty times more

---

[181] Quoted by Nadra Kareem Nittle, in "Five Ways to make Your Racially Segregated Church More Diverse," June 30, 2016. https://www.thoughtco.com/nadra-kareem-nittle-2834471.

[182] Id. In addition, Nadra Kareem Nittle reported that "only 5 to 7.5 percent of churches in the U.S. are considered to be racially diverse. *Id.*

segregated than the public schools in the same areas.[183] This situation highlights the continuing racial strife in America. The Constitution does not mandate integration in private churches. Consequently, in 2019 in the Christian community in America, for the most part blacks and whites continue to segregate. What Martin Luther King, Jr., stated in 1963, is still true in America today: "The most segregated of Christian America is 11 o'clock on Sunday morning."[184]

With this backdrop, the integration of blacks that exists in The Church of Jesus Christ of Latter-day Saints stands in sharp contrast to this entrenched and continuing segregation in American Christianity. There are no segregated Mormon congregations. Mormons attend the congregation organized for their particular geographic boundaries, rather than based upon what pastor they would prefer. And the lay priesthood leadership of Mormon congregations usually mirrors the racial composition of the members within those boundaries. The integration of blacks in the Mormon church in America and throughout the world is a model of good integration. It stands in contrast to many congregations in America that continue to be segregated.

# I. EQUAL OPPORTUNITY FOR EXALTATION

### All Mankind Have Equal Opportunity for Eternal Life, but Earth Experiences and Opportunities Are Not Equal

God is no respecter of persons—meaning that He loves each and every human being equally and that He will judge each and every person with perfect fairness and justice. It also means that every human being who has entered this world has a full and fair opportunity to attain exaltation in God's highest kingdom of glory. But it does not mean that every human being will

---

[183] Reported in Sam Fulwood, III, "Stepping Away from Racism" (September 2, 2016). Retrieved February 25, 2016, from https://www.americanprogress. org/issues/race/news/.../stepping-away-from-racism/
[184] Id.

have the exact same opportunities and trials in this life. Each of us have different talents, different capacities, different weaknesses, different challenges, different life situations, different trials and different opportunities and missions in life. God's plan does not guarantee equal opportunities and blessings in this life, but it does guarantee equal opportunity to secure Exaltation with God in the next life.

Equal opportunity for Eternal Life is an important part of God's law of justice. But this is different from equality in all things. There is no inalienable right of human beings to have equality in everything. Our gifts and opportunities and trials and experiences are all different. Similarly, the levels of work, commitment, sacrifice, creativity, initiative and efficiency that we each bring to our own circumstances and endeavors are also very different. The eternal law of the harvest properly rewards those whose work and efforts are better than others. Thus, humans in mortal life will always have great diversity in their conditions and in the things of life that they acquire. But the purpose and potential for all mankind is to return to live with God and to attain exaltation in the celestial kingdom of God. Ultimately, attaining that will depend upon how well we endure our particular trials and tribulations—how well we develop our characters. But the level of temporal success and comfort that we attain in this life is not the gauge for determining our eternal reward.

In contemplating God's eternal purposes for all mankind, it must be noted that billions of people have lived on the earth without having the opportunity to receive the blessings of the fullness of the gospel of Jesus Christ while they were alive. In the six thousand years since Adam and Eve were placed on the earth, most of their descendants have not had this opportunity, including the billions that lived from 100 A.D. until the restoration of the gospel in 1830, and even continuing until today. That the fullness of the gospel has been denied to these people during their earthly probation cannot be denied. But the fact that others have had the opportunity to have the gospel during their earth life is no reason to condemn God because some do not; everyone will ultimately have the opportunity to learn and receive all the blessings of the gospel. God will judge us according to how we lived with the knowledge and opportunities given to us. None of us will be condemned for matters beyond our control. The Apostle Peter taught this when he said: "For for this cause was the gospel preached also to them that are dead, that they might be judged according to men in the flesh, but live according to God in the spirit" (1 Peter 4:6). And in our day this eternal principle of justice was stated with even better clarity in a revelation given to Joseph Smith in January 1836:

> Thus came the voice of the Lord unto me, saying: All who have died without a knowledge of this gospel, who would have received it if they had been permitted to tarry, shall be heirs of the celestial kingdom of God; Also all that shall die henceforth without a knowledge of it, who would have received it with all their hearts, shall be heirs of that kingdom; For I, the Lord, will judge all men according to their works, according to the desire of their hearts. (D&C 137:7-9)

This is a beautiful truth, and it helps us to understand that mankind's eternal reward is not denied because of limited opportunities in this life. The fact is that the preaching of the gospel is one of the main activities that is taking place in the world of the spirits who have departed this life. After death, we leave our bodies on earth until the resurrection. But our spirits continue to exist and to associate with other spirits. As spirits we do not continue to experience the heightened blessings that attend the mortal experience, but we do continue to converse, discuss, debate and otherwise influence one another in that realm. There, all will eventually be taught the gospel of

Jesus Christ in its fullness. There, those who did not have the opportunity to embrace the gospel of Jesus Christ on earth will have the full opportunity to do so. It was this ultimate, eternal justice to which the Apostle Paul referred when he said that "[i]f in this life only we have hope in Christ, we are of all men most miserable" (1 Corinthians 15:19). There is a resurrection of the dead, and there is a final judgment that will be perfectly fair and just, and all mankind will have the opportunity to enter into the kingdom of greatest glory prepared for God's children.

A vision of the celestial kingdom of heaven was revealed to Joseph Smith and other brethren on the top floor, west end (back) of the Kirtland Temple in January 1836.

But all will not receive an equal reward. Absolute equality may sound good to superficial thinkers, but it would deny the justice of God and it would undermine the law of the harvest and the agency of man. Justice will require different rewards and blessings based upon the efforts and work and character of each individual. Equality of eternal opportunity is a part of God's plan; but equal rewards without equal effort and equal obedience is Satan's proposal—it is not God's way.

## II. GOD CHOOSES WHO WILL RECEIVE HIS PRIESTHOOD

### A. "Ye Have Not Chosen Me, But I Have Chosen You."

God controls the selection of the parents to whom His spirit children are sent when they begin their earth life at birth. Similarly, He also controls who will receive His priesthood on earth. From the very beginning of earth life for Adam's posterity, God has called prophets to reveal His messages to mankind and to do His work. God decides who He calls to do his work, and He does not give reasons for whom He calls. At least as early as the days of Noah, the posterity of some people were given certain blessings, while the posterity of others were cursed. This developed into some racial divisions—although that is not what it was called then. Such family heritages continued for four thousand years, becoming an established norm throughout the world.

God chooses those on whom He bestows His priesthood. There is no individual right of any person to dictate to God who will hold God's priesthood. The mere statement of such a thing should be sufficient to highlight its absurdity. For any human being to assert that he knows better than God who should hold God's priesthood is a totally illogical and pretentious position. By definition, true priesthood is God's authority and is therefore subject to His control—and it is not bestowed by the whims of man or according to whatever may be politically correct at the time. If God gives His authority to humans, it is absurd for humans to presuppose that they can dictate to God if and when and to whom He should bestow His authority.

Jesus told His apostles, "Ye have not chosen me, but I have chosen you and ordained you" (John 15:16). And the Apostle Paul wrote that "no man taketh this honour unto himself, but he that is called of God, as was Aaron" (Hebrews 5:4). Through the ages, God has called certain men to be His prophets, but He doesn't share with the world the reasons why one person is called but others are not. Similarly, there have been times in the history of the world when the gospel and God's priesthood have been extended to one people but not to another. For example, for over a thousand years the Lord only allowed the people of the Tribe of Levi to hold the Aaronic Priesthood. This was the situation among the Jews when Jesus was born. Jesus changed this when He called His twelve apostles. During Jesus' life, He said that His Father sent him only to the House of Israel (Matthew 15:24). And when Christ called and ordained His apostles, He told them specifically not to go to the "Gentiles." He said: "Go not into the way of the Gentiles, and into any city of the Samaritans enter ye not: But go rather to the lost sheep of the house of Israel" (Matthew 10:5-6). However, after Jesus' resurrection He sent them to all the world, and this commenced the preaching of the gospel to the gentiles. These historical accounts show that God controls the work of His servants by limiting the scope of their work at certain times, and that He sometimes limits who is to receive His gospel and His priesthood until it is appropriate to extend such blessings and opportunities to others. While we do not always know the reasons for what triggers these changes, we do know that historically this has been God's pattern.

## B. Special Blessings for Abraham's Seed.

When the Lord blessed Abraham, He made promises to Abraham and "thy seed after thee in their generations for an everlasting covenant" (Genesis 17:7). That this blessing was to extend to Abraham's seed was emphatically repeated four additional times in this chapter (verses 8, 9, 10 and 19). Later, when Jacob blessed his grandson, Ephraim, he promised blessings for him and for his "seed after him" (Genesis 48:4). With regard to the blessing that the Lord promised to Abraham's seed, the Lord revealed to the Prophet Joseph Smith that this blessing included the right to hold God's priesthood (Abraham 2:9 & 11). This indicates that God was giving the opportunity to hold the priesthood to Abraham's posterity. By implication, this opportunity would not be extended to some others; were it not so, the blessing to Abraham would be meaningless. Thus, in the days of Abraham the Bible teaches that the opportunity to hold the priesthood was given only to one particular family, or "race," if you will.

These positive blessings for Abraham and his posterity seem good and proper, but down through the ages such a blessing actually becomes a racial preference. Nevertheless, it is well established that God extended great blessings to the seed of Abraham. In addition, in biblical times it was also sometimes said that wicked people and their seed would be cursed. For example, when the prophet Elisha cursed his servant Gehzi (who had betrayed him), Elisha said: "The leprosy therefore of Naaman shall cleave unto thee, and unto thy seed for ever" (2 Kings 5:27). Similarly, the psalmist wrote: "The seed of the wicked shall be cut off" (Psalm 37:28). To bless or curse one person's posterity was a concept that was accepted by some people in biblical times. It is not fair to punish a person for the sins of his/her parents, but the extending of opportunities to one person's descendants—and not to others— does not punish one person for the sins of another; it is nothing more than a type of inheritance that a person can bestow on his descendants— not punishment of the others; it is merely the controlling and limiting of certain opportunities and blessings. Although such restrictions can deprive some people of certain earthly opportunities on earth, they do not deprive anyone of any heavenly reward or opportunity. In any event, the practice of giving or denying a person's seed of certain earthly opportunities was practiced by prophets in biblical days.

Humans have limited understanding of why God does what He does. We only know what He reveals to us. We do know that some persons were foreordained to receive God's priesthood and to do His work. Such persons include Abraham, Jeremiah, Isaiah, Moses, John the Baptist, Joseph Smith, and, of course, the Great High Priest, Jesus Christ. But even with these prophets, the Holy Scriptures give almost no information about why God chose them. However, we do know one eternal principle that pertains to this; it is articulated by the prophet Alma in these words:

> And this is the manner after which they were ordained—being called and prepared from the foundation of the world according to the foreknowledge of God, on account of their exceeding faith and good works; in the first place being left to choose good or evil; therefore they having chosen good, and exercising exceedingly great faith, are called with a holy calling, yea, with that holy calling which was prepared with, and according to, a preparatory redemption for such.
>
> And thus they have been called to this holy calling on account of their faith, while others would reject the Spirit of God on account of the hardness of their hearts and blindness of their minds,

while, if it had not been for this they might have
had as great privilege as their brethren.

Or in fine, in the first place they were on the same
standing with their brethren; thus this holy calling being prepared from the foundation of the
world for such as would not harden their hearts,
being in and through the atonement of the Only
Begotten Son, who was prepared. (Alma 13:3-5)

Despite the biblical precedence for restricting the priesthood
of God to certain people in the past, this opportunity is now
extended to all worthy males. In the future we will know more
about the reasons for the practice that had its origin in biblical
days. In the meantime, we will have to be content living with
some unanswered questions. But the fact that we don't know all
the answers does not mean that we cannot know whether it was
God's will to limit the people who would have the opportunity
to hold the priesthood while on earth.

## C. The Long-Awaited Day.

On June 8, 1978, the Lord inspired His prophet, Spencer W.
Kimball, to begin to make the priesthood available to all worthy
males. The announcement did not come with an explanation of
why the change was being made at that time, nor did it come
with an explanation of why the priesthood had been withheld
in the past. What we do know is that the previous withholding
of the priesthood did not prevent anyone from receiving the
highest of all possible blessings of God. And we also know that
the timing of the change came at a time in American history
where the predominant national attitude towards race had finally reached a point where the majority embraced people of all
colors and nationalities as people of equal value in society. By
1978 America had finally turned the corner on racial matters;
the nation reached a point where prejudices against blacks had

become unacceptable for most of society. The social forces that polarized the nation for two hundred years had then reached a point of widespread consensus—that equal political rights should be extended to all, without limitation based upon race or color. The wide-spread, intense, pro-longed political divisiveness was decreasing. And the effect of this change on Christ's church was to greatly facilitate the taking of His gospel to all the world without the missionaries being targeted as political revolutionaries. Thus, while the Church of Christ may not have taken the lead in the important advances in bringing equal rights to people of all races, the Church nevertheless embraced these improvements. And when the revelation on the priesthood was announced, the response of all faithful disciples of Christ was one of gratitude and happiness that the long-awaited day had arrived.

## III.  RACIAL RELATIONS IN AMERICA

When Mormon Mitt Romney became the Republican nominee for President of the United States in 2012 this precipitated a flood of new criticisms of racism against the Church because of its previous practice of withholding the priesthood from blacks of African descent. Although that practice had ceased 34 years earlier (1978), accusations of racism against Mormonism became useful in 2012 to the opponents of Mitt Romney as an attack against his political campaign. The attacks were successful in helping to defeat Mitt Romney, and they were also successful in turning some people against the Church. Then, subsequent to the election of 2012, there has developed in many people a hyper-sensitivity to matters of race that approaches that which existed in America in the 1960s and 1970s. Although America elected a black President in 2008 and 2012, Barack Obama's presidency did not bring about improvement in race relations. To the contrary, many believe that racial relations deteriorated during his administration, and with the election of Donald

Trump in 2016 as President Obama's successor, some people in America attributed Trump's election to racism in America. Even if this accusation is without merit, it does appear that race issues are almost as intense and divisive today as they were in the 1960s.

Because God and the Church do not have prejudices against anyone, it can properly be stated that neither have ever been racists. But it cannot be denied that God and His Church have discriminated. Discrimination is disparate treatment of people. But discrimination can be totally right and proper when it is based on good reasons. For example, our society only imprisons people after they have been proven guilty in courts of law. Conduct-based discrimination is perfectly accepted in America and around the world. It was okay for the Cleveland Cavaliers to play LeBron James more than other players because he is a better player than they are. It is good to give an "A" grade to excellent students, and to give lower grades to other students based upon their lesser performances. Not all discrimination is bad or wrong. Discrimination can be justified and proper when based upon sufficient facts and reason. Admittedly, however, it is difficult to explain why God did something when He does not reveal His reasons. We will return to this question after we review the history of racism in America.

## A. The Original National Sin.

America was closely divided on the issue of slavery during the Constitutional Convention in 1787 and continuing through Joseph Smith's day and through the Civil War. And even after the war, despite the passage of the Thirteenth, Fourteenth and Fifteenth Amendments (in 1865, 1868 and 1870), volatile racial tensions and strife between blacks and whites continued in America through the end of the Nineteenth Century and most of the way through the Twentieth Century. Hatred, violence, anger, prejudice and injustice continued to plague America in the 1940s, 1950s and 1960s. Lest one forget how vast and intense and polarizing this situation was through the 1960s and beyond, let me point out some historical facts that help portray the powerful political wars that existed right here in the United States through the end of the 1960s.

In April of 1865, the surrender of General Robert E. Lee to General Ulysses Grant in Virginia at Appomattox Court House brought an end to the Civil War, but the hearts of the nation were not unified in embracing equal rights for blacks. Many, many people in America remained ardent in their opposition to the liberation of blacks and the end of slavery. Just two days after Lee's surrender, the belligerent southern sympathizer, John Wilkes Booth assassinated President Lincoln as he watched a play at Ford's Theatre in Washington, D. C. The war had ended, but animosity and prejudice and anger continued. The federal government's control and regulation of the southern states during the Reconstruction era was marked with continued polarization of many people. The passage of the Civil War Amendments laid the legal groundwork to eradicate slavery and its attendant prejudices, but it would be many decades before the blacks obtained widespread acceptance as equals throughout America.

## B.  Separate But Equal.

Not only did the Reconstruction period in the late 1800s fail to bring healing to America, but the political unrest was extended and made worse by the Supreme Court ruling in *Plessy v. Ferguson* (163 U.S. 537) in 1896 that held that it was proper and legal for the government to establish separate accommodations for blacks. This resulted in a period of segregation in America that actually stifled improved race relations—this situation continued for almost sixty years, and it resulted in heightened racial tensions, and discrimination became firmly entrenched throughout America, and especially in the southern states.

Black children were excluded from schools with white children. There were separate restrooms for blacks, separate water fountains, separate restaurants, and separate hotels. All of this sent the unmistakable message that blacks were inferior to whites. Segregation was somewhat difficult to maintain in some things, such as on buses and in sports arenas. But even there it could be accomplished by making blacks sit only in certain areas—like the back of buses.[185] Segregation was also maintained by laws prohibiting interracial marriage and by excluding blacks from major league football, basketball and baseball teams.

## C. Racism in Sports Reflected National Attitudes.

1. *Baseball—Jackie Robinson*. For many years major league baseball owners intentionally kept blacks off their teams. A year or two before Jackie Robinson joined the Brooklyn Dodgers in 1947, the major league owners did a study that concluded that the presence of black players on teams would cause attendance and revenues to drop. Actually, the exact opposite happened to the Brooklyn Dodgers during Jackie's first year. But the racial unrest in America after World War II was extensive and ugly.

When Jackie Robinson became the first black major league baseball player on April 15, 1947, this was not greeted with widespread celebration—it was greeted with anger and rudeness and protest by many people. Racial prejudice continued to be a volatile and polarizing reality in America. When word spread that a black player was on the Dodgers team, all but one of the other major league teams voted to walk off the field if Jackie took the field against them. Fortunately, no such boycott

---

[185] In July of 1944, when travelling with his Army group on a bus, someone directed Jackie to move and sit in the back of the bus. Jackie refused, which led to his arrest, and a military trial for insubordination. Jackie was found not guilty, but soon thereafter he was allowed to be honorably discharged from the military. At that time Jackie was an officer (a Lieutenant). Jackie was a man of strong character as well as a gifted athlete. He had played college football at UCLA, where he was a very good running back.

ever materialized. But there was still a lot of abuse and prejudice. One opposing manager would taunt and mock Jackie, calling him "boy" and telling him to "Come here and shine my shoes." When Jackie went on road trips, usually he could not stay at hotels with the other players, and often he could not eat where the other players ate. Even some of the principal starters on the Dodger team were racists; two of them insisted on being traded from the Dodgers, and others treated him coldly. Jackie took a lot of abuse, as he broke the color barrier in baseball. The process of changing from segregation to integration was underway—but progress was made slowly and begrudgingly on the part of many.

A television documentary was made of Jackie Robinson in 2017, celebrating the 70th anniversary of his breaking the color barrier in baseball. The documentary highlighted the character and strength of Jackie Robinson and of his wife, Rachel Robinson. Because of their great personal strength, Jackie was able to survive the severe racism and to achieve greatness in the sport that for years had specifically and intentionally excluded blacks. The documentary is a powerful reminder of the ugly racism that continued to exist in America in the 1940s and into the 1950s.

Seventy years later (2017), integration has been attained in all major league sports and in most schools and universities, and in most of American society. But this volatile and emotional social change was very slow in coming. Now, every year on April 15th, every player on every major league baseball team wears a jersey numbered "42" (Jackie Robinson's number) in celebration of Jackie Robinson's breaking the color barrier on that day in 1947.

2. _Basketball and Football_. The NBA did not have any black players until 1950. The first black professional basketball players joined the NBA in 1950. Bill Russell joined the Boston Celtics in 1956, and he was one of the early black pioneers. In the NFL, a few blacks played beginning in the 1920s, but there was a

league boycott from admitting blacks from 1934 to 1946. And while most teams came to have black players in the 1950s, the Washington Redskins did not have a black player until it signed running back Bobby Mitchell from Cleveland in 1962. (Bobby was a running back with Jim Brown, before he was traded to Washington.) The Redskin owner, George Marshall, had openly opposed and resisted segregating his team. And even after all NFL teams became integrated, there was still widespread prejudice that discouraged and resisted allowing blacks from filling the more "intellectual" positions of Center, Middle Linebacker and Quarterback. It was not until the late 1970s and into the 1980s that the NFL and society came to acknowledge that blacks could be great quarterbacks, just like the whites. In 1970 Joe Gilliam (with the Pittsburgh Steelers) became the first black quarterback to start a game in the NFL. In the late 1970s and into the 1980s, Warren Moon was acknowledged to be one of the game's best quarterbacks, and in 1988 the Washington Redskins won the Super Bowl with black quarterback Doug Williams at the helm.

I mention this slow progress in professional sports for two reasons. First, it is a good indicator of the condition of race relations in America. Second, sports have been one of the most effective instruments for improving race relations in America. To this day Jackie Robinson, Roy Campanella, Jim Brown, Bill Russell, Mohammad Ali, and many other blacks were pioneers who played a major role in helping America to accept and embrace blacks as equals. Major league sports were in the forefront of this progress. These great advances in sports were not accomplished until the 1960s, 1970s and 1980s; American society basically mirrored the racial attitudes in professional sports.

### D. Racism in Entertainment.

Racism was also prevalent in American entertainment well into the Twentieth century. In the 1950s, the television variety show of the great singer Nat King Cole was cancelled for racial reasons—the advertisers would not support the show. In the late 1960s, Sidney Poitier starred in the movie, "Guess Who's Coming to Dinner." The plot of that movie was about a white woman who brought a black boy friend to her parents' home for dinner. This plot was timely and provocative then. But only a few years later things began to change, and blacks became integrated in American sports, entertainment and even politics. America eventually elected a black President in 2008 and 2012—President Barack Obama. Most Americans are no longer prejudiced about race. Today (2019), some people do not realize how polarized American society was with respect to blacks in the 1940s, 50s, 60s and 70s. Even today many people claim that racism is pervasive in America, but compared to the serious racism of the mid-Twentieth Century, things are very good today.

### E. Brown v. Board of Education.

In 1954 the Supreme Court ruled in the case of *Brown v. Board of Education*, 347 U.S. 483, that segregation in schools was unconstitutional. This caused a dramatic change in America, as the nation had functioned for over fifty years as a segregated society (pursuant to the *Plessy v. Ferguson* case), where blacks and whites were separated in schools, bathrooms, restaurants, buses and sports teams. American society was racist. But the *Brown v. Board of Education* case was a key in breaking down continuing racial prejudices and barriers.

### F. The 1960s.

As late as the 1960s, some colleges still refused to admit blacks. When James Meredith applied for admission to the University of Mississippi in 1961, he was denied admission because he was black. He sued, and his case went to the U. S. Supreme Court, which on September 10, 1962, ruled that the university must admit him. Even after the Supreme Court had ruled, Mississippi Governor Ross Barnett tried to block Meredith's admission, which led to some violence where two people were killed, 206 people were wounded, and 200 people were arrested. Martin Luther King, Jr., became a prominent national civil rights leader at this time, leading civil protests, including one that landed him in jail in Birmingham, Alabama. In 1963, King led a civil rights march in Washington, D.C. to bring attention to the injustices of racial discrimination. And King was assassinated on April 4, 1968 in Memphis, Tennessee. This led to the riots in Washington, D.C. for four days. I remember this personally, being a high school student in the Metropolitan Washington D. C. area at that time.

Several other historical events from the 1960s point out the extreme racist views that were held by a large part of America, even into the late 1960s. It was not until 1961 that the 23$^{rd}$ Amendment to the Constitution was ratified, which allowed residents of the District of Columbia to vote in Presidential Elections. Beginning in the 1950s, the District of Columbia was a majority black city, so extending to them the right to vote in Presidential elections was a major improvement in racial relations. Similarly, the 24$^{th}$ Amendment was not ratified until 1964. This Amendment abolished the poll tax, which had been used to restrict blacks from voting. Also in the mid-60s, Congress passed and President Johnson signed the Civil Rights Act of 1964 and the Voting Rights Act of 1965. These two laws were very powerful in eliminating various practices in many states that were blocking the integration of blacks into society. It was not until 1967 that the Supreme Court struck down the Virginia law that prohibited interracial marriage. *Loving v. Virginia,* 388 U.S. 1. And it was not until 1967 that the first black was appointed to be a Justice of the Supreme Court (Thurgood Marshall). And finally, former Alabama Governor George Wallace, an overt segregationist, ran for President of the United States in 1964, 1968 and 1972, under the banner of promoting segregation. All of these things show how deep and entrenched racism was in

America at that date; and it shows that these racial issues were political, emotional and volatile at that time, and that these forces against integration were very strong.

In addition to these major societal changes in the 1960s, there were also great technological advances occurring. Travel by jet plane around the globe became common place. In July of 1969 NASA sent men to the moon and back. In the early 1960s satellite communication was established that allowed instantaneous communication around the world. This instantaneous communication created a more unified world than was ever before thought possible. These advances helped to bring most of the world to accept all peoples as equals. These advances were especially rapid and significant in the United States of America, and they contributed to ending segregation and in extending equal rights to blacks.

There were two black players on my high school football team in the late 1960s. I played at Wheaton High School, in Maryland, where today (2018) white students are probably a minority. In 1968-69 there were very few blacks in our school. But we did not regard the blacks as lesser or inferior. I have no feelings of racism today, and I didn't have any when I was a youth. But as a youth, and later as a missionary for The Church of Jesus Christ of Latter-day Saints, I was confronted with the Church's ban on giving the Priesthood to blacks, and I sought then to understand it and to respond to accusations of prejudice that were hurled at me because of the Church's policy. I was a freshman at BYU in the fall of 1969 when students at other universities protested against the BYU basketball team because blacks were denied the Priesthood. I also recall the arm band protests that two black sprinters (Tommie Smith and John Carlos) made at the 1968 Olympics in Mexico, where these runners raised their arms with black wrist bands as they were awarded medals on the podium. The point is that much racism existed in America in the mid-twentieth century. Society was changing, but the changes were slow in coming.

I remember one time listening to WTOP radio in Washington, D. C., when Robert W. Barker was on the air, responding to questions about the Church's policy of not ordaining blacks to the priesthood. (This would have been either the late 60s or early 70s.) Robert Barker was a prominent Washington, D. C. attorney, who represented the Church in many legal matters.[186] He was confronted on the radio with the accusation that the Church was prejudiced. The response that I recall him giving was that if people do not believe that the Church possesses the priesthood of God, then those people should not be concerned as to whether or not the Church gave the priesthood to blacks. But if the Church was operating under God's authority, then we must do as God directs through His prophet; the priesthood is God's priesthood, and He directs who is to receive it and who is not to receive it, whether or not we understand why.[187] I submit that is still good doctrine and reasoning. As a member, I don't tell God what to do. As Jesus said to his Apostles, "you have not chosen me, but I have chosen you and ordained you" (John 15:16).

Such reasoning is certainly good for a member. The prophet, however, has the responsibility to obtain the mind and will of the Lord and to implement the policies that God wants. I was reluctant then to criticize either Brigham Young or any of the prophets who succeeded him for not lifting the ban. Who was I to dictate what the prophet should do and when to do it. If I

---

[186] He was called to be one of the first Regional Representatives in 1967. He was Secretary of Bonneville International, where he worked closely with Gordon B. Hinckley for many years. At his death, Robert Barker was President of the Washington D. C. Temple, and President Hinckley spoke at his funeral.

[187] Brother Barker echoed the statement of the First Presidency dated December 15, 1969, regarding those who criticized the Church for not extending the priesthood to blacks. They said: "Those individuals, we suppose, do not believe in the divine origin and nature of the Church, nor that we have the priesthood of God. Therefore, if they feel we have no priesthood, they should have no concern with any aspect of our theology on priesthood so long as that theology does not deny any man his Constitutional privileges."

have a view on the matter, I have the right to share that view with the prophet. But I am reluctant to condemn a prophet for saying that the blacks should or should not be given the priesthood during a period of time. This was the issue that I faced in the 1970s. It was not within my purview to dictate what the Church should do on this matter. Rather, I followed the Prophet and my priesthood leaders because I knew that they were in fact God's chosen leaders.

## G. Heightened Racial Tensions beginning in 2012.

Criticism of the Church for withholding the priesthood from blacks had all but ended in 1978. Thereafter the issue rarely surfaced. But when the Republican Party nominated Mormon Mitt Romney to be its candidate in August of 2012, Mitt Romney was viciously labeled by some to be a racist because of his support of the Church when it withheld the priesthood from blacks. Suddenly the Church again became a target of criticism by a segment of America—once again the Church was accused of racism because of the priesthood policy that was in place prior to 1978. From then until the present, there has emerged on the part of some people an intense condemnation of acts and attitudes (including those of the past) that are or were related to discrimination against blacks. This hyper-sensitivity includes the following: (1) a condemnation of any display of the Stars and Bars (the Confederate flag); (2) efforts around the nation to remove from government properties statues that honored pro-slavery people and confederate troops; (3) many accusations by blacks in America of discriminatory and racist treatment by the police—many of which are false and were generated by people who were too anxious to find racism where it did not exist;[188] and (4) widespread allegations that those who

---

[188] Two examples of this are the riots in Ferguson, Missouri (2015) and Baltimore, Maryland (2015), following two separate incidents where a black person was killed by the police. In both cases, the facts ultimately confirmed

voted for Donald Trump for President are racist. All of this creates a very intense, polarizing, irrational, political environment in America.

## IV.  JESUS DECLINED TO PARTICIPATE IN VOLATILE POLITICAL MOVEMENTS

Jesus told Pontius Pilate, "My kingdom is not of this world: if my kingdom were of this world, then would my servants fight, that I should not be delivered to the Jews: but now is my kingdom not from hence" (John 18:36). As Jesus came into Jerusalem on Palm Sunday, though crowds of people hailed him and praised him, yet this royal reception was not about any effort on his part to change either the political powers that be or, in particular, to attempt to end slavery of either the Jews or any other people. Jesus proceeded into Jerusalem riding on a donkey—a gesture of peace, not a threatening action such as could be conveyed had he been riding on a horse. Jesus' message was for individuals to be kind and to help others. "Render therefore unto Caesar the things which are Caesar's; and unto God the things that are God's" (Matt. 22:21). Jesus' message was to turn the other cheek—to submit to some injustices rather than to fight. Jesus recommended against suing one who has wronged another.

Jesus did not encourage the people to revolt against political injustice; his teachings focused more on what was within their total control—they can always be good and kind and compassionate toward others. Jesus neither encouraged nor incited the people to revolt or to engage in any social revolution or any political confrontations. The significance of this, as applied to slavery is that Jesus never led any revolution against it—not by his words and not by his actions. This was not to condone

that these killings were both justified and that they were not racist actions by the police.

slavery, rather Jesus' non-confrontational approach to slavery was protective of those who were slaves and of those who could be endangered by attacking or challenging the institution. Jesus sought to help people, including slaves, to engender and promote goodness, being kind to their enemies or oppressors.

Thus, in Jesus' day, and in the first century of the church of Christ, neither the Apostles nor the church were proponents of challenging either slavery or other political oppression. (See, e.g., 1 Peter 2:18; Ephesians 6:5-9; Colossians 3:22; 1 Timothy 6:1; & Titus 2:9.) And again—this was not to condone such evils. The Church of Christ just did not participate in political unrest or activism or revolution, and this was not and should not be regarded as supportive of the institution of slavery.

## A. The Church of Christ Is Not a Political Activist Organization.

Those who would contend that the Church of Jesus Christ should take the lead in bringing about needed political changes in the world do not understand the primary purpose of the Church. Such is not the Church's role. The Church needs to be helpful to peoples in all nations—including to those who live under dictatorships, under repressive regimes, under communism, under monarchies and in slavery, as well as to those who live in democratic nations with equal political rights for all of its citizens. Thus, when Hitler came to power in Germany and exercised abusive power in that nation, the Church did not direct its people to challenge the Third Reich. This was not to condone Hitler, but it did allow the Church to continue to serve and bless the people until the political issues were resolved. The same principles apply to the Church's functioning around the world. Had the Church prematurely taken the lead in advocating for political reforms in civil rights, this could have brought death to members, and it could have impaired the Church's ability to accomplish its more important mission. It was appropriate and proper for the Church to decline to take the lead in civil rights reform; and it is proper for the Church to now praise those who helped to bring about these tremendous reforms. It is not inconsistent or improper for the Church not to have taken the lead in these important reforms.

Thus, accusations made in 1969 and 1977 and 2012 and even in 2019 that The Church of Jesus Christ of Latter-day Saints used to be racist or still is racist are totally unfounded. Such accusations are a gross misrepresentation of the Church. A full understanding of God's plans and purposes presents The Church of Jesus Christ of Latter-day Saints in a good and noble light.

# V. STATEMENTS OF JOSEPH SMITH REGARDING SLAVERY, BLACKS AND THE PRIESTHOOD

### A. Priesthood in the Abrahamic Covenant.

The Mormons were persecuted politically in the 1830s and 1840s because they, as a group, were anti-slavery. This was one of the factors that brought persecution on the Church in both Missouri and Illinois.[189] In April of 1836, the Prophet Joseph Smith counseled the missionaries to not "interfere with slaves, contrary to the mind and will of their masters" (HC 2:263-64 (1835)). (See also HC 2:440 (April 9, 1836).) The Prophet spoke

---

[189] For example, in 1836, citizens in Clay County, Missouri accused Mormons of being "non-slaveholders, and opposed to slavery," and the citizens demanded that the Mormons leave the county. The local leaders of the Church agreed to leave, but they responded to the charges saying, among other things: "We have no part for or against slavery; but are opposed to the abolitionists, and consider that men have a right to hold slaves or not, according to law. . . . [W]e do not believe it right to interfere with bond-servants, nor preach the gospel to them." HC 2:453-4. While I do not believe this statement accurately presents the official position of the Church, it does illustrate the types of pressures that were put on the saints in that period of time.

about slavery and racial matters a number of times. See, e.g., HC 1:375-79; 2:369; 2:436-40; 4:445-46; 5:217-18; and 6:197-210 & 244.) Joseph said that the institution of servitude was present in biblical times, including being practiced by Abraham, and that God did not chastise Abraham for it. He pointed out that servitude continued to exist in New Testament times, and that the prophets did not condemn it, but rather encouraged the masters to be kind and the servants to be good and loyal (HC 2:438-40).

## B. Racial Problems in the Early Days of America.

In 1835 and 1836 Joseph Smith gave directions to the missionaries about what they should and should not do regarding the institution of slavery. The directions he gave the early leaders and missionaries were very similar to the Savior's approach eighteen hundred years earlier. Joseph directed the Elders to avoid aligning with the abolitionists. He instructed them to not teach slaves without the consent of their masters (HC 2:263-64; and 2:437-40). This direction was also given in *The Doctrine and Covenants*, Section 134:12: "[W]e do not believe it right to interfere with the bondservants, neither preach the gospel to, nor baptize them contrary to the will and wish of their masters."[190] While the Prophet Joseph Smith taught the principles of equality of all peoples, he advised the missionaries to avoid aligning themselves too closely with political activists, whether or not the cause was just. The Prophet gave reasons for this approach, which can be summed up as the need for the Elders to focus on their divine mandate to bring the blessings of the gospel of Jesus Christ to as many people as possible. Without either criticizing or advancing the institution of slavery, his divine mission, like that of Jesus, was to uplift and save mankind whatever their station in life may be (HC 2: 262-64). He proposed to leave to God the task of ending or changing the institution of slavery

---

[190] In the 1835 edition of *The Doctrine and Covenants* this statement on government was section 102. It became section 134 in later editions.

(HC 2:438 and 4:445-46). In other words, the purpose of The Church of Jesus Christ of Latter-day Saints was not to lead the world in political activism or revolution. And therefore, both in the days of Jesus and in the last dispensation the Church has not been the leader of political change in the world. The Church can operate under slavery and oppression, as well as in a society where all races and peoples have freedom and equal rights under the law. Thus, the Church can and has often adapted to the laws and social customs of the nations where it exists. There is no need for the Church to be the first organization to embrace new and good social changes; rather the Church has demonstrated great resiliency and adaptability, as it helps the people live righteously, in whatever political system they may be—whether in slavery or freedom. And those who would desire to transform the kingdom of God into one of political activism—they would be mistaken. And those who would criticize the Church for not being sufficiently active in promoting and advancing political purposes—they would show a lack of understanding of the purposes of God's church.

However, by the year 1844, Joseph's views on how the Church should address the slavery issue had changed somewhat. On February 8, 1844, Joseph announced that he was running for President. He said that none of the other candidates were proposing to do the things that would protect and safeguard the saints, and therefore he decided to run for the office to secure for the saints the protection of their rights and liberties (HC 6:210). One of the main planks in his platform was to free the slaves. Whereas in 1835 and 1836 the Prophet had encouraged the missionaries to avoid aligning with the abolitionists, in 1844 he commenced a campaign that involved the missionaries in proposing to end slavery. Joseph proposed freeing the slaves, and paying the slave owners for the loss of their "property." His proposal was set forth in his "Views of the Powers and Policy of the Government of the United States" (HC 6:197-209). The prophet gave directions to advance this campaign by directing the Quorum of the Twelve and 337 missionaries to take the message throughout the States. By 1844, the Church had grown stronger, such that it could better handle any opposition that might materialize for this politically active stance.

But even though the Church began to take a more active position in working for the liberation of slaves, there were some aspects of racial discrimination that the prophet implicitly condoned, and which apparently escaped his comment: First, the Nauvoo Charter denied blacks the right to vote (section 7), and second, the applicable laws in Nauvoo made it a crime for a black to marry a white. In February 1844, as Chief Judge of the Nauvoo Municipal Court, Joseph convicted and fined two black men for attempting to marry white women (HC 6:210).

In the 1800s there were many people who opposed slavery personally, but who nevertheless thought that various types of segregation were proper, including in marriage. Several states (including Illinois) in the 1800s had laws against interracial marriage.[191] Many who held such views felt that blacks were equal in the sight of God, but nevertheless felt it better for men and women of different races not to marry.[192] And while this point of view is unacceptable in society today, until the latter part of the Twentieth Century this view was widely held in America. Thus, as was pointed out above, in 1844, when Joseph Smith was acting in his official capacity of a judge in Nauvoo, he fined two negroes for attempting to marry white women (HC 6:210). In addition, as a candidate for President of the United

---

[191] In the 1600s Virginia and Maryland enacted laws prohibiting interracial marriages with blacks (called anti-miscegenation laws). This was partly done to prevent rebellion and to preserve the institution of slavery. I understand that all of the thirteen colonies had anti-miscegenation laws. In 1924 Virginia re-affirmed this policy in that state by passing its "Racial Integrity Act of 1924." In 1967, when the Supreme Court struck down this Virginia law (in *Loving v. Virginia*, 388 U.S. 1), 16 states still had anti-miscegenation laws.
[192] The Prophet Joseph was also of this point of view. In January of 1843 he said the negroes "have souls, and are subjects of salvation." He said he favored "national equalization" for them, but he said he "would confine them by strict law to their own species" (HC 5:217-18).

States in 1844, Joseph Smith proposed that after liberating the slaves and compensating the slave owners, then the government should send the slaves to live in Texas or Mexico, where there would be a better chance for them to be fully accepted in society (HC 6:244). While this approach to the slavery issue would be criticized today, it was a reasonable and acceptable position in the 1840s. Similarly, during the 1800s, the withholding of priesthood from blacks was typical of national racial attitudes in America at that time. In the 1840s, many churches in America were segregated.[193] Interestingly, however, Mormon congregations were never segregated. And the withholding of the priesthood from blacks was a matter of insignificance in America at that time.

But dealing with the institution of slavery is different from the policy of withholding the priesthood from blacks. The fact that Joseph Smith advised against being abolitionists does not mean the priesthood could not be extended to blacks. Nevertheless, the ban did serve to protect the Elders from attacks from pro-slavery forces as they preached the gospel throughout the nation. And the ban did serve to give the Church a measure of insulation from political attacks. And again, it seems clear that the time for extending the priesthood to blacks was a part of God's own timetable. And while the two issues are technically separate, they are also related in that they both pertain to blacks. Advising the Elders to avoid aligning with abolitionists does not answer why the Lord's prophets withheld the priesthood from blacks, but it could very well be a timing issue—that it was not yet time to undertake a major

---

[193] In the 1800s segregated congregations existed in most of the major religions, including Catholics, Methodists, Lutherans, Presbyterians, Episcopalians and Baptists. Racial issues were a major cause of the split in the Baptists that created the Southern Baptist Convention. But the segregation was not solely the result of whites seeking to exclude blacks; both blacks and whites seemed more comfortable segregating. In the late 18th century the African Methodist Episcopal Church (AME) was established in a split from the Methodist Church over racial issues.

missionary effort to the blacks until the 1970s. The accelerated emphasis on bringing the gospel to the black nations was inaugurated in 1978.

## C. Newly Revealed Ancient Scriptures Comment on Who Could Hold the Priesthood.

While God has not revealed all the reasons for withholding the priesthood from blacks for a period of time, the Prophet Joseph Smith did receive some new revelations that shed some light on this. In December of 1830 the Lord revealed the following new scriptures to the Prophet Joseph Smith, as recorded in Moses 7:8 & 12:

> [T]here was a blackness came upon all the children of Canaan, that they were despised among all people. . . . And it came to pass that Enoch continued to call upon all the people, save it were the people of Canaan to repent.[194]

Describing the people of Enoch who were "taken up to heaven," verse 22 states: "they were a mixture of all the seed of Adam save it was the seed of Cain, for the seed of Cain were black, and had not place among them." On January 25, 1841, Joseph said that negroes are the "sons of Cain" (HC 4:501). Not only did the Prophet know this, but he was also familiar with teachings in the Book of Abraham that provided further insight on this matter. Shortly after the Egyptian papyri was obtained in the summer of 1835, the Prophet announced that it included some writings of Abraham. The Prophet's translation

---

[194] Enoch refers to this people as the people of Canaan, even though Canaan had not been born yet. (Canaan is the fourth son of Ham and Egyptus, and he was born after the flood.) This chapter explains that Enoch was shown in vision Canaan and his posterity, and therefore he knew that descendants of Cain would survive the flood and that some of them would become the people of Canaan, whose name would be widely known in a later time.

of The Book of Abraham was not published until 1842, and the following is included in that account, at Abraham 1:21-24, 26-27, which is now a part of our canonized scripture:

> Now this king of Egypt was a descendant from the loins of Ham, and was a partaker of the blood of the Canaanites by birth.
>
> From this descent sprang all the Egyptians, and thus the blood of the Canaanites was preserved in the land.
>
> The land of Egypt being first discovered by a woman, who was the daughter of Ham, and the daughter of Egyptus, which in the Chaldean signifies Egypt, which signifies that which is forbidden;
>
> When this woman discovered the land it was under water, who afterward settled her sons in it; and thus, from Ham, sprang that race which preserved the curse in the land. . . .
>
> Pharaoh [the oldest son of Egyptus], being a righteous man, established his kingdom and judged his people wisely and justly . . . . Noah . . . blessed him with the blessings of the earth, and with the blessings of wisdom, but cursed him as pertaining to the Priesthood.
>
> Now, Pharaoh being of that lineage by which he could not have the right of Priesthood, notwithstanding the Pharaohs would fain to claim it from Noah, through Ham. . . .

These recently revealed ancient scriptures lend support and

provide explanation for the episode about Noah and his grand-son Canaan that is recorded in Genesis chapter 9. In Genesis, after the flood, Noah pronounced a curse upon Canaan and his posterity following an incident where Ham discovered Noah naked in his tent. This event can be puzzling, and the curs-ing of Canaan (Ham's son) sounds unreasonable unless one understands that Canaan was of the lineage that was denied the priesthood. Scholars suggest that this incident involved an attempt by Ham to secure for Canaan Noah's priesthood gar-ment, by which Canaan might contend that he held the priest-hood. Joseph Smith apparently understood this episode in that way because (1) he added some wording to Genesis, chapter 9 that conveyed this message, and (2) he revealed verses in the Book of Abraham which also confirm this meaning.

### D. Limited Scope of Missionary Work in the 1800s.

The above referenced verses of scripture teach that anciently the blacks who descended from Egypt were of a race that was denied the priesthood. The Prophet's writings indicate that he understood that blacks might properly be in the Kirtland Temple HC 2:369, but that reference does not shed any light on whether he thought that such participation extended to the priesthood ordinances. It is recorded in *History of the Church*, 2:440 that in April of 1836 Joseph Smith said that "the curse is not yet taken off from the sons of Canaan, neither will be until it is affected by as great a power as caused it to come." Later, in November of 1841, the Prophet again stated that "the curse remains on the posterity of Canaan" (HC 4:445-46).[195] A fair

---

[195] In writing about this in 1951, Milton R. Hunter wrote that withholding of the priesthood from negroes was taught to Brigham Young by Joseph Smith. In support of this he referred to minutes of a meeting of Church general authorities on August 22, 1895, which state: "President George Q. Cannon remarked that the Prophet taught this doctrine: That the seed of Cain could not receive the Priesthood nor act in any of the offices of the Priesthood un-til the seed of Abel should come forward and take precedence over Cain's

interpretation of this is that Joseph Smith confirmed that the withholding of the priesthood from the descendants of Canaan had not yet been lifted. The Prophet took the position that if the institution was to be changed or stopped, then God would attend to it. That is what happened in 1978.

In writing about the policy of withholding the priesthood from negroes, Milton R. Hunter wrote in 1951 that Joseph Smith taught this to Brigham Young. In support of this, Hunter referred to minutes of a meeting of general authorities of the Church on August 22, 1895, which state:

> President George Q. Cannon remarked that the Prophet taught this doctrine: That the seed of Cain could not receive the Priesthood nor act in any of the offices of the Priesthood until the seed of Abel should come forward and take precedence over Cain's offering.[196]

George Q. Cannon would not have personally heard this from the Prophet, but at the time he made this remark, Elder Cannon had served in the First Presidency with four different prophets—Brigham Young, John Taylor, Wilford Woodruff and Lorenzo Snow. It is a good assumption that all of these men had heard the same report from Brigham Young.

America was a very racially-charged nation in the Nineteenth

---

offering." George Q. Cannon would not have personally heard this from the Prophet, but at the time he made this remark, Elder Cannon had served in the First Presidency with Brigham Young, John Taylor, Wilford Woodruff and Lorenzo Snow, one or more of whom would have heard it from the Prophet. Milton R. Hunter, *Pearl of Great Price Commentary* (Salt Lake City: Bookcraft, 1951), 142, quoting Joseph Fielding Smith, *The Way to Perfection* (Salt Lake City: originally published by the Genealogical Society of The Church of Jesus Christ of Latter-day Saints, 1931), 111.

[196] Milton R. Hunter, *Pearl of Great Price Commentary* (Salt Lake City: Bookcraft, 1951), 142, quoting Joseph Fielding Smith, *The Way to Perfection* (Salt Lake City: The Genealogical Society of The Church of Jesus Christ of Latter-day Saints [and later published by Deseret Book Co.], 1931), 111.

and Twentieth Centuries. The former slave Frederick Douglass gained some national prominence in the latter half of the Nineteenth Century. But racial unrest was strong and pervasive in the United States throughout the Nineteenth and into the Twentieth Century. Prior to the Civil War, slavery was regarded as an acceptable practice by many people. Initially, the Church did not seek to buck the system, and Joseph Smith directed that missionaries not attempt to preach the gospel to slaves without their owners' consent (HC 2:263; & 438-40). This approach was a reasonable, conservative approach to this issue. Similarly, the Savior did not encourage his disciples to instigate political unrest with regard to slavery issues in his day. *Id.* The slavery issue was a major societal problem in the Nineteenth Century, but it was not an issue that the Church was forced to address. The Prophet directed the Elders to steer clear of causing agitation and unrest on this issue. The Church's subsequent withholding of the priesthood from the blacks was consistent with this policy that was quite reasonable in the 1830s and 1840s. With the Mormons settling the west—being a mostly white community—and following the norms of American society on the black issue, the priesthood ban was essentially a non-issue until the late 1960s.

## VI. CONCLUSION

As a missionary in France in the early 1970s, there were a number of times when I had to answer accusations that the Church's ban was wrong. In response we would explain that no eternal blessing is denied to any individual because of his race; we know that in God's timetable all worthy individuals can be exalted in the celestial kingdom if they live worthily. I did not understand why the Priesthood was not made available to them then, but I knew that if they would live worthily they would later receive it and all the attendant blessings. I also knew that God frequently discriminated in deciding who could and who could not receive certain blessings and certain priesthood authority.[197] The timing of things is often a factor in God's directives. Thus, there is precedent for the Lord's directive that the Priesthood be restricted to a particular race or people for a period of time. All of these reasons remain valid today, even though the need to give them rarely surfaces any more. But for those today who are sincerely seeking for answers to some of these historical questions, the foregoing explanations can help to understand the perspective of the ancient prophets Noah, Abraham, Jacob and of Jesus, himself. God has a long history of bestowing earthly blessings on the descendants of his righteous prophets, like Abraham. But former restrictions on holding the priesthood were lifted in these last days, as the gospel is being preached in all the world. And regardless of whether a man had the opportunity to hold God's priesthood on earth, he will have that opportunity before the final judgment. God extends to all of his children the equal opportunity to obtain exaltation with Him and to be joint heirs with Christ.

---

[197] Historically, offices in the priesthood were restricted to the seed of Abraham and to men, and at various times limited to the tribe of Levi and to the House of Israel. After Christ's resurrection, the priesthood was extended to the Gentiles.

# Chapter 9

# Alleged False Prophecies
# of Joseph Smith

Those who are anxious to discredit Joseph Smith sometimes argue that he was not a true prophet because he made some false prophecies. In support of this they often identify one or more of six prophecies made by him which they allege did not come to pass. Based upon this, they argue that Joseph Smith was a false prophet. We will examine six such statements, as well as a test proposed by Joseph Smith's critics, which they contend should be applied to determine whether Joseph Smith was a true prophet of God.

Joseph Smith made more than a thousand prophetic statements that are recorded in scripture. In addition to that he made hundreds of other predictions.[198] In light of this, the very prospect of reaching a conclusion that he was a false prophet based upon a few prophecies that allegedly did not come to pass, at the same time ignoring hundreds that did come to pass, seems to be most unreasonable. Basically, such an approach starts with the premise that if one can find even one prophecy of Joseph Smith that did not come to pass, then this would prove that he

---

[198] See, e.g., Truman Madsen, *Joseph Smith the Prophet* (Salt Lake City: Bookcraft, 1989), 37.

was not a true prophet. Again, it is absolutely illogical to construct such a test. If ninety-nine percent of Joseph's prophecies
came to pass, the inescapable conclusion would be that he was
a true prophet. Therefore, if a handful of prophecies could be
identified that did not come to pass, the most negative conclusion that one could possibly make from this would be that
Joseph was mistaken in a very small number of his prophetic
statements.

It is not within the scope of this book to list or discuss the
thousand plus prophecies of Joseph Smith.[199] But they are inter-
spersed throughout his writings and throughout the journals
of those who observed and recorded what he said—you literally can't miss them if you undertake a serious examination of
Joseph Smith. Among those who are unaware of these prophecies are the lazy critics of Joseph—those who have pre-judged
him to be a false prophet, and who then look to find support
for their prejudices. Hundreds of Joseph's prophecies are found
in *The Book of Mormon*, the *Doctrine and Covenants*, the *Pearl of
Great Price*, and in many of the serious works that have been
published about Joseph Smith. See, for example, Ivan J. Barrett's
book, *Joseph Smith and the Restoration*, and Truman G. Madsen's
book, *Joseph Smith the Prophet*. In particular, I would recommend
the reading of chapter 3 in Madsen's book (pp. 35-49) as a great
introduction to the study of the prophecies of Joseph Smith. The

---

[199] Such a study would be marvelous. Just to whet your appetite a little bit:
Lillie Freeze reported that Joseph said "the time would come when none
but the women of the Latter-day Saints would be willing to bear children."
*Young Woman's Journal* 2, November 1890, 81. In a general sense, this is being fulfilled today. It has been well known for years in America that large
families have been generally Catholic or Mormon. However, recently there
have been fewer and fewer Catholics in this special group. Joseph prophesied that Eliza R. Snow would visit Jerusalem; that Brigham Young's name
would be known for good or evil; that Dan Jones would fulfill a mission to
Wales; and that the Saints would "be driven and would suffer" and "go to
the Rocky Mountains and there become a great and mighty people." All
of the above prophecies have been fulfilled and are discussed by Truman
Madsen, at 39-40, with sources given there.

chapter is entitled, "Joseph Smith and Spiritual Gifts." This is a wonderful chapter to give the flavor and a small sampling of Joseph's many prophecies. My study of this chapter and these books, including the 872 pages of scripture produced by Joseph Smith, supports the divine witness that I have received that Joseph Smith was God's choice prophet and seer of the restoration, in preparation for the triumphal return of our Lord and Savior Jesus Christ.

After a few more introductory comments, I will identify the specific alleged false prophecies, and I will give my comments about them—I conclude that none of them is a false prophecy. And while some critics argue that one or more of these prophecies were not fulfilled within the time period that Joseph stated, I disagree with such conclusions. The following discussion will address these timing arguments.

Joseph Smith has produced 872 pages of scripture (531 from the Book of Mormon; 280 from the Doctrine and Covenants; and 61 from the Pearl of Great Price). This is almost three times as much as the next most prodigious prophet, Moses, who produced 308 pages of scripture. Next to Moses would be the Apostle Paul (122 pages)—Joseph Smith produced seven times as much scripture as Paul. Luke produced 103 pages; Isaiah 80 pages; Samuel 80 pages; Jeremiah 78 pages; and Ezekiel 72 pages. Joseph Smith produced more pages of scripture than all of these great prophets combined. Even if one false statement could be found in the 872 pages of scripture produced by Joseph Smith, this would never be a sufficient basis to conclude that he was a false prophet. If one is to conduct a proper, thorough examination of the Prophet Joseph Smith, the main examination of him would have to include all of his words which he identified as scripture. If this main body is not included, then the review becomes nothing but an anecdotal glimpse, focusing on lesser or minor matters, that may or may not have been accurately stated or accurately recorded. Such analysis can never have validity as a proper examination and evaluation of whether Joseph Smith was a prophet of God.

## The One Mistake Test

As I understand it, Joseph's critics argue that if they can show even one prophecy made by him that never came to pass, then they assert that this would prove him to be a false prophet. In support of such a test, critics of Joseph Smith like to use verse 22 from the eighteenth chapter of Deuteronomy to establish it. But as you will see that would be a misapplication of verse 22, which states:

> When a prophet speaketh in the name of the
> LORD, if the thing follow not, nor come to pass,
> that is the thing which the LORD hath not spoke,
> but the prophet hath spoken it presumptuously:
> thou shalt not be afraid of him.

Now that's some pretty reasonable advice. Basically, Moses tells the people not to worry about a prophet who predicts things that don't come to pass. But this verse does not say that if a man makes even one prophecy that does not come to pass, then he is a false prophet. Those who assert such an interpretation are misrepresenting Moses' words.

But what about a prophet who predicts one hundred things to come to pass, and ninety-nine do come to pass, but one does not—what did Moses say about that situation? And what about a prophecy that is proven mostly correct, but which contains one part that does not seem correct? Verse 22 doesn't address these questions either. I submit that God wants us to use good judgment, and he wants us not to lose sight of the important things because of minor mistakes and flaws in his chosen servants. To do otherwise will inevitably lead one to reject the larger good because of a tiny flaw. It would be a big mistake to reject a prophet of God because of a minor mistake that the prophet made. And prophets, being human, will certainly make some mistakes.

As we move on to analyze the six, alleged false prophecies, it will be shown that those criticizing these prophecies have incorrectly interpreted the meaning of some of Joseph's words. But they are not entitled to do this. They are not allowed to pick and choose the way they wish to interpret his words. In interpreting a prophecy of Joseph Smith, the person critiquing is not entitled to ascribe his own interpretations to words and phrases, but rather it must be determined what Joseph understood and what he meant. In other words, the critic is not entitled to misinterpret the statement and then conclude it to be false when the interpretation meant by Joseph Smith would support the prophecy being true. To emphasize the importance of this previous sentence, let me state it again in slightly different words: A prophecy stated by Joseph Smith must be interpreted by giving his words HIS meaning. It is bad reasoning to ascribe different meanings to Joseph Smith's words in order to conclude a certain prophecy to be false.

Applying an erroneous test to determine whether a man is a prophet will invariably be more misleading than helpful. A prophet is not God. God is infallible, but man is not, and neither is a prophet. "A prophet is a prophet only when acting as such" (HC 5:265). If someone were to reject all of the words of Joseph Smith because one percent of them were found to have a flaw or error, this would mean rejecting all of Joseph's words because of a minor error or flaw. No reasonable person applies this type of an excessively rigid standard in dealing with family, friends, and business associates; on the contrary, we recognize that people are imperfect, and we do not discard people and things of great value because of minor imperfections. We recognize that it is irrational, unjust, unreasonable, overly harsh, and usually counter-productive to reject something of great value because of an insignificant flaw. Thus, to apply a standard of infallibility to the Prophet Joseph Smith will always be more harmful than helpful. Joseph himself acknowledged having flaws and weaknesses (HC 5:401 & 6:366). But when the identification of a minor flaw or mistake by Joseph Smith causes one to conclude that he was not a prophet of God, then I must point out that the conclusion is wrong; the standard applied to reach that conclusion is flawed; the great body of inspiring teachings and prophecies of Joseph are ignored or mistakenly denied; and the confirming witness of the Holy Ghost that Joseph Smith is a prophet of God is rejected.

The Savior, Jesus Christ, loves Joseph Smith, and He called Joseph Smith to be His prophet. The Prophet Joseph Smith delivered to the world 872 pages of the word of God, and the Holy Ghost bears witness to their truthfulness. In addition to those 872 pages, Joseph Smith said many other things, and some of them are also marvelous and inspiring. But to reject Joseph Smith as the prophet of Jesus Christ because of one or two minor misstatements of opinion is a totally unreasonable standard to apply. There is just no need to be fanatical in scrutinizing God's messengers. Every man and woman who comes into this world is born with the light of Christ, by which he or she can recognize the truth and God's messengers. And while some people like to use Deuteronomy 18:22 to rationalize their belief that Joseph Smith is not God's prophet, I would point out that there is another test given by Moses in this chapter which applies to Joseph Smith, and by this test if they reject Joseph Smith as God's prophet, they are rejecting God himself. Here is the prophecy:

> I will raise them up a Prophet from among their
> brethren, like unto thee, and will put my words
> in his mouth; and he shall speak unto them all
> that I shall command him.

And it shall come to pass, that whosoever will not
hearken unto my words which he shall speak in
my name, I will require it of him. (Deuteronomy
18:18-19)

This is the prophecy referred to by Peter in speaking to
the Jews as recorded in Acts, chapter 3. On the one hand, Peter
confirmed that Jesus was the prophet spoken of by Moses who
had been "raised up." But on the other hand, Peter also made
it clear that the people are responsible to hear and heed the
words of Christ as delivered by Jesus' prophets, including from
Peter and the Apostles and including all messengers sent by the
Lord. Peter prophesied that those who will not hear the words
of Jesus Christ, as delivered by his servants, the prophets—they
"shall be destroyed" (Acts 3:23).

So while Joseph Smith's critics are looking for any and every
error they can find to attempt to discredit him, it is actually they
who are being tested, for Moses' prophecy makes it clear that
it is the people who have the duty to recognize and respond to
the words of God's prophets.

There are at least two examples in the Bible of prophecies
by true prophets which did not come to pass. Perhaps one of
the best-known examples of this is Jonah, who prophesied that
the City of Nineveh would be destroyed (Jonah 3:4). In that
interesting account, no one seemed more disappointed than
Jonah when the Lord spared Nineveh after the city repented.
The point of that story was that God sometimes has some un-
stated qualifications and conditions that can prevent a prophecy from coming to pass. In the case of Jonah's prophecy about
Nineveh's destruction, the prophecy was true and would have
come to pass, but its fulfillment was altered when the people
repented. Another example of a prophecy that did not come to
pass is Isaiah's prophecy that King Hezekiah would shortly die
(2 Kings 20:1). But after hearing this prophecy, Hezekiah prayed
for God to prolong his life, and God granted his petition and

extended his life an additional fifteen years (2 Kings 20:2-6). Again, the point is that there are multiple principles and conditions that apply when prophecies are given, and sometimes true prophecies do not come to pass when other superseding conditions occur.

Finally, I would note that because I have received the witness from God that Joseph Smith was His prophet, I am hesitant to be too quick in finding fault with his words. I am reluctant to criticize a prophecy that to me may not seem to be true, but which could be fulfilled in a way that does not presently occur to me. In other words, we can sometimes be confronted with a prophecy that does not seem to be true, but which may nevertheless be true. Those who have predetermined that Joseph Smith is a false prophet are prone to jump to the conclusion that a particular prophecy was wrong. I choose a more cautious approach; I will extend the benefit of the doubt to Joseph Smith and allow for every possible reasonable interpretation for his prophecies. There is no virtue in making a hasty and erroneous judgment that a particular prophecy is false, when in fact it is true.

Now, having made the foregoing introductory comments about examining and judging Joseph Smith, let's move on to the six specific, alleged "false" prophecies of Joseph Smith that someone has identified—two of which are found in the *Doctrine and Covenants*, and four in the *History of the Church*:[200]

---

[200] Joseph did not have the opportunity to review those reports for accuracy. Hearsay is routinely inadmissible in our courts of law (with various exceptions) because it is second-hand information which is known to be susceptible to error, and because the person quoted is not available for cross-examination or clarification. Thus, with regard to the 3,000 pages of statements in the seven volumes of *History of the Church*, Joseph Smith did not proof-read those materials for correctness. This is unlike his statements in the scriptures. Further, the statements in the scriptures have been accepted by the Church as scripture—meaning that the saints regard those writings as the word of God. No such stature is attached to the 3,000 pages of statements in History of the Church, except for those portions that have been canonized as scripture.

1. The coming of the Lord is nigh, 56 years "should wind up the scene" (HC 2:182);

2. Wars shall be poured out upon all nations (D&C 87:1-3);

3. In a few years the government shall be overthrown (HC 5:394);

4. Congress will be broken up (HC 6:116);

5. Death of the wicked (HC 1:315); and

6. Temple to be built in Missouri (HC 1:286-95; D&C 84:4-5).

We will review these alleged "false prophecies" one by one to see what if any parts of them are not fulfilled and for which the time of their fulfilling has passed.

## 1. "Fifty-six years should wind up the scene."

This prophecy was made in 1835 and is found recorded in *History of the Church*, vol. 2, page 182. The larger prophecy, which the critics apparently do not take issue with, is that in speaking about Zion's Camp, Joseph said:

> [I]t was the will of God that those who went to Zion, with a determination to lay down their lives, if necessary, should be ordained to the ministry, and go forth to prune the vineyard for the last time, or the coming of the Lord, which was nigh—even fifty-six years should wind up the scene.

The allegation is that the Second Coming was predicted to happen within 56 years, but that it did not happen. While critics may want to interpret this statement to mean that "the Second Coming will occur within 56 years," the words do not actually state this. The coming of the Lord to His temple did occur the next year, when the Savior did "suddenly come to His temple" (Malachi 3:1), as was witnessed by Joseph Smith and Oliver Cowdery (D&C 110). But the appearance spoken of in Matthew

24:30 that Jesus will come "in the clouds of heaven" and that "all people would see him together" (1 Thessalonians 4:16-17)—that has not yet taken place. What specifically Joseph was referring to by the words "wind up the scene" no one knows, so it is impossible to state that this has not happened. Perhaps Joseph meant that the work of these brethren would be completed within 56 years. The "scene" for Joseph Smith ended at his death in 1844—9 years later—long before 56 years. In any event, Joseph did not say that winding up the scene "**will**" happen, rather he said that he thinks it "**should** wind up" within 56 years. Thus, this as a statement of Joseph Smith's opinion, but not a statement of absolute prophecy. The word "will" is definitive in meaning, while the word "should" is an opinion word that conveys the possibility that the thing might not happen. Joseph did not know when the Second Coming would occur. On another occasion, Joseph wrote that he asked the Lord about when the Second Coming would occur, and he said he was led to believe that it would not occur before he would reach the age of 85 (1890), if he were to live that long (D&C 130:14-17). Just because Joseph Smith made some prophecies does not mean that he could not also have opinions about some things, including some opinions that may not have turned out to be totally correct.

In conclusion, the coming of the Lord is nigh at hand; the Savior did suddenly come to his temple one year later (fulfilling the prophecy in Malachi 3:1). The main thrust of this prophecy was that men would be ordained from the ministry from among those who were willing to join in "Zion's Camp" and give their lives for the Lord. And that is what happened; it was from among those faithful brethren who "went to Zion" and were willing to give their lives for the Lord that most of the original members of the Quorum of the Twelve Apostles were called and "ordained to the ministry." This part of the prophecy was fulfilled right after it was given. But Joseph's statement that "fifty-six years should wind up the scene" was a vague statement of opinion. It cannot be proved that it did not come to pass. Therefore, it cannot be regarded as a false prophecy.

## 2. Wars shall be poured out upon all nations.

The next alleged, false prophecy is taken from a prophecy made by Joseph Smith in 1832 about the civil war; it is found in section 87 of the Doctrine and Covenants, verses 1-4, which states the following:

> Verily, thus saith the Lord concerning the wars that will shortly come to pass, beginning at the rebellion of South Carolina, which will eventually terminate in the death and misery of many souls;
>
> And the time will come that war will be poured out upon all nations, beginning at this place.
>
> For behold, the Southern States shall be divided against the Northern States, and the Southern States will call on other nations, even the nation of Great Britain, as it is called, and they shall also call upon other nations, in order to defend themselves against other nations; and then war shall be poured out upon all nations.
>
> And it shall come to pass, after many days, slaves shall rise up against their masters, who shall be marshaled and disciplined for war.

This is a prophecy that was clearly fulfilled—Joseph prophesied in 1832 that the civil war would occur; that it would begin with the rebellion of South Carolina; that it would result in the death and misery of many people; that the Southern States would call upon Great Britain for aid; that slaves would rise up against their masters and be marshaled for war; and that "then war shall be poured out upon all nations" (D&C 87:1-4). This is one excellent example of a prophecy of Joseph Smith that has been fulfilled. However, for some reason, some critics want to take issue with the fulfillment of one part of this prophecy—the part about war being poured out upon all nations. Note, there is no time limit involved by which this prophecy must be fulfilled, so even if someone today might contend that war has not **yet** been poured out on **all** nations, there is still time remaining for this to happen. However, this type of nit-picking criticism of this prophecy should be embarrassing to any who would seriously make it. America's civil war was not an international war, but shortly thereafter international conflicts resulted in World Wars I and II that were clearly a fulfillment of the prediction that "war shall be poured out upon all nations." All major nations in the world were directly involved in these wars, and those who were not directly at war were nevertheless impacted by these wars.

This prophecy has been mostly fulfilled, and some of it remains to be fulfilled. There is no reasonable basis for concluding that this is a false prophecy; rather this is clearly a prophecy that includes several specifics that have been fulfilled. There is no basis to call this a false prophecy.

## 3. "In a few years the government will be utterly overthrown."

The third alleged false prophecy is from a statement by Joseph Smith in 1843, when he is reported to have said:

> [U]nless the United States redress the wrongs committed upon the Saints in the state of Missouri and punish the crimes committed by her officers that in a few years the government

will be utterly overthrown and wasted, and there
will not be so much as a potsherd left. (HC 5:394)

This prophecy has two parts—(1) some conditions, and (2)
consequences if the conditions are not met. Then, with regard to
the consequences, the statement is made that they would occur
within a "few years." The condition is that "unless the United
States redress the wrongs committed upon the Saints in . . .
Missouri and punish [the perpetrators of] the crimes." These
conditions were never met. Therefore, assuming the statement
was recorded correctly, we turn to the meaning of the predicted
consequence and whether it was fulfilled within the time al-
lotted. The prediction given was to take place "in a few years."
My review of history shows that the predicted consequence
occurred within 25 years, which satisfies the time factor.

The consequences predicted in this prophecy were substantially fulfilled with the occurrence of the civil war and the
resulting disruption of both the federal government and the
Missouri State government. Nevertheless, we will examine the
statement a little more closely. To re-state the quote: If the U.S.
doesn't both give the saints a remedy for wrongs they suffered
in Missouri, and if the Missouri officers who inflicted these
wrongs are not punished, then "in a few years the government
will be utterly overthrown and wasted, and there will not be
so much as a potsherd left."

Some critics may feel that the word "government" should
apply to the United States government, rather than to the
Missouri government. But Joseph never explained which government would be overthrown if the conditions were not met.
When the southern slave states seceded from the union this
resulted in a substantial disruption of the federal government
and its operations, but ultimately the U. S. government survived, despite its existence being challenged and seriously
damaged. "Overthrown" is not a word that I would normally
have used to describe what happened to the United States, but

such a word could be an accurate word to describe what happened to the governments of those states which seceded. But the United States government was also disrupted; it was tipped over, toppled, divided, challenged, threatened, attacked and devastated—and thus, in a sense, "overthrown." At the end of the war the Confederate States of America was "overthrown" as well as the governments of every State that was a part of it. Nevertheless, something else happened to the Missouri government that clearly fulfills this prophecy.

"Overthrown" is one word that would aptly describe what happened to the government of Missouri in 1861.[201] As soon as South Carolina seceded from the Union in December of 1860, the Missouri government was immediately put into chaos. Missouri citizens were divided in their support for the North and for the South. Control over the state of Missouri was critical to both sides because it was a border state and because control of the Mississippi River (Missouri's eastern border) was strategically critical to both sides. The debate over whether Missouri should secede was so divisive and violent that the state government was put in disarray and confusion.

Missouri's recently elected governor, Claiborne Fox Jackson, wanted Missouri to secede, but in early 1861 he had difficulty getting any legislators to support this—at the time, most citizens wanted to remain neutral and not join either side. Federal troops in Missouri backed those Missourians who wanted to stay in the Union. On May 10, 1861, in St. Louis, federal troops led by Captain Nathaniel Lyon captured some secessionists and paraded them down the street in a show of strength and submission. This exhibition led to violence, where 28 civilians were killed. This event is referred to as the Camp Jackson Massacre. Captain Lyon followed up this skirmish by capturing Jefferson

---

[201] A concise summary of the governmental chaos in Missouri in 1861 can be found on *Wikipedia*; see "Missouri secession" and "Missouri in the American Civil War." The following historical summary comes primarily from these sources.

City (the State capital) on June 15th. Those Missouri legislators siding with the South were driven out of town. Then, in late July the Union faction called and convened a Missouri State Convention and declared the Governor's office to be vacant. On July 28th the Union faction appointed Hamilton R. Gamble to be the military governor. About the same time, Federal General John Fremont declared martial law. Governor Jackson disputed these actions, and on August 10, 1861, Missouri secessionist troops led by former governor Sterling Price took back control over the state government at the battle of Wilson's Creek. In this battle, federal troops suffered 1,300 casualties and Southern troops suffered 1,200 casualties. But Price's victory was short-lived. On September 26th, General Fremont drove Price and his troops out of the state. This effectively secured federal control over Missouri for the rest of the war. On October 28th, Governor Jackson assembled a session of the State legislature at Neosho, Missouri, where on October 30th the Legislature passed a bill seceding from the Union, and Governor Jackson signed it the next day. Governor Gamble (the Union faction's governor) did not recognize this action as valid, and regardless of whether or not the vote was legally sufficient to make Missouri secede, Governor Gamble maintained control over the state during the war. Thus, while there were both North and South factions asserting control over Missouri, the state effectively was supporting the North. But the division in Missouri was so intense that there were more battles fought in Missouri in the Civil War (1,000 – 1,200) than in any other states except Virginia and Tennessee. The Missouri secessionists never conceded that Gamble was governor. In 1864, Sterling Price led another attempt to regain control of the State, but this attempt also failed.

The above account of Missouri state history clearly shows how the government of Missouri, led by Governor Claiborne Fox Jackson was overthrown by the pro-Union citizens that were backed by federal troops. Governor Jackson and his supporters did not submit and relinquish control to the Union faction; rather, Jackson's government was forcefully overthrown.

This prophecy also uses the word "wasted" to describe the results from the government's being overthrown. The word "wasted" does not seem like a word that would normally be used in describing the toppling of a government. One meaning of "wasted" is "desolate." But that is not a normal meaning to be applied to a government—it more readily applies to a destruction of plants, animals and people. This meaning of "wasted" certainly applied to many cities and places in Missouri following the many battles fought there. Another meaning of the word "wasted" is that it literally means that something that had value and use was allowed to become useless. The statement is that the "government" would be both "overthrown" and "wasted." Thus, while the adjective "wasted" is not a term that one would normally use to describe a defeated and toppled government, it could make sense here.

The prophecy about the government being utterly overthrown, found in HC 5:394, has clearly been fulfilled.[202] As long as there is one reasonable interpretation that was fulfilled,

---

[202] While not directly pertinent to this discussion, it is interesting to note that Jackson County, Missouri suffered an extraordinary amount of destruction during the civil war.

N. B. Lundwall,, *The Fate of the Persecutors of the Prophet Joseph Smith* (Salt Lake City: Bookcraft Publishers, 1952). Lundwall wrote that the area along the Blue River (which had been inhabited by the Mormon settlers in the early 1830s) was destroyed. Lundwall quoted a man named Mason, who stated that this area of land "was destroyed during the guerrilla and bushwackers' campaign of terror in the time of the late civil war. It was a war between neighbors and neighborhoods, and the whole section of country was laid waste." Lundwall, 312. Lundwall also included a statement made by A. Saxey in 1902 that the destruction in Jackson County was vast and complete; Saxey wrote: "I remember very well that the county looked a veritable desolation." Lundwall, 331.

Another interesting aspect of the devastation that took place in Jackson County is that Joseph prophesied of this. Lundwall includes a statement by Alexander Doniphan that Joseph warned him not to accept payment from a client of some real property in Jackson County because that particular

then the prophecy was fulfilled. In this case we have a couple of plausible interpretations of how the prophecy was fulfilled. The enemies of Joseph Smith do not have the right to interpret Joseph's words only in a way that would preclude the prophecy from being fulfilled.

The concluding phrase, "there shall not be so much as a potsherd left," does not seem to fit in meaning in describing the overthrow of a government. A "potsherd" is a broken piece of ceramic material, but governments are organizations, not pieces of tangible property. Therefore, the precise meaning of this phrase is difficult to pinpoint. If the meaning is symbolic, then this phrase would seem to be an additional modifier, similar in meaning to the word utterly, and it would be an accurate description of what happened. If the meaning was literal then there are certainly many pieces of pottery that were totally demolished in connection with the civil war battles in Missouri that accompanied the toppling of its government. In Psalm 2:9 the prophecy is made that the Lord would "dash them [the wicked] in pieces like a potter's vessel." If the statement by Joseph Smith about a "potsherd" was intended to echo the psalmist's prophecy, then it was certainly fulfilled, because many people were "dashed into pieces" and killed in Missouri in connection with the Civil War battles there, and with the toppling of the Missouri government at the start of the war. Other verses in the Bible also use terms describing the breaking of pottery to describe the destruction that is to precede the Lord's Second Coming. (See e.g., Rev. 2:27; Isaiah 29:16 and 30:14.)

It is interesting to note that while the critics of Joseph Smith are over-anxious to find minor flaws in him and his words, they are not interested in noting some of the other wonderful and remarkable things that he said on the same occasion when he made the prophecy that the government would be "overthrown." On that occasion Joseph went on to make a remarkable

property would become wasted (Lundwall, 330). This prophecy was fulfilled, and Doniphan remembered it for years.

prophecy about Stephen A. Douglas that was fulfilled. Joseph told Mr. Douglas this:

> Judge, you will aspire to the presidency of the United States; and if you ever turn your hand against me or the Latter-day Saints, you will feel the weight of the hand of the Almighty upon you; and you will live to see and know that I have testified the truth to you. (HC 5:394)

While the meaning of the Almighty's turning his hand against Mr. Douglas was not stated with great specificity, what later transpired was indeed devastating to Mr. Douglas. In a speech by Douglas in 1857, he knowingly and wrongly charged the Mormons with numerous depredations. Thereafter, in 1860, when Douglas was running for president, and when there was good reason to expect him to win, he ended up with a dismal result—receiving only one electoral vote, and losing to Abraham Lincoln. (See HC 5:394-98.) Because Douglas wrongfully turned against the Mormons, he then did feel the weight of the hand of God, as he suffered a crushing defeat in the presidential election of 1844. The effect on Douglas was so severe that he died within a year of this defeat.

### 4. "Congress will be broken up."

The fourth alleged false prophecy comes from a statement made by Joseph Smith in 1843. It is interesting to note that this alleged, "false" prophecy is not even accurately quoted by the critics. Joseph never stated that "Congress" will be broken up; the prophecy is that "they" will be broken up. Nevertheless, let us examine the specific words of the prophecy given in 1843, and then analyze them: "[I]f Congress will not hear our petition and grant us protection, they shall be broken up as a government" (HC 6:116).[203]

This prophecy also has two parts—a condition and a consequence. In my opinion, Congress did not satisfy the condition—to "hear our petition and grant us protection."[204] Therefore we may properly look to see whether the predicted consequences occurred. The consequence is that "they . . ., a government," would be "broken up." This was absolutely fulfilled with the secession of the southern states in 1861 and with the federal government's taking control over the southern states after the war. Let us review more closely four possible interpretations of this prophecy. First, if "government" referred to the U. S. federal government, then it was literally "broken up" with the secession of the southern states in 1861 and the ensuing war. Second, if "government" referred to the Confederate States of America, then it was broken up when the North conquered the South, right after Lee's surrender at Appomattox Court House. Third, if "government" referred to the "Tyler Administration," then that "government was put out of office ("broken up") in the November 1844 election. Fourth, if "they" refers to the several

---

[203] Immediately following the stating of this prophecy, Joseph wrote: "I informed the Council that it was my wish they should ask the privilege of calling on Government for the United States troops to protect us in our privileges, which is not unconstitutional, but lies in the breast of Congress." *Id.*

[204] I am of the opinion that the United States never granted the Mormons' petition for redress for the wrongs they suffered at the hands of Missouri, and the government did not give the saints protection. But there are instances of some help from the federal government for the saints. One such example is the government's raising a battalion of about 500 men to assist in the war with Mexico in 1846. The federal government paid the men for this service, and the funds were of tremendous benefit to the Mormons at that time, when they were again refugees at Winter Quarters, preparing to make the trek west to the Great Salt Lake. If such aid satisfied the condition part of the prophecy, then the analysis is ended. At this point, I am personally of the opinion that the U.S. never did sufficiently grant the saints protection, and therefore I believe it proper to look for a fulfillment of the consequence part of the statement, for which there are three or four possible fulfillments which may properly apply.

members of Congress, then of course this is fulfilled literally every two years when the composition of Congress changes with new people elected and with the departure of some members of Congress. In this sense, Congress is broken up every two years. Specifically, this is what happened in the 1844 General Election when many Democrat Congressmen lost, such that the party in control (the Democrat Party) was broken up. Perhaps all four of these possible meanings were intended.

With regard to the third possible interpretation, according to B. H. Roberts, this prophecy was fulfilled by the defeat ("breaking up") of the "Tyler Administration" in the national election in November of 1844. The Democratic Party had been in power for 24 years, but it lost badly in the 1844 election, thereby fulfilling this prophecy because the Tyler Administration was indeed broken up. To this day (2019) the terms "Trump Administration," "Obama Administration," etc. are used to mean government in many contexts. The same applied in 1843, such that one legitimate meaning of who "shall be broken up as a government" could properly be applied to the demise of Tyler's Democratic Administration, which was replaced with the election of James Polk as President in 1844.

### 5. Death of the wicked.

The fifth alleged false prophecy of Joseph Smith is a statement made by Joseph Smith in 1833 that the wicked would be swept off the face of the land, preceding the Second Coming (HC 1:315). There are multiple biblical prophecies of the same thing. (See e.g., Malachi 4:1-3; Isaiah 47:10-14; and Jude 1:14-15.) The ultimate fulfillment of these prophecies has yet to occur—the earth has yet to be cleansed by fire. Thus, there can be no legitimate dispute about this aspect of Joseph's prophecy. Here is a fuller rendition of the prophecy:

> [N]ot many years shall pass away before the United States shall present such a scene of bloodshed as has not a parallel in the history of our nation; pestilence, hail, famine, and earthquake will sweep the wicked of this generation from off the face of the land, to open and prepare the way for the return of the lost tribes of Israel from the north country. (HC 1:315)

This prediction is stated without any conditions. The unparalleled "scene of bloodshed" occurred during the civil war, which started 28 years after the prophecy was given. This time period is certainly within the limitation that it would happen before "not many years shall pass away." The scene of bloodshed that did ensue in America was without a parallel in the history of our nation." There were over 600,000 deaths from the civil war, but the end of the civil war did not mark the end of "this generation." This generation—meaning the era of the dispensation of the fullness of times—is still not yet ended, 158 years after the beginning of the civil war.

Today, the number of American deaths from World Wars I and II and all the other intervening wars has just recently exceeded 600,000. This puts into perspective the enormous scene of bloodshed and horror that resulted from the civil war—the nation suffered as many deaths in the four years of the civil war as it suffered in the next 150 years from all the wars combined during that period of time. Many people have died and been swept off the earth, including many wicked people. But all of "the wicked of this generation" have not yet been swept off the earth. However, the prophecy does not state that "all" "the wicked of this generation" would be swept off within "not many years." Neither does the prophecy state that there would be no other wicked people on earth after the scene of bloodshed and pestilence that would take place within "not many years." There has indeed been considerable pestilence, hail, famine and earthquakes that killed millions of people in the world, including many wicked people, since this prophecy was pronounced.[205] And many people from the lost tribes of Israel have returned from the north countries. Most of the converts to the Church were either living in Europe or were descendants of Europeans. Europe is comprised of northern countries, and many of those who joined the Church were indeed descendants of the twelve tribes of Israel. Thus, the prophesied events did happen. Nevertheless, the ultimate fulfillment of this prophecy will not occur until the final destruction of "the wicked of this generation" by the cleansing fire just before the Savior's triumphal return.

The second clause of the prophecy describes separate, additional causes of destruction that would sweep wicked people of this generation off the earth: "pestilence, hail, famine and earthquake." All of these destructive agents had already begun by the time of the civil war, but they did not end when the civil war ended—they continued. Does the time limitation of the first clause ("not many years . . . before . . . a scene of bloodshed [would occur]") also apply to this later destruction? I don't think so; the order of the two statements could mean that the

---

[205] It is a well-known historical fact that since the date of this prophecy there has been pestilence, hail, famine and earthquakes that have killed millions of people. The deaths from hail are the fewest; deaths from earthquakes have been considerable; but deaths from famine and pestilence have been enormous. A brief review of *Wikipedia* articles lists millions of deaths from various pestilences—cholera, influenza, plague and others. 75 million people died from the world-wide flu pandemic from 1918-20; and over 30 million people have died from the HIV/AIDS pandemic from 1960-present. (See "List of epidemics," *Wikipedia*.) Similarly, millions have died from famine since the pronouncement of this prophecy. More than 60 million people in China died from famine between 1850 and 1873, and another 18 million people died from famine in China and India from 1873-79. Another 25 million people died of famine in China between 1907 and 1911. 8-10 million people died of famine in Iran from 1917-19. 5 million people died of famine in Russia in 1921. From 1928 to present there have been at least another 50 million people around the world who died of famine. Even as late as 1961 there is reported to have been between 15 and 43 million deaths from famine in China. (See "List of famines," *Wikipedia*.)

"pestilence, hail, famine and earthquake" will occur some time after the scene of bloodshed from the civil war. Additionally, the meaning of "not many" is so vague and relative that even two hundred years can be "not many years" in some contexts.

It is true that sometimes the time limit of a preceding clause can also apply to the following clause. But such application is not automatic; it is not required; and in this case the time limit may not fully apply to the second phrase. Nevertheless, pestilence, hail, famine and earthquakes did occur within "not many years," and some, but not all, of the wicked were swept off the land. Thus, by applying the time limit of the first clause to the following clause would add a meaning that may never have been intended. Critics have no right to ascribe a limiting meaning to Joseph's words that he did not intend, and then use such a changed meaning to conclude that the prophecy was not fulfilled.

Moving on to another part of this prophecy—later, in the same reported speech, Joseph reportedly stated: "[F]lee to Zion, before the overflowing scourge overtake you, for there are those now living upon the earth whose eyes shall not be closed in death until they see all these things, which I have spoken, fulfilled" (HC 1:316). Assuming this statement was properly recorded, and assuming the words were what Joseph intended to say, this sounds like the fulfillment would have to occur before the death of the last person who was living on the earth at that time. Joseph knew very well that John the Revelator and the three Nephite disciples were living somewhere "upon the earth." So, if they were "those" to whom he was referring it was easy for him to say that "their" "eyes shall not be closed in death before all these things" would happen. If Joseph was referring to others, we don't know. But I would note that Joseph did not say that there were any people who were listening to him then, who would still be alive; neither did he say that there were any Missourians nor any Americans who would live to see these things—rather he said that there are "those now living upon the earth [somewhere]" who would live to see it. Thus, he clearly used words that encompassed the whole world. This would be broad enough to make sure that John and the three Nephites were included.

Now, 184 years later, it appears that all the predicted events preceding the Second Coming did not occur within the lifetime of most of the people living in 1833, but all the events spoken of either have been fulfilled or will be fulfilled before the Savior's return to the earth.

### 6. Temple to be built in Missouri in this generation.

The sixth alleged false prophecy of Joseph Smith was a statement in 1832 (recorded in Section 84 of the Doctrine and Covenants) regarding the building of a temple in Independence, Missouri that was to occur before "this generation" should have "passed away." Here is the specific wording for this prophecy:

> Verily this is the word of the Lord, that the city New Jerusalem shall be built by the gathering of the saints, beginning at this place, even the place of the temple, which temple shall be reared in this generation.
>
> For verily this generation shall not all pass away until an house shall be built unto the Lord, and a cloud shall rest upon it, which cloud shall be even the glory of the Lord, which shall fill the house. (D&C 84:4-5; see also HC 1:286-95)

I don't see any stated conditions in connection with this prophecy, thus the prophecy is that a temple will be built in Independence "in this generation."

So, was the prophecy a false prophecy because the temple has not already been built? I don't think so. The time limit mentioned was that it would be built in this "generation," whatever that means. One meaning of generation is similar in meaning to "era" or "time period" or "dispensation." Meaning number

4 in *Webster's Universal Collegiate Dictionary* (Random House, copyright 1997) is this: "a group of individuals belonging to a specific category at the same time." Jesus is reported to have used "generation" in this way when he said: "An evil and adulterous generation seeketh after a sign" (Matt. 12:39). But more specifically, in Matthew 24, this is the meaning that Jesus gave to the word when he made a prophecy about the tribulation and signs that would occur in the last days; with respect to those many events He said: "This generation shall not pass until all these things be fulfilled" (Matthew 24:34). Just as Jesus used "generation" to mean "the people of a certain era of time," so did Joseph use the word "generation" in his 1832 prophecy. In fact, it is clear that Joseph was aware of the very issue about the meaning of "generation," for in his inspired translation of Matthew 24:34 Joseph rendered it as follows: "[T]his generation, *in which these things shall be shown forth*, shall not pass away until all I have told you shall be fulfilled" (Joseph Smith—Matthew 1:34 [italics added]). The additional modifiers added by Joseph Smith (italics) show that he understood that when Jesus said "this generation" he was not referring to the generation of Peter, James and John, but rather the people of the dispensation of the fullness of times in the latter days.

Based upon the foregoing, it appears that in this 1832 prophecy that Joseph used the word "generation" to identify the people living in the last days, the "dispensation of the fullness of times" that was spoken of by the Apostle Paul (Ephesians 1:9). Thus, while Joseph's detractors may wish to limit the time for this prophecy to be fulfilled to a shorter one, in order to attempt to make this a "false" prophecy, they cannot legitimately do this, for there is a valid and reasonable definition of "generation" that is consistent with the prophecy's having continued validity.

A number of people who heard this prophecy in 1832 believed that the Independence temple would be built in just a very few years. Perhaps that was a possibility, but it did not happen. Based upon subsequent revelations to Joseph Smith, we understand that the building of that temple was delayed for two reasons—because mobs were interfering (D&C 124:49-51) and because the saints had not kept commandments that were given to them (D&C 105:1-9).[206] Thus, the day will come when the temple will be built in Independence, but it was not built as soon as many had expected. Nevertheless, this generation has not all passed away, so the time for fulfillment has not expired.

Those who may be fixated on disproving any and every prophecy of Joseph that they can, will likely miss some of the more pertinent parts of this prophecy for which disciples of Christ continue to anticipate its fulfillment. This prophecy also predicts that after the temple is built that the glory of God would rest upon this temple in an actual "cloud." This will be marvelous to behold. This temple is prophesied to occupy a key role and be a key place in the New Jerusalem, which is to be built in this area. This, too, is a fantastic development to take place during the dispensation of the fullness of times. The Church of Jesus Christ of Latter-day Saints looks forward with anticipation for these events to unfold.

It is interesting to note that two other churches also regard this prophecy about the Independence Temple to have continued validity and to be of great importance. The Church of Christ—Temple Lot (also called, "Hedrickites") owns this site, and they continue to look for a temple to be built on it. The Community of Christ (formerly The Reorganized Church of Jesus Christ of Latter Day Saints [RLDS Church]) also believes that the building of a temple on or near the original site in Independence is very important. These two churches engaged in litigation over ownership of the temple site in a federal law suit, which was finally concluded in 1896 when the Church of Christ prevailed, and the RLDS Church's petition for *certiorari* to the U. S. Supreme Court was denied. (See chapter 6.) Eventually,

---

[206] An excellent discussion about the redemption of Zion being delayed because the saints were not prepared is given in Whitney, *The Life of Heber C. Kimball*, 57-58, 63-66.

the RLDS Church decided to build a temple on the lot adjacent to the one that had been dedicated by Joseph Smith for the temple. The RLDS Temple was completed in 1994.

## Conclusion

Some people are so set on finding fault with Joseph Smith that they become blinded to messages and meanings that are clear and inspiring. It does not help to be overly anxious to find fault with Joseph Smith and his prophecies. Joseph made enough prophecies that have come to pass to clearly prove him to be a prophet. Of the six alleged false prophecies that were identified in this chapter, all six of them are true prophecies, some of which have yet to be fulfilled. These prophecies are evidence that Joseph Smith was a true prophet of God. The criticisms respecting the timing of some of the prophecies are minor matters at best, and it cannot be conclusively proven that Joseph's statements respecting timing were not true. Those whose fanaticism impels them to accuse Joseph Smith of being a false prophet are themselves fulfilling the prophecy from March of 1839, when Joseph wrote that the Lord said to him that "fools shall have thee in derision" (D&C 122:1).

So, where does this leave us? Even if one could prove that Joseph Smith stated one or two opinions that turned out to be wrong, would this prove him to be a false prophet? Of course not! That would be a ridiculous conclusion, if those were the only mistakes you can find from a man who produced 872 pages of scripture, including dozens and dozens of prophecies. Proving that Joseph Smith stated one or two opinions that turned out to be wrong, would prove only that he held one or two opinions that turned out to be wrong; this would not prove Joseph Smith to be a false prophet. No reasonable, intelligent person could draw such a conclusion. The great weight of evidence from these six prophecies and the dozens of others that he made shows that Joseph Smith was a true prophet of God.

# Part IV–Joseph Smith, the Messenger of Jesus Christ

On the morning of June 24, 1844, Joseph and Hyrum Smith stopped briefly at the Nauvoo Temple, overlooking the Mississippi River, as they rode to Carthage to be arrested on specious charges, under the guarantee of protection from Illinois Governor Thomas Ford. Statue is the work of Stan Watts and Kim Corpany.

The chapters of this book provide information and insights to help understand the Prophet Joseph Smith and some important historical events that are a part of the restoration of the gospel of Jesus Christ. This information can help one better understand important issues about the restoration. This information refutes some accusations made against Joseph Smith and it explains others. While Joseph's enemies have relentlessly sought to demonize and besmirch him, no material character flaw has yet to be proven. After an extensive examination, I have not found one claim of a major moral flaw in Joseph Smith that has been proven to be true. None of those accusations stick.

If Joseph's enemies can smear and malign him enough, then this can divert some of his adherents to second-guess their spiritual witnesses, and then to doubt the character of the Prophet, and then in some cases to join in condemning him. But a thorough knowledge of Joseph's history exposes and diffuses most of the attacks made on his character.

But as long as the character of Joseph Smith is an issue, then one must consider the testimony of those who knew Joseph well. And those testimonies are not only impressive, they describe a magnificent, charismatic man. One of the best sources of such testimonies is found in the collection of testimonies compiled by Hyrum and Helen Mae Andrus, *They Knew the Prophet* (Salt Lake City: Bookcraft, 1974). Included in these eight dozen testimonies are the following, many of which repeat and confirm the same wonderful descriptions of Joseph:

> His countenance was ever mild, affable, beaming with intelligence and benevolence . . . cheerfulness . . . .
>
> *Parley P. Pratt*

> The Prophet was incomparably the most God-like man I ever saw. . . .His kind manner and

gentle words . . . . his easy, jovial appearance . . . his firm dislike of that which was degrading.

*Edward Stevenson*

Joseph Smith was one of the most engaging personalities it has ever been my good fortune to meet. . . . Socially he was an ideal of affability and always approachable to the humblest of his acquaintances.

*Jane Snyder Richards*

Much has been said of his geniality and personal magnetism. I was witness of this—people, old and young, loved him and trusted him instinctively.

*William Taylor*

General Smith is naturally a man of strong mental powers, and is possessed of much energy and decision of character, great penetration, and a profound knowledge of human nature. . . . He is kind and obliging, generous and benevolent, sociable and cheerful . . . . He is a true lover of his country and a bright and shining example of integrity and moral excellence.

*John M. Bernhisel*

The Kindness he manifested in all the walks of life cause him to be beloved by the little boys and girls, who often sought his company, as well as by the many thousands of his people . . . .

*James Palmer*

He possessed the most indomitable persever-ance . . . . His views were so strange and striking, and his manner was so earnest and apparently so candid that you could not but be interested. There was a kind, familiar look about him that pleased you. He was very courteous in discus-sion, readily admitting that he did not intend to controvert, and would not oppose you abruptly, but had due deference to your feelings.

*Peter Hardeman Burnett*

[H]e was an extraordinary man, a man of great penetration; was different from any other man I ever saw; had the most heavenly countenance; was genial, affable and kind; and looked the soul of honor and integrity.

*Bashsheba W. Smith*

To me, Joseph Smith seemed to possess more power and force of character than any ordi-nary man.

*Daniel D. McArthur*

During a period of about seven years I had fre-quent opportunities of continuing my acquain-tance with Joseph Smith, seeing him nearly every day. From my actual knowledge, I can testify to the purity and uprightness of his life, and I know that he was a man of God.

*Benjamin Brown*

Joseph was a prophet of God, and a friend of man. His was a noble character. All who knew him can testify to that assertion. He was all that the word *gentleman* would imply—pure in heart, always striving for right, upholding innocence, and battling for the good of all.

*Emily Partridge Young*

The power of God rested upon him to such a degree that on many occasions he seemed transfigured. His expression was mild and almost childlike in repose; and when addressing the people, who loved him it seemed to adoration, the glory of his countenance was beyond description.

*Emmeline Blanche Wells*

He boldly and bravely confronted the false traditions, superstitions, religious bigotry and ignorance of the world—proved himself true to every heaven-revealed principle—true to his brethren and true to God, then sealed his testimony with his blood.

*Eliza R. Snow*

For some of Joseph Smith's heavenly manifestations he was accompanied by witnesses; other times he was alone. But as to all of them, those to whom Joseph declared his messages must make a judgment as to his credibility. During Joseph's short life, as the above statements show, there are many people who not only had the absolute highest regard for the character of Joseph Smith, but who also held him to be a prophet of God. Joseph made dozens of prophecies which were subsequently fulfilled, and which bear witness that he was a prophet of God. Joseph was an instrument of the Lord in healing dozens of people, and he even raised William Huntington from the dead (Andrus, 128-29). There exist ample reasons to believe that Joseph was a prophet of God, just as he said he was.

Sculpture at the Nauvoo LDS Visitors Center, depicting Joseph Smith's first vision in 1820, at Palmyra, New York, when God the Father and His Son, Jesus Christ, appeared to Joseph. Sculpture is the work of D. J. Bawden.

Eliza R. Snow wrote this about her initial encounters with Joseph Smith:

In the autumn of 1829, I heard of Joseph Smith
as a prophet to whom the Lord was speaking
from the heavens; and that a sacred record containing a history of the origin of the aborigines
of America was unearthed. A prophet of God,
the voice of God revealed to man as in former
dispensations—this was what my soul had hun-
gered for. But could it possibly be true? I considered it a hoax—too good to be true. In the winter
of 1830 and 31, Joseph Smith called at my father's
home. As he sat warming himself, I scrutinized
his face as closely as I could without attracting
his attention, and decided that this was an honest
face. My adopted motto, "Prove all things and
hold fast to that which is good," prompted me
to investigation, as incredulous as I was. On the
5th of April, 1835, I was baptized by a Mormon
"Elder." (Andrus, 56)

Eliza eventually received her own witness from God that
Joseph was His prophet. Today there are millions of people who
have done what Eliza R. Snow did and reached the same conclusion. As this book demonstrates, there is substantial evidence
that Joseph Smith was indeed a prophet of God. Many good,
God-fearing people have so concluded, as have I.

One final individual who knew Joseph Smith extremely
well was Brigham Young. Here is what Brigham said about the
Prophet (taken from several of Brigham's discourses):

Who can justly say aught against Joseph Smith? I
was as well acquainted with him, as any man. . . .
I do not think that a man lives on the earth that
knew him any better than I did; and I am bold
to say that, Jesus Christ excepted, no better man
ever lived or does live upon this earth. I am his

witness. (John A. Widtsoe, *Discourses of Brigham Young* (Salt Lake City: Desert Book Co., 1926, 1941 and 1954), 459)

We can find no person who presents a better character to the world, when the facts are known, than Joseph Smith, Jr., the Prophet, and his brother, Hyrum Smith, who was murdered with him. . . . But let his enemies give his character, and they will make him out one of the basest men that ever lived. . . . [H]e was defendant in forty-six lawsuits, and every time Mr. Priest [i.e., some minister] was at the head of and led the band or mob who hunted and persecuted him. And when Joseph and Hyrum were slain in Carthage jail, the mob, painted like Indians, was led by a preacher. . . . Joseph Smith, in forty-six prosecutions, was never proved guilty of one violation of the laws of his country. (*Id.*, 466)

Why did people hate him? Because of his influence. Did he gain or exercise an unrighteous influence? By no means. He possessed a righteous influence over the spirits, feelings, passions, and dispositions of all who delighted in truth and goodness. . . . I never saw any one, until I met Joseph Smith, who could tell me anything about the character, personality and dwelling-place of God, or anything satisfactory about angels, or the relationship of man to his Maker. Yet I was as diligent as any man need to be to try to find out these things. . . . When I saw Joseph Smith, he . . . opened up, in plainness and simplicity, the things of God. . . . I honor and revere the name of Joseph Smith. . . . I feel like shouting Hallelujah, all the time, when I think that I ever knew Joseph Smith, the Prophet whom the Lord raised up and ordained, and to whom he gave keys and power to build up the Kingdom of God on earth. (*Id.*, 464, 458)

While some of Joseph's teachings and actions were controversial and sometimes provocative, a full examination of Joseph's words and actions demonstrate that he was a good and loving man, a bright man of exceptional initiative, a hard worker, and a dynamic leader. Joseph testified that he received dozens of revelations from God, and many of these revelations were witnessed by others. Joseph Smith produced hundreds of pages of inspired writings—more than twice as many as any other biblical prophet. Joseph shared these messages with the world, as prophets of God do. The reading of those words has brought the confirming witness of the Holy Ghost that the messages are of divine origin. Joseph was a courageous, devoted disciple of Christ, who died as a martyr at the hands of wicked, hateful men. A thorough examination of Joseph Smith's life and messages provides abundant evidence that he was a valiant witness of the Lord Jesus Christ, and that he was God's chosen prophet, foretold in the Bible, to preside over the restoration of the gospel of Jesus Christ in preparation for the Lord's Second Coming.

# BIBLIOGRAPHY

Anderson, J. Max, *The Polygamy Story: Fiction and Fact* (Salt Lake City: Publishers Press, 1979)

Anderson, Richard L., and Faulring, Scott, "The Prophet Joseph Smith and His Plural Wives," Oct. 2, 1998. Retrieved February 19, 2018, from https: //scholarsarchive.byu.edu/cgi/viewcontent. cgi?article=1362&context=msr

_____, "The Second Witness of Priesthood Restoration," *Improvement Era*, Nov. 1968, p. 19

Andrus, Hyrum L. and Helen Mae, eds., *They Knew the Prophet* (Salt Lake City: Bookcraft, 1974).

Austin Cowles. (n.d.). In *Wikipedia*. Retrieved February 18, 2018 from https://en.wikipedia.org/wiki/Austin_Cowles

Backman, Milton V., Jr., "The Keys Are Right Here" (1995), in S. E. Black & L. C.

Porter,(in *Lion of the Lord--Essays on the Life and Service of Brigham Young* (pp. 107-127) (Salt Lake City: Deseret Book Co.)

Barrett, Ivan J., *Joseph Smith and the Restoration* (Provo: Brigham Young University Press, 1967).

Bennett, John C., *History of the Saints* (1842).

Bergera, Gary James. Identifying the Earliest Mormon Polygamists, 1841-44, in *Dialogue: A Journal of Mormon Thought* (Smith-Pettit Foundation, 2005). Retrieved in 2017 from https://www.dialoguejournal.com/wp-content/uploads/sbi/.../Dialogue_V38N03_13.pd...

Berrett, William E., *The Restored Church* (Salt Lake City: Deseret Book Co., 1965).

Black, Susan Easton, *Who's Who in the Doctrine & Covenants* (Salt Lake City: Deseret Book Co., 1997).

Black, Susan Easton and Porter, Larry C., eds., *Lion of the Lord--Essays on the Life and Service of Brigham Young* (Salt Lake City: Deseret Book Co., 1995).

Book of Abraham. (n.d.). In *Wikipedia*. Retrieved June 3, 2016, and February 18, 2018, from https://en.wikipedia.org/wiki/Book_of_Abraham

Brewster, Hoyt W., Jr., *Prophets, Priesthood Keys and Succession* (Salt Lake City: Deseret Book Co., 1991).

Brodie, Fawn M., *No Man Knows My History--The Life of Joseph Smith, the Mormon Prophet* (New York: Alfred A. Knopf, 1946)

Bushman, Richard L., *Joseph Smith--Rough Stone Rolling* (New York: Alfred A. Knopf, 2005).

Cannon, Donald Q. and Cook, Lyndon W., eds., *Far West Record: Minutes of the Church of Jesus Christ of Latter-day Saints* (Salt Lake City: Deseret Book Co., 1883).

Carpenter, Samuel R., *Facts about differences that persist* (Salt Lake City: Deseret News Press, 1958).

Children of Joseph Smith. (n.d.). In *Wikipedia*. Retrieved August 24, 2017, from https://en.wikipedia.org/wiki/Children_of_Joseph_Smith

Clark, E. Douglas, *The Blessings of Abraham--Becoming a Zion People* (Salt Lake City: Covenant Press, 2005).

Community of Christ. (n.d.). In *Wikipedia*. Retrieved February 18, 2018, from https://en.wikipedia.org/wiki/Community_of_Christ

Community of Christ. (n.d.). In *Wikipedia*. Retrieved in 2017, from https://en.wikipedia.org/wiki/Community_of_Christ

Community of Christ, *The Book of Mormon* (Independence, MO: Board of Publications of the Reorganized Church of Jesus Christ of Latter Day Saints, 1966).

Compton, Todd, *In Sacred Loneliness: The Plural Wives of Joseph Smith* (Salt Lake City: Signature Books, 1997).

Cook, Lyndon W., "William Law, Nauvoo Dissenter," *BYU Studies Quarterly*: Vol. 22: Iss. 1, Article 5 (1982). Available at: https://scholarsarchive.byu.edu/byusq/vol22/iss1/5

Corbett, Don Cecil, *Mary Fielding Smith, Daughter of Britain, Portrait of Courage* (Salt Lake City: Deseret Book Co., 1966).

Critical appraisal of the Book of Abraham. (n.d.). In *Wikipedia*. Retrieved February 18, 2018 from https://en.wikipedia.org/wiki/Critical_appraisal_of_the_Book_of_Abraham

Dahl, Larry E. and Cannon, Donald Q., eds., *Encyclopedia of Joseph Smith's Teachings* (Salt Lake City: Bookcraft, 1997).

Draper, Richard D., Brown, Kent S. and Rhodes, Michael D., *The PEARL of GREAT PRICE, A Verse-by-Verse Commentary* (Salt Lake City: Deseret Book Co., 2005).

Ehat, Andrew F., *Joseph Smith's Introduction of Temple Ordinances and the 1844 Succession Question* (Master's Thesis, Dept. of History, BYU 1982).

Esplin, Ronald K., "Brigham Young and the Transformation of the 'First' Quorum of the Twelve" (1995), in S. E. Black & L. C. Porter,(in *Lion of the Lord--Essays on the Life and Service of Brigham Young* (pp. 54-84) (Salt Lake City: Deseret Book Co.)

Faulring, Scott, ed., *An American Prophet's Record: The Diaries and Journals of Joseph Smith* (Salt Lake City: Signature Books, 1989).

Fluhman, J. Spencer, "A Subject that Can Bear Investigation," in Robert L. Millet, ed., *No Weapon Shall Prosper* (Salt Lake City: Deseret Book Co., 2011)

Fulwood, Sam, III, "Stepping Away from Racism" (Sept. 2, 2016). Retrieved Feb. 25, 2018, from https://www.americanprogess.org/issues/race/news/.../stepping-away-from-racism/

Garr, Cannon & Cowan, *Encyclopedia of Latter-day Saint History* (Salt Lake City: Deseret Book Company, 2000).

Gee, John, "A Guide to the Joseph Smith Papyri" (Provo: FARMS, 2000).

_____, "An Egyptian View of Abraham," in Andrew C. Skinner, D. Morgan Davis and Carl Griffin, eds. *Bountiful Harvest: Essays in Honor of S. Kent Brown* (Provo: Maxwell Institute, 2011).

_____, *An Introduction to the Book of Abraham* (Salt Lake City: Religious Studies Center, BYU and Deseret Book Co., 2017).

_____, "The Facsimiles of the Book of Abraham, " linked from footnote 3, retrieved February 18, 2018, from https://www.fairmormon.org/answers/Book_of_Abraham/.../Facsimiles/Facsimile_3

Hales, Brian C., "Encouraging Joseph Smith to Practice Plural Marriage: 'The Accounts of the Angel with a Drawn Sword,' Mormon Historical Studies 11, no.2 (Fall 2010):69-70." Retrieved Feb. 19,

2018, from mormonhistoricsites .org/.../Encouraging-Joseph-Smith-to-Practice-Plural-Marriage-Th

_____, "Joseph Smith's Practice of Plural Marriage" in Laura Harris Hales, ed., *A Reason for Faith* (Provo: Religious Studies Center, BYU and Salt Lake City: Deseret Book Co., 2016), pp. 129-141.

Hales, Brian C. & Laura H., "Biographies of Joseph's Plural Wives-- Marinda Nancy Johnson," in *Joseph Smith's Polygamy*. Retrieved February 19, 2018, from www.josephsmithspolygamy.org

Hales, Brian C. and Smith, Gordon L., "A Response to Grant Palmers Sexual Allegations Against Joseph Smith and the Beginnings of Polygamy in Nauvoo." Retrieved February 19, 2018, from www. mormoninterpreter.com /a-response-to-grant-palmers-sexual-allegations-against-j

Holzapfel, Neitzel and Shupe, R. Q., *My Servant Brigham - Portrait of a Prophet* (Salt Lake City: Bookcraft, 1997).

Hunter, Milton R., *Pearl of Great Price Commentary* (Salt Lake City: Bookcraft, 1951).

Jesse, Dean C., Esplin, Ronald K. and Bushman, Richard L., *The Joseph Smith Papers* (Salt Lake City: The Church Historians' Press, 2008).

Joseph Smith Papyri. (n.d.). In *Wikipedia*. Retrieved February 18, 2018 from https://en.wikipedia.org/wiki/Joseph_Smith_Papyri *Journal of Discourses* (1854-1886).

Kirtland Temple Suit. (n.d.). In *Wikipedia*. Retrieved February 18, 2018, from https://en.wikipedia.org/wiki/Kirtland_Temple_Suit

Koury, Aleah G., *The Truth and the Evidence* (Independence, MO: Herald Publishing House, 1965). Plural Marriage in Kirtland and Nauvoo. (n.d.). Retrieved February 18, 2018, from https://www.lds.org/topics/plural-marriage-in-kirtland-and-nauvoo?lang=eng

Larson, Charles M., *By His Own Hand–A New Look at the Joseph Smith Papyrus* (Grand Rapids, Michigan: Institute for Religious Research, 1985, 1992).

Legg, Phillip R., *Oliver Cowdery, the Elusive Second Elder of the Restoration* (Independence, MO: Herald Publishing House, 1989).

Lightner, Mary Elizabeth Rollins, *Autobiography*. Retrieved February 19, 2018, from https://www.boap.org/LDS/Early-Saints/MLightner.htm

List of epidemics. (n.d.). In *Wikipedia*. Retrieved February 18, 2018, from https://en.wikipedia.org/wiki/List_of_epidemics

List of famines. (n.d.). In *Wikipedia*. Retrieved February 18, 2018, from https://en.wikipedia.org/wiki/List_of_famines

Ludlow, Daniel H., *Encyclopedia of Mormonism*, 5 vols. (New York: Macmillan Publishing Co., 1992).

Lundwall, N. B., *The Fate of the Persecutors of the Prophet Joseph Smith* (Salt Lake City: Bookcraft, 1952).

Madsen, Truman, *Joseph Smith the Prophet* (Salt Lake City: Bookcraft, 1989).

"Marinda Johnson Hyde." Retrieved February 19, 2018, from www.wivesofjosephsmith.org/11-MarindaJohnsonHyde.htm

McConkie, Bruce R., *The Millennial Messiah* (Salt Lake City: Deseret Book Company, 1982).

McConkie, Bruce R., *Mormon Doctrine* (Salt Lake City: Bookcraft., 1958, 1966 & 1978).

McConkie, Mark L., *Remembering Joseph* (Salt Lake City: Deseret Book, 2003).

McKiernan, Mark, *The Voice of One Crying in the Wilderness: Sidney Rigdon, Religious Reformer (1793-1876)* (Coronado Press, 1971; Herald House, 1979, 1986).

*Millennial Star* (Great Britain, 1845).

Millet, Robert L., ed., *No Weapon Shall Prosper--New Light on Sensitive Issues* (Salt Lake City: Deseret Book Co., 2011)

Millet, Robert L. and Jackson, Kent P., eds. *Studies in Scripture, Volume Two: The Pearl of Great Price* (Salt Lake City: Randall Book Co., 1985).

Missouri in the American Civil War. (n.d.). In *Wikipedia*. Retrieved Feb. 18, 2018 from https://en.wikipedia.org/wiki/Missouri_in_the_American_Civil_War

Missouri secession. (n.d.). In *Wikipedia*. Retrieved February 18, 2018, from https://en.wikipedia.org/wiki/Missouri_secession

Mormonism and Polygamy. (n.d.). In *Wikipedia*. Retrieved in 2017, from https://en.wikipedia.org/wiki/Mormonism_and_polygamy

Morris, Larry E., "The Book of Abraham: Ask the Right Questions and Keep on Looking (Review of: "The Breathing Permit of Hor Thirty-four Years later" (*Dialogue*, 2000).

Muhlestein, Kerry, "Egyptian Papyri and the Book of Abraham," in Robert L.

Millet, ed., No Weapon Shall Prosper (Salt Lake City: Deseret Book Co., 2011).

_____, "The Explanation-Defying Book of Abraham," in Laura Harris Hales, ed., *A Reason for Faith* (Provo: Religious Studies Center, BYU and Salt Lake City: Deseret Book Co., 2016).

*Nauvoo Expositor* (Nauvoo, June 7, 1844).

Nibley, Hugh, *Abraham in Egypt* (Salt Lake City: Deseret Book Co. and Foundation for Ancient Research and Mormon Studies [FARMS], 2000).

_____, *An Approach to the Book of Abraham - The Collected Works of Hugh Nibley: Volume 18* (Salt Lake City: Deseret Book and FARMS, 2009).

_____, *Collected Works of Hugh Nibley: Volume 5, The Book of Mormon* (Salt Lake City: Deseret Book Co., 1988).

_____, *Enoch the Prophet* (Salt Lake City: Deseret Book Co., 1986).

_____, *The Message of the Joseph Smith Papyri, An Egyptian Endowment* (Salt Lake City: Deseret Book Co., 1975 and later Deseret Book Co. and FARMS, 2005).

_____, "Three Facsimiles from the Book of Abraham" (1980). Retrieved February 19, 2018, from www.boap.org/LDS/Hugh-Nibley/TrFac.html

Nittle, Nada Kareem. Five Ways to Make Your Racially Segregated Church More Diverse. (June 30, 2016). Retrieved February 18, 2018, from https://www.thoughtco.com/nadra-kareem-nittle-2834471

Osiris myth. (n.d.). In *Wikipedia*. Retrieved February 18, 2018, from https://en.wikipedia.org/wiki/Osiris_myth

Peterson, H. Donl, *The Pearl of Great Price: A History and Commentary* (Salt lake City: Deseret Book Co., 1987).

_____, "Book of Abraham," in *Encyclopedia of Mormonism*, 5 vols. (New York: Macmillan Publishing Co., 1992).

Potter, Charles Francis, *Did Jesus Write This Book?* (Greenwich, CT: Fawcett Publications, Inc., 1965).

Price, Richard and Pamela, *Joseph Smith Fought Polygamy*, Vol. 1 (Independence, MO: Price Publishing Co., 2000).

Race and the Priesthood. (2014). Retrieved February 18, 2018, from https://www.lds.org/topics/race-and-the-priesthood

Reimann, Paul E., *The Reorganized Church and the Civil Courts* (Salt Lake City: Utah Printing Company, 1961).

Rhodes, Michael D., "Why doesn't the translation of the Egyptian papyri found in 1967 match the text of the Book of Abraham in the Pearl of Great price?" *Ensign*, July 1988.

————, "Facsimiles from the Book of Abraham," in "Book of Abraham," in *Encyclopedia of Mormonism*, 5 vols. (New York: Macmillan Publishing Co., 1992).

Ritner, Robert K., *A Response to "Translation and Historicity of the Book of Abraham"* (Salt Lake City: Signature Books, 2017).

————, *The Joseph Smith Papyri: A Complete Edition* (Salt Lake City: Signature Books, 2013).

Roberts, B. H., ed., *A Comprehensive History of the Church* (Salt Lake City: Deseret Book Co., 1930).

————, *History of The Church of Jesus Christ of Latter-day Saints* (7 vols.) (Salt Lake City: Deseret Book Co., 1902-1951).

Sarah Marinda Bates Pratt. (n.d.). In *Wikipedia*. Retrieved February 18, 2018, from https://en.wikipedia.org/wiki/Sarah_Marinda_Bates_Pratt

Shields, Steven L., *Latter Day Saint Beliefs - A Comparison Between the RLDS Church and the LDS Church* (Independence, MO: Herald Publishing House, 1986).

Smith, Arthur M., *A Brief History of The Church of Christ (Temple Lot)* (Fourth Edition, 1971).

Smith, Joseph F., *Gospel Doctrine* (Salt Lake City: Deseret Book Co., 1975 ed. first published 1919)

Smith, Joseph F., Jr., see Smith, Joseph Fielding

Smith, Joseph Fielding, *Blood Atonement and the Origin of Plural Marriage* (Salt Lake City: Deseret Book Co., 1905).

————, *Doctrines of Salvation*, compiled by Bruce R. McConkie, 3 vols. (Salt Lake City: Bookcraft, 1954).

————, *Origin of the "Reorganized" Church and the Question of Succession* (Independence, MO: Press of Zion's Printing and Publishing Co., 1929).

————, *The Way to Perfection* (Salt Lake City: The Genealogical Society of The Church of Jesus Christ of Latter-day Saints, 1931).

The Book of Abraham. (n.d.). Retrieved February 18, 2018, from thebookofabraham.blogspot.com/2011/.../theodule-deveria-memoires-et-fragments.ht...

The Church of Jesus Christ of Latter-day Saints, *The Doctrine and Covenants* (Salt Lake City: The Church of Jesus Christ of Latter-day Saints, 1979).

_____, *The Pearl of Great Price* (Salt Lake City: The Church of Jesus Christ of Latter-day Saints, 1979).

_____, *Doctrine and Covenants Student Manual, Religion 324 and 325* (Salt Lake City: The Church of Jesus Christ of Latter-day Saints, 2001)

The Church of Jesus Christ of Latter-day Saints membership history. (n.d.). In *Wikipedia*. Retrieved February 19, 2018, from https://en.wikipedia.org/ wiki/The_Church_of_Jesus_Christ_of_Latterday_Saints_membership_history *Times and Seasons* (Nauvoo, 1842)

Webster's Universal Collegiate Dictionary (Random House, 1997)

Whitney, Helen Mar Kimball, *Plural Marriage as Taught by the Prophet Joseph:*

*A Reply to Joseph Smith, Editor of the Lamoni (Iowa) "Herald"* (Salt Lake City: Juvenile Instructor Office, 1882).

_____, *Why We Practice Plural Marriage* (Salt Lake City: Juvenile Instructor Office, 1884).

Whitney, Orson F., *The Life of Heber C. Kimball* (Salt Lake City: Bookcraft, 1945).

Widtsoe, John A, *Discourses of Brigham Young* (Salt Lake City: Deseret Book Co., 1926, 1941 and 1954).

_____, Gospel Interpretations (Salt Lake City: Bookcraft, 1947).

William Law. (n.d.). In *Wikipedia*. Retrieved February 18, 2018, from https://en.wikipedia.org/wiki/William_Law_(Latter_Day_Saints)

# INDEX

Aaronic Priesthood 186

Abolitionists 204-205, 207-208

Abraham 2, 74, 85, 137-178, 188, 204, 213

Abraham, Book of: see Book of Abraham

Abraham, covenant of 17, 20, 85, 203-204

Abraham, seed of 179, 187-189

Abrahamic test 36

Abraham 148

Adam 132

Adams, James 53

Adultery 14, 15, 17, 18, 44, 70, 87, 107

African Methodist Episcopal Church (AME) 297

Aikens, Mary 53

Alger, Clarissa 13

Alger, Fanny 13-17, 56

Ali, Mohammad 195

Alley, Sarah B. 53

Amendments to Constitution 40, 191, 192, 197

Andrus, Pamela 53

Anti-miscegenation laws 206

Apostasy 18, 19, 44

Apostles 22

Appomattox Court House 232

Assistant President 18, 21

Astronomy 156, 176

Babbot, Ammon W. 37

Baldwin, Caleb 112

Ballantyne, Jane 53

Baltimore, MD 201

Baptism for the dead 20, 21, 86, 113, 118, 125, 129

Barker, Robert W. 199

Baseball, major league 193-194

Basketball, NBA 194-195

Beaman, Louisa 56

Bennett, John C. 23-27, 32, 33, 36, 37, 77, 84, 85, 87, 104, 143

Benson, Ezra Taft 32, 53, 71

Blacks and the priesthood xvi, xx, xxi, 179-213

Bliss, Nancy 53

Boggs, Gov. Lilburn 25, 83, 87

Book of Abraham xvi, xx, 131, 136-178, 208-210

*Book of Breathings* 144

Book of Enoch 150

Book of Mormon xviii, 63, 115-117, 127, 128, 142, 167, 215

*Book of the Dead* 144

Booth, John Wilkes 192

Booth, Linda L. 118

Boston Celtics 194

Briggs, Jason W. 31, 104, 111
Brodie, Fawn 64, 166-167
Brooklyn Dodgers 193-194
Brotherton, Elizabeth 53
Browitt, Martha R. 29, 30, 53
Brown, Jim 195
Brown v. Board of Education, 196
Brunson, Seymour 17, 18
Buchanan, Mary Ann 53
Buell, Norman 56
Buell, Oliver 65
Buell, Presendia Huntington
    56, 65
BYU basketball team 198
Cahoon, Reynolds 53
Cain, descendants of 136, 208-211
Camp Jackson Massacre 227
Campanella, Roy 195
Campbell, Alexander 23
Canaan, and descendants of
    208-211
Cannon, George Q. 211
Carlos, John 198
Carthage Jail 4, 48, 79, 99, 241, 248
Catholicism xv
Celestial kingdom 2, 12-13, 17, 46,
    66, 72, 184
Celestial marriage 8, 20, 45, 94,
    129, 130, 132, 212
Church of Christ – Temple Lot
    105, 123-126, 131-133, 239
Church of Jesus Christ of Latter-
    day Saints, The throughout
Civil Rights Act of 1964 197
Civil War 191-192, 212, 224-231,
    233-235
Clark, E. Douglas 143-144, 156,
    160, 171
Clark, Harriet 53
Clawson, Catherine Reese 53

Clayton, William 32, 53, 71
Cleveland Browns 195
Cleveland Cavaliers 191
Cleveland, John 56
Cleveland, Sarah Kingsley 56, 61
Clift, Eliza 53
Clift, Mary 53
Cobb, Augusta Adams 53
Cole, Nat King 196
Community of Christ 49, 50,
    110-131
Confederate States of America
    227, 232
Congress 231-232
Constitutional Convention 191
Cook, Harriet Elizabeth 53
Coolbrith, Agnes 56
Coolidge, Joseph 53
Cowdery, Oliver 3, 14-19, 21, 39,
    45, 63, 66-72, 77, 85, 92, 124,
    126, 135, 146
Cowdery, Jane 124
Cowdery, John 124
Cowdery, Joseph Smith 124
Cowles, Austin 41, 61, 68, 94, 104,
    106, 107
Cowley, Matthias 52
Custer, Solomon 14
David 2
Dead Sea Scrolls 150, 156
Decker, Clarissa Caroline 53
Decker, Harriet P. wheeler 53
Defamation 108-109
Deveria, Theodule 155, 177-178
District of Columbia, right to
    vote 197
DNA 62-65
Doctrine and Covenants, The
    xviii, 16, 115, 204, 215, 216,
    221, 224

Doniphan, Alexander 229
Douglas, Stephen A. 230-231
Douglass, Frederick 212
Durfee, Elizabeth Davis 56, 61
Durfee, Jabez 56
Eaton, Mary 31
Edmunds-Tucker Act 51
Egan, Howard 53
Elias 17, 20, 21, 85
Elisha 187
Elijah 17, 20, 21, 85
Elkanah 2
Elkenah 139, 174
Ells, Hannah 56
Egyptian xvi, 137-178, 208-210
Egyptian Alphabet and
    Grammar 146
Egyptologist 144, 146, 152-155,
    157-170
Egypts 209-210
Eighth Circuit 125
Emmerson, Michael O. 180
Emmons, Sylvester 44
Endowment 22, 28, 40, 72, 86-89,
    93, 94, 130, 131, 142, 143
England 84
Equal Opportunity 181-185
Eternal marriage xvi, 8, 21, 129
Exaltation 132, 181-185
Extermination Order 19, 83
Extradition 87
Facsimiles 1, 2 and 3 137-178
False prophecies (alleged) xxi,
    214-240
Families xvi
Far West, MO 18, 83, 84
Felshaw, William 53
Ferguson, MO 201
Fielding, Mercy 53
First Amendment 4-5, 50-51

First Presidency 24, 37, 40-41, 43,
    51-52, 83-85, 93, 94, 96, 98,
    106, 132, 211
First Vision 129
Football, NFL 194-195
Ford, Gov. Thomas 241
Fordham, Elijah 21
Ford's Theatre 192
Fornication 16
Foscutt, Mark 119
Foster, Charles 44, 68, 94, 107
Foster, Robert D. 42, 44, 68, 75,
    106, 107
Freemont, John 228
Frost, Olive 56
Fullmer, Desdemona 56
Gamble, Hamilton R. 227-228
Gee, John 143-144, 146, 149, 153-
    159, 162-163, 170
Gehzi 187
Germany 202
Gideon 2
Gilliam, Joe 195
God the Father 10, 116, 129, 246
Grant, Ulysses 192
Great Britain (or British Isles) 32,
    34, 224
Grove 95, 98
Guardian 48, 95
Gurley, Zenos H. 104, 111, 113
Gynecologist 24
Habeas corpus 23
Ham 208-210
Hancock, Levi 13
Hancock, Mosiah 13
Harmony, PA 135
Harris, Dennison 75, 94
Harris, George W. 18, 56
Harris, Lucinda Morgan 18, 56, 62
Harris, Martin 19

Hawley, Mary 53
Heaven 10-13
Hedrick, Granville 104, 131, 132
Hedrickites: 128, 239; see also
	Church of Christ –
	Temple Lot
"Helping Hands" xv
Hezekiah 220
Higbee, Chauncey 41, 44, 68,
	75, 107
Higbee, Elias 124
Higbee, Francis 44, 68, 107
Hitler 202
Hobart, Mary Ann 53
Hoffmann, Mark 112
Holmes, Elvira Cowles 56, 61
Holy Ghost 77, 249
Hôr papyrus 145, 157-161, 165-166
Hunter, Milton R. 210-211
Huntington, William 53, 246
Hurricanes xv
Hyde, Frank Henry 62, 65
Hyde, Nancy Marinda Johnson
	29, 30, 56, 61, 63, 65
Hyde, Orson 19, 25, 29, 30, 53, 56,
	61, 68, 69, 95, 99, 103
Hyde, Orson Washington 62, 65
Independence, MO 7, 123, 130, 131,
	133, 237, 239
Interracial marriage 206-207
Irvins, Charles 44
Isaiah 188, 220
Isis, wife of Osiris 155
Jackson, Joseph 41, 44, 75, 107
Jacob 2, 74, 213
Jacobs, Henry 56
Jacobs, Zebulon 65
Jacobs, Zina Huntington 56, 62, 65
James, LeBron 191
Jeremiah 188

Jesus Christ throughout
Jackson, Claiborne Fox 227-228
Johnson, Almira 56
Johnson, Lucinda Roberts 53
Johnson, Luke 19
Johnson, Lyman 7, 19
Johnson, Lyndon B. 197
John the Baptist 188
Jonah 220
Jones, Dan 215
Jones, Mary 53
Kaighan, Elizabeth 53
Kelley, E. L. 122
Kelting, Joseph A. 53
Keys of the Priesthood 40, 89-94
Kimball, Heber C. 3, 25, 26, 53, 59,
	60, 89, 99
Kimball, Helen Mar 56, 58-60
Kimball, Spencer W. 189
Kimball, Vilate 26, 59
King Follett Discourse 42-43,
	94, 108
King, Martin Luther, Jr. 181, 197
Kirtland, OH 13, 14
Kirtland Temple 66, 119-123, 184
Knight, Marth McBride 56
Knight, Vinson 53
Law, Jane 43, 93, 106
Law, William 23, 37, 41-45, 61, 68,
	70, 71, 75, 77, 93, 94, 103, 104,
	106, 107, 110
Law, Wilson 42, 44, 53, 68, 75, 107
Lawrence, Maria 56
Lawrence, Sarah 56
Lee, Robert E. 192, 232
Levi, Tribe of 186, 213
Libby, Hannah 30, 53
Libby, Sarah 30, 53
Libel 108-109
Liberty Jail, MO 83

Lightner, Adam 56
Lightner, George Algernon 63, 65
Lightner, Mary Elizabeth Rollins
  56, 62, 63, 65
Lincoln, Abraham 192, 231
Liptrot, Susannah 53
Longstroth, Nancy 53
Longstroth, Sarah 53
Lott, Melissa 56
*Loving v. Virginia* 197, 206
Lyman, Amasa 43
Lyon, Josephine Rosetta 63-65
Lyon, Capt. Nathaniel 227
Lyon, Sylvia Sessions 56, 63-65
Lyon, Windsor 56, 64
M., Precilla 53
Mackay, Lachlan 130-131
Manifesto 51, 52
Mansion House 28, 89, 130
Markham, Stephen 32
Marks, William 41, 94, 95, 104,
  106, 111
Marriott, Bill xv
Marsh, Thomas 19
Marshall, George 195
Marshall, Thurgood 197
Mayor of Nauvoo 24
McLellin, William E. 19, 104
McMurray, W. Grant 115, 127, 128
McRae, Alexander 112
Melchisedec(k) Priesthood
  132, 135
Mengel, Gail E. 118
Meredith, James 196
Metropolitan Museum of Art
  136-137
Miller, Bishop George 35, 99
Missionary(ies) xvi, 40
Missouri government over-
  thrown 225-230

Mitchell, Bobby 195
Moon, Margaret 53
Moon, Warren 195
Morley, Isaac 32, 53, 63, 71
Mormon battalion 232
Mormon Church xv
Moroni 74
Morris, Larry E. 160, 170
Moses 2, 20, 21, 74, 85, 188, 216-219
Muhlestein, Kerry 143, 144, 153,
  155-156, 158-160
Myrick, Philinda C. 53
Naaman 187
Nauvoo Charter 23, 45, 108, 109
*Nauvoo Expositor* 41, 44-45, 107-109
Nauvoo House 21
Nauvoo Legion 23
Nauvoo Temple 21, 72, 130, 241
New and everlasting covenant 22
New Jerusalem 123, 237, 239
"New Organization" 132
Nibley, Hugh 137, 143-145, 149-150,
  153-154, 157, 158, 161, 164,
  170, 172
Nineveh 220
Noah 213
Noble, Joseph B. 53
Noon, Sarah Peak 53
Nuisance 108
Obama, Barack 190, 196, 233
*Obergefell v. Hodges* 5
Official Declaration 1 52
Official Declaration 2 136, 189
Olympics 198
One mistake test 217
Osiris myth 155, 177-178
Osmond, Marie xv
Owens, Jedediah 131, 132
Page, John E. 25, 30-32, 48, 53, 95,
  99, 103-104

*Painesville Republican* 167
Palestine 29, 32
Papyri xvi, 136-178
Parrish, Warren 158, 162, 164,
     166, 168
Partridge, Edward 123-24
Partridge, Eliza 27, 56, 88
Partridge, Emily 27, 56, 88, 245
Patriarch 21, 31
*Pearl of Great Price, The* xviii,
     138-139, 146-147, 152, 156,
     215, 216
Perjury 44, 107
Peter 183, 220
Peter, James and John 135
Pharaoh 171, 174, 176
Phelps, W.W. 7, 19, 40, 77, 112, 146
Philips, Judge John F. 125-126
Phillips, Catherine 53
Pittsburgh, PA 40, 69
Pittsburgh Steelers 195
*Plessy v. Ferguson* 192, 196
Plurality of Gods Discourse 43
Plural marriage xvi, 1-77, 85, 87,
     93, 94, 106, 107, 109, 110, 113,
     115, 118, 127, 131
Poitier, Sidney 196
Polk, James 233
Poll tax 197
Polygamy: see plural marriage
Pontius Pilate 201
Pratt, Mary Ann Frost Stearns
     62, 65
Pratt, Moroni 65
Pratt, Orson 7, 16, 25, 32-34, 36, 49,
     53, 94, 127
Pratt, Parley P. 25, 39, 53, 62, 63,
     90, 91, 168, 242
Pratt, Sarah 32, 33
Presidential campaign 40-41, 93

President of the United States
     40-41
Price, Mary Ann 29, 53
Price, Sterling 228
Priesthood xvi, 89
"Quorum" 88, 89
Quorum of the Twelve Apostles 3,
     9, 23, 25-27, 32-34, 40, 43, 47,
     49, 52, 58, 71, 73, 82-86, 89-
     103, 206, 223
Racism xvi, 179, 190-201
Reconstruction 192
Red Brick Store 22, 130-131
Reformed Mormon Church 44,
     106, 107
Reid, Harry xv
Relief Society 131
Reorganized Church 31, 49, 50,
     105, 110-131, 239-240; see
     also Community of Christ
Repsher, Roxena Higby 53
Restored gospel xvii
Resurrection 8
Revelation 117
Reynolds, George 50-51
*Reynolds v. United States* 4, 50-51
Rhodes, Michael D. 145, 149, 153-
     154, 158, 168
Rice, Chris 180
Richards, Franklin D. 139
Richards, Rhoda 56
Richards, Willard 25, 41, 53,
     95, 112
Rigdon, John W. 35
Rigdon, Nancy 34-37, 54-55
Rigdon, Sidney 3, 7, 10-12, 23, 34-
     40, 45, 47-49, 66-72, 77, 84,
     89, 95-101, 104, 112
Rising, Louisa Chapin Gordon 53
Ritner, Robert K. xx, 157-170,

RLDS Church see Reorganized
    Church
Robinson, Jackie 193-195
Robinson, George W. 35
Robinson, Rachel 194
Rocky Mountains 215
Romney, Mitt xv, 190, 200
Russell, Bill 194, 195
Salt Lake 47, 101, 232
Same-sex marriage 117
Samuel 2
*Sangamo Journal* 55
Savage, Becky L. 118
Sayers, Edward 56
Sayers, Ruth Vose 56, 61
Scott, Robert 75, 94
Sealing powers 14, 21, 91
Sealings 14, 60, 86, 90
Secession 226-229
Second Coming 38, 39, 78, 222-223,
    230, 233, 237, 249
Second Elder 15
Seeley, Lucy Ann Decker 53
Segregation 192-198
Separate but equal 192-198
Sessions, David 56
Sessions, Patty Bartlett 56, 62
Seventies Hall 95, 97
Sheffield, Mary Ann
    Covington 53
Sherman, Delcena Johnson 56
Sherman, Judge 122
Shields, Steven L. 116
Slavery 180, 202-208, 212
Smith, Arthur M. 128, 131
Smith, Emma Hale 14, 27, 28, 56,
    87, 88, 95
Smith, Frederick M. 114-115
Smith, George A. 25, 49, 53, 94
Smith, Howard 106

Smith, Israel A. 114-115, 121
Smith, Hyrum 21, 26-28, 31, 37,
    41, 47, 48, 53, 61, 71, 94, 106,
    112, 241
Smith, Jerusha 27
Smith, John 32, 53, 71
Smith, Joseph throughout
Smith, Joseph III 104-105, 111-112,
    114-115, 119-121
Smith, Mary Fielding 27
Smith, Precilla M. 30
Smith, Tommie 197
Smith, Wallace B. 114-115, 128
Smith, W. Wallace 114-115
Smith, William 25, 30, 31, 48, 53,
    95, 99, 103-104, 110, 111, 132
"Smoking gun" 163
Snow, Abigail Leonora 53
Snow, Eliza R. 56, 215, 245-247
Snow, Erastus 32, 53, 71
Snow, Lorenzo 49, 212
Solomon 2
South Carolina 224, 227
Southern Baptist Convention
    xv, 207
Splinter churches/groups xx, 82
Spokesman 48, 95
Sports, racism in 193-195
Strang, James J. 23, 31, 104,
    110, 111
Succession xx, 42, 81-134
Super Bowl 195
Supreme Court, U.S. 4-5, 13, 50-
    51, 239
Taylor, John 25, 34, 39, 41, 53, 95,
    99, 112, 120-121, 138, 212
Taylor, John W. 52
Telestial kingdom 46
Temple 20, 85-90, 93, 118, 129, 130,
    142, 175, 222, 239-240

Temple Lot 123-126, 143, 222

Terrestrial kingdom 46

Texas 103

Third Reich 202

Thompson, Charles B. 104

*Times and Seasons, The* 35-36, 138, 141, 144, 152, 168

Translation xvi

True Church of Jesus Christ of Latter Day Saints 44, 105-110

Trinity 116, 129

Trump, Donald 191, 201, 233

Turley, Theodore 32, 53, 71

Twelve Apostles: see Quorum of Twelve Apostles

Tyler, President 232-233

United Methodist Church xv

United States 4-5

University of Mississippi 197

Urim and Thummim 141, 168

Veazey, Stephen A. 115, 117, 128

Victorian 9

Vision 10

Voting Rights Act of 1965 197

Walker, Lucy 56

Wallace, George 198

Walters, Charlotte 53

Wars 224-231

Washington Redskins 195

Wheaton High School 198

White, Minerva 53

Whitmer, David 18, 19, 68-69, 104

Whitmer, John 19

Whitney, Horace 59

Whitney, Orson F. 60

Whitney, Sarah Ann 56

Wight, Lyman 25, 30, 31, 48, 53, 99, 103-104, 112

Wilding, Ellen 53

Williams, Doug 195

Winchester, Nancy 56, 58-59

Wisconsin 103, 111, 132

Women, ordained to priesthood 117, 118

Woodruff, Flora Ann 56

Woodruff, Wilford 25, 39, 49, 51, 53, 90, 91, 94, 100, 212

Woods, Minerva O. 53

Wooley, Edwin D. 53

World Wars I and II 225, 234

WTOP radio 199

Young, Brigham 3, 25-27, 31, 48-50, 53, 81, 82, 89-92, 94-101, 110, 113, 131, 200, 210-212, 247-249

Young, Emily Partridge: see Partridge, Emily

Young, Fanny 56

Young, Lorenzo D. 53

Young, Steve xv

Zion 7, 222, 239

Zion's Camp 222-223